CHOOSING YOUR BATTLES

CHOOSING YOUR BATTLES

AMERICAN CIVIL-MILITARY RELATIONS AND THE USE OF FORCE

Peter D. Feaver and Christopher Gelpi

PRINCETON UNIVERSITY PRESS

PRINCETON AND OXFORD

PUBLISHED BY PRINCETON UNIVERSITY PRESS, 41 WILLIAM STREET,
PRINCETON, NEW JERSEY 08540
IN THE UNITED KINGDOM: PRINCETON UNIVERSITY PRESS,
3 MARKET PLACE, WOODSTOCK OXFORDSHIRE OX20 1SY

LIBRARY OF CONGRESS CATALOGING-IN-PUBLICATION DATA

FEAVER, PETER.
CHOOSING YOUR BATTLES : AMERICAN CIVIL-MILITARY RELATIONS AND
THE USE OF FORCE /PETER D. FEAVER AND CHRISTOPHER GELPI.
P.   CM.
INCLUDES BIBLIOGRAPHICAL REFERENCES AND INDEX.
ISBN 0-691-11584-2 (ALK. PAPER)
1. CIVIL-MILITARY RELATIONS—UNITED STATES. 2. WAR AND EMERGENCY
POWERS—UNITED STATES. I. GELPI, CHRISTOPHER, 1966– II. TITLE.
JK330.F434   2004
322'.5'0973—dc21   2003043344

THIS BOOK HAS BEEN COMPOSED IN POSTSCRIPT SABON

PRINTED ON ACID-FREE PAPER. ∞

WWW.PUPRESS.PRINCETON.EDU

PRINTED IN THE UNITED STATES OF AMERICA

1   3   5   7   9   10   8   6   4   2

CONTENTS

FIGURES AND TABLES

Figures

Tables

PREFACE

THIS BOOK began as a series of papers commissioned for the Triangle Institute for Security Studies (TISS) Project on the Gap between the Military and American Society, as explained more comprehensively in Feaver and Kohn (2001b). The TISS project set out to provide systematic data on and analyses of a debate that has been prominent since the mid-1990s—whether inherent differences between the military and American society had grown into a troublesome gap that might compromise military effectiveness and civil-military cooperation. Of course there have and always will be differences between military and civilian institutions. But during the stormy tenure of the Clinton administration, many argued that those differences had so sharpened that they were affecting the way national security policy was made and implemented. The TISS project commissioned twenty-one different studies analyzing this issue from a variety of perspectives. Our task was to see whether there was such a gap on matters pertaining to the use of force and, if so, whether it mattered for the actual conduct of American foreign policy.

In this book we show that civil-military differences on the use of force are systematic and, at points, profound, and that these differences shape the behavior of the United States in important ways.

We were attracted to this topic for several reasons. First, it was precisely the kind of policy-relevant question on which good scholarship might make a contribution. There are many policy questions that leave academics out in the cold, and there are probably even more academic topics that have only marginal utility for policymakers. But the nexus of civil-military relations and the use of force brings the academic and policy worlds together. And as we brought this book to completion, the daily headlines on our topic—"Two Retired Generals Voice Doubts over Bush's Plan to Attack Iraq," "Be Cautious on Iraq, Say War Vets in Congress," and so on—convinced us that our argument could not be more timely.

Second, the project allowed us to blend our separate strengths and interests together in a way that would be better than anything we could do on our own. It is a cliché that coauthorship is meant to be coequals generating a product that is considerably superior to what the individuals would have produced on their own. In this case, at least, we are convinced this is true. We have enjoyed a felicitous collaboration matching our various skills and interests. We followed an alphabetical rule in listing authorship, and neither is the "lead author" in the traditional sense. The basic topic grew directly out of Feaver's prior work on civil-military relations theory, but we approached it in a way that lies more squarely in the tradition of Gelpi's prior work on American conflict behavior. Feaver could not have written this book without Gelpi; Gelpi would not have thought to write the book without Feaver.

Third, the project allowed us to bring together various questions, methods, and approaches that are rarely combined: civil-military topics, survey research, statistical analysis of conflict behavior, and hypotheses generated from the historical case study literature and the op-ed pages of the leading newspapers. We recognize that such a bouillabaisse may not be to everyone's personal taste. But we have tried to blend advanced methods and real world problems in a way that will appeal to the broadest possible audience.

We broke our TISS mandate down into two discrete subtopics: civilian versus military attitudes about the use of force generally (Feaver and Gelpi 1999a) and civilian versus military attitudes about casualties in particular (Feaver and Gelpi 1999b). We quickly discovered that the TISS data were so rich—and they led us on such fruitful excursions—that the papers could be expanded and then combined into a separate book. We have separately published earlier versions of some of our findings (Feaver and Gelpi 1999c, 2000; Gelpi and Feaver 2002), and through the public dissemination of the overall TISS study, we have presented portions of our argument in over sixty briefings to a wide spectrum of policy and academic audiences. Our findings have also been discussed and debated in scores of media reports over the past several years. We have benefited from every exchange, especially from the focused critiques and challenges, and this book supersedes the earlier versions of our arguments and represents our definitive statement on the topic.

Our basic argument has not changed substantially since we first released it in 1999, but we have refined it and, we believe, improved it considerably. We hope that people who found the earlier work unpersuasive will find this more so. And those who were already convinced, may nevertheless appreciate the more extensive and nuanced treatment we provide here.

Because of this long genesis and extensive public vetting, we cannot possibly thank all who improved this book with their comments. Richard H. Kohn, who co-directed the overall TISS project and provided extensive (and often trenchantly critical) feedback at every step of the way, deserves singular mention. Equally, Janet Newcity was indispensable—she secured the vital TISS data, her advice was instrumental in the construction of the casualty questions and scenarios, and she provided innumerable comments, suggestions, and critiques, especially regarding the survey analysis, that have greatly improved this work. At the risk of inadvertently omitting someone who aided and abetted our venture, we also want especially to credit Deborah Avant, Andrew Bacevich, Richard Betts, John Brehm, Risa Brooks, Cori Dauber, Hein Goemans, Joseph Grieco, Paul Gronke, John Hillen, Ole Holsti, Bruce Jentleson, Robert Keohane, Eric Larson, Sean Lynn-Jones, Charles Moskos, Dan Reiter, Tom Ricks, Glenn Snyder, and Allan Stam. We also thank the anonymous reviewers for Princeton University Press, the *American Political Science Review*, and *International Security*. And of course we thank the entire team, authors and advisors, who put together the original TISS study and served as regular sounding boards and sources of inspiration.

We were ably assisted by an extraordinary group of research assistants who logged countless hours on our behalf, especially Erin Abrams, Lindsay Cohn, and Christine Young. We also thank Philip Demske, William Grimsley, and Andrew McKinley. Several classes of Duke students gave comments as well, and we thank you for affording us the privilege of learning with and from you. We thank William Bianco for sharing with us his data on veterans in the political elite, and we credit him for helping us solve the thorny measurement problem that enabled us to do a time-series analysis of the influence of civil-military variables over time.

We thank the team at Princeton University Press who guided us to the finish line: Chuck Myers, Kevin McInturff, Elizabeth Gilbert, and Sara Lerner. We thank Anne-Marie Boyd for preparing the index.

An earlier version of chapter 3 was published in the *American Political Science Review* as "Speak Softly and Carry a Big Stick? Veterans in the Political Elite and the American Use of Force." We thank Cambridge University Press for granting us copyright release to publish it in revised form here. A small portion of chapter 1 is adapted from *Soldiers and Civilians: The Civil-Military Gap and American National Security*. We are grateful to the Belfer Center for Science and International Affairs for permission to publish it in revised form here.

Finally, we thank our families, who let this become more than just a work project. Karen, Samuel, and Ellie—Janet, Mitchell, and Grace—you are our sweetest inspiration and we dedicate the book to you. May our earnestness inspire you to read it someday!

CHOOSING YOUR BATTLES

Chapter One

INTRODUCTION

FOR MONTHS after the September 11th terrorist attacks in 2001, a vigorous debate raged within the Bush administration: should the war on terrorism be expanded to go after well-known state sponsors of terrorism, especially Saddam Hussein's regime in Iraq? By the summer of 2002 the internal debate had spilled out onto the front pages of the major newspapers, culminating in a historic congressional debate and vote in favor of the Joint Resolution to Authorize the Use of United States Armed Forces against Iraq.

The public debate was lively and wide-ranging, but many commentators focused on one curious feature: how the principals in the debate tended to fall into two camps, one military and the other civilian. Within the administration, the strongest proponents of going to war with Iraq were the civilians, especially those who had never served in the military: Vice President Dick Cheney, Deputy Secretary of Defense Paul Wolfowitz, and chairman of the Defense Policy Board Richard Perle; they argued that creative uses of special forces and limited strikes could topple the Hussein regime and eliminate Iraq's weapons of mass destruction (WMD). At the same time, the strongest opponents of going to war were the senior military leaders and the most prominent veteran, former chairman of the Joint Chiefs and current secretary of state Colin Powell; they considered the innovative war plans too risky, while the more prudent military option of a massive buildup to a second Desert Storm was too costly. Accordingly, they argued, diplomacy and deterrence were the best way to deal with Iraq's WMD threat. Outside the administration, the pattern seemed to replicate itself. Some of the staunchest critics were retired senior military officers, and for a while the leading congressional critics included some of the most decorated war veterans in office. Of course there were prominent exceptions; for instance, Senator John McCain, the former Vietnam War POW, was a vocal hawk, whereas the late Senator Paul Wellstone, a well-known nonveteran liberal, was a prominent critic, but the pattern was too pronounced to ignore (Dewar 2002; Kiely 2002; McGregor 2002). In the words of retired four-star general Anthony Zinni, "It's pretty interesting that all the generals see it the same way and all the others who have never fired a shot and are hot to go to war see it another way" (Salinero 2002).

This marked civil-military subtext was matched by another at work in the Iraq debate: would the American public be willing to pay the human costs of a war against Iraq, or would support collapse when body bags showed up on CNN? Opponents of the war, military or otherwise, emphasized that Hussein could be expected to do everything possible to make a war bloody for Americans. Although polls showed consistent and fairly strong support among the general public for war, the support eroded somewhat when pollsters talked about "thousands of U.S. casualties" (see figure 6.2). Even without analyzing specific polls, some pundits were convinced that the body-bag syndrome would sink a war in Iraq. As one retired Marine officer worried aloud, "How long will public support last when hundreds, possibly thousands, of body bags start arriving home? Desert Storm and Afghanistan make war look so easy, with so few casualties. When support at home wanes, how will you turn back the clock?" (Raspberry 2002).

This book argues that the Iraq debate is not exceptional. On the contrary, the debate's civil-military and casualty sensitivity subtexts fit a pattern. The pattern is evident in systematic surveys of civilian and military opinion, shows up in case studies of decision making on the use of force since World War II, and shaped American foreign policy in both the nineteenth and twentieth centuries.

Do civilians and the military in the United States differ in their attitudes about when and how force should be used? Do they differ about the appropriate human costs that the use of force should entail? And do these attitudes, however differentiated, affect the propensity of the United States to use force in international disputes? We answer yes to all three questions, and demonstrate this with original survey data as well as with systematic analysis of the historical record of U.S. involvement in foreign disputes since 1816.

Civil-Military Gaps and the Use of Force

The debate over Iraq recalls the civil-military turmoil of the 1990s. In his autobiography, General Colin Powell relates his difficulty in dealing with the academic and "nonmilitary" style of the Clinton foreign policy team. He describes his patient efforts early in President Bill Clinton's first term to instruct civilian leaders on when and how to use force. During one such session, Madeleine Albright, then ambassador to the UN and later secretary of state, asked General Powell in frustration, "What is the point of having this superb military that you're always talking about if we can't use it?" Powell reports that he thought he "would have an aneurysm.

American GIs were not toy soldiers to be moved around on some sort of global game board" (Powell 1995, 576–77).

The Powell-Albright exchange cannot be dismissed as merely a contretemps between two powerful and idiosyncratic personalities. Nearly every post–cold war use of U.S. military force was conducted against the backdrop of some sort of civil-military dispute, and these disputes in broad brush seemed to conform to the Powell-Albright pattern: civilian leaders seemed more willing than military leaders to deploy the military in Bosnia, Somalia, Haiti, Rwanda, Kosovo, and so on (Desch 1999; Feaver 2003). Nor is this simply an artifact of partisanship, with a Democratic administration flummoxed by a Republican-leaning senior military. During the debate over Iraq, Senator Trent Lott, then the Republican leader in the Senate, was asked about the apparent hesitation on the part of the Joint Chiefs of Staff to embrace the Iraqi mission; Lott averred that the chiefs would end up backing the Bush administration in a war, but then went on to express his frustration in Albrightesque terms: "If the military people don't want to fight, what is their role? Do they want to be people that clean up after natural disasters?" (Gertz and Scarborough 2002). Something deeper than personalities or partisanship is at issue—a basic civil-military divide on how force should be integrated into American foreign policy.

It is conventional wisdom that military experience colors people's attitudes about America's role in the world. The scholarly literature on civil-military relations argues that there are important differences of opinion between civilian and military leaders (Huntington 1957; Betts 1991; Holsti 1999; Feaver and Kohn 2001b; Kohn 2002; Feaver 2003). At the colloquial level of the media pundit, the insight seems obvious. Of course we should expect civilian and military leaders to approach foreign policy and the use of force differently (Bamford 2002; Kessler 2002c; Van Deerlin 2002). There is even a popular slur—chicken hawk—directed at one of the apparently persistent features of American politics: non-veterans who are gung-ho on the use of force (Cohen 2002a; Kelly 2002). To be sure, exceptions abound, with some prominent civilian politicians showing reluctance and some prominent military officers showing a greater willingness in a given case (Avant 1996/97). At the most senior policymaking levels, the civil-military distinction is blurry and only awkwardly fits the neat categories of classical civil-military relations theory (Roman and Tarr 2001). Nevertheless, reports persist that post–cold war civil-military relations in the United States are characterized by repeated clashes between promiscuous civilians and reluctant warriors (Mandelbaum 1996; Weigley 2001). Even or perhaps especially in the post-September 11th world, many of the most important debates in American foreign policy—how to conduct the war in Afghanistan, whether to attack Iraq, or how to attack

Iraq—seem to crystallize along broadly defined civil-military lines (Dowd 2002; Kessler 2002a,b; Landay 2002; Marquis 2002; Milbank 2002a,b; Ricks 2002a,b; Webb 2002).

At some level, this makes common sense. Like any other profession, the military immerses its members in a set of beliefs, traditions, and experiences that those outside the institution do not share. Many of these relate to the military's most central mission: fighting and winning wars. Lawyers undoubtedly differ from the general public in terms of their attitudes toward the legal system. Academics surely have distinct views regarding universities. But in the case of civil-military relations, it is important to know what those gaps are and whether even understandable gaps have an impact on U.S. foreign policy.

This book is a follow-on project to a larger study of the so-called culture gap between civilians and the military in the United States and what that gap might mean for national security (Feaver and Kohn, 2001a; b). The earlier study responded to concerns that a gap was emerging between the military institution and civilian society that was harmful for military effectiveness and civil-military cooperation; it concluded that as the twenty-first century began, the gap between the military and society in values, attitudes, opinions, and perspectives presented no compelling need to act to avert an immediate emergency. However, there were problems that, if left unaddressed, would over time undermine civil-military cooperation and hamper military effectiveness. The earlier study identified the interface between differing civilian and military worldviews and the actual use of force as a priority for research—hence the need for the separate, sustained, and systematic analysis of the issue presented in this book.

In a similar way, the "casualty phobia" question raised by the Iraq case—does the U.S. public have the stomach for war or is it a paper tiger?—was only the continuation of a longer debate that has dominated U.S. post–cold war foreign policy. Certainly the last three tyrants to directly challenge the United States—Saddam Hussein in 1991, Slobodan Milosevic in 1999, and Osama bin Laden in 2001—all believed that the United States could be successfully defied. The key to each of their military strategies was not outright defeat of the U.S. military on the battlefield, a task made hopeless by the United States' unmatched technical prowess. Rather, the key was to defeat the U.S. will, by raising the costs of war beyond what the American public would be willing to pay—something that each of the challengers thought was within his grasp. As one Iraqi general captured during the Gulf War told U.S. intelligence officers, "Saddam Hussein, the man is a gambler. He was certain that you would not attack, and if you did, it would only be by air. He kept telling the Iraqi people that airpower had never won a war in the history of warfare and that Americans would never have the nerve to engage the Iraqi army on the ground. I remember him saying that Americans would not be able to stand the loss of even hundreds of soldiers, that Iraqis were prepared to sacrifice thousands" (Gordon and Trainor 1995). Similarly, in 1999, Slobodan Milosevic referred to the U.S.-led NATO force's reluctance to take casualties in Kosovo when he told German foreign minister Joschka Fisher, "I can stand death—lots of it—but you can't" (Daalder and O'Hanlon 2000). And bin Laden made a similar calculation in 1998 when he told a reporter, "America is a paper tiger that runs in defeat after a few blows" (Strobel 2001). The disastrous Ranger raid in Mogadishu in 1993 seemed to confirm this basic American weakness: if you kill enough Americans, they will go home.

Pundits recognized that September 11th may have changed the stakes for the American public, but they still worried that a new war with Iraq might founder on this same body-bag syndrome. After all, the American public might have been willing to pay a huge price to wipe out the perpetrators, Al Qaeda and the Taliban in Afghanistan, but in fact no such price was needed. Once again the Cassandras in the arm-chair strategist community were proved wrong, and after a year of heavy action the U.S. military had suffered only fifty-three casualties in the Afghan war. The real question of how the public would react if casualties ever did start to mount was left begging, even while September 11th brought home the priority of national security. And although the question was usually left hanging, at least since Vietnam the conventional wisdom has supplied only one answer: the American public only wants war on the cheap and will not accept even moderate levels of U.S. casualties.

The Basic Argument

In this book we show that the conventional wisdom about civil-military relations and the use of force is right in some respects and wrong in others. We present evidence to show that civilians and the military do differ in systematic ways in their attitudes concerning whether and how to use force and in their professed willingness to bear the human costs of war. Moreover, these different opinions seem to have had a profound effect on the propensity of the United States to initiate the use of force for most of its history, from 1816 to 1992.

Compared with mid-career active duty military officers, civilian elites who have no military experience are somewhat more interventionist with regard to the range of issues over which they will support the use of force by the United States. Military officer respondents report what may be called a "realpolitik" approach to the issue, one that reserves the use of force for interstate issues that represent a substantial threat to national security such as control of territory, the maintenance of geostrategic access and position, and the defense of allies. Civilian elites who have no military experience are somewhat more likely than military officers to report an "interventionist" opinion, advocating foreign policy goals that do not fit within the realpolitik interstate security paradigm, including responses to human rights abuses and the internal collapse of governance in other countries, or the desire to alter a state's domestic regime. Thus interventionists will generally have a wider set of issues across which they will support the use of force, while realpolitik thinkers will only support force over a narrower range of issues. In other words, civilian and military views converge somewhat when considering potential realpolitik uses of force but diverge more sharply when considering potential interventionist uses of force. Veterans in the civilian elite give responses that track more closely with active duty military officers than with nonveterans in the civilian elite.

At the same time, however, nonveteran civilians express a greater willingness to place constraints on the manner in which force is used, whereas the military respondents are more likely to endorse a position that has come to be known as the Powell Doctrine of overwhelming force (Stevenson 1996; Dauber 1998). The doctrine calls for using force only in circumstances where the political will is present to use force essentially without restrictions, or with only very broad restrictions such as no use of nuclear weapons. Again veterans in the civilian elite give responses that track more closely with active duty military officers than with nonveterans in the civilian elite.

These opinion differences are not dramatically large and to some extent they merely confirm the expectations of the case study literature that has examined civilian and military attitudes during cold war uses of force. Nevertheless, confirming this pattern with more systematic opinion data sets the stage for linking the opinion gap to actual foreign policy behavior.

The record of how the United States has engaged the world from 1816 to 1992 matches to a remarkable degree the pattern one would expect if one extrapolated directly from opinion to behavior. Since veteran opinion corresponds with military opinion, we can use veterans' presence in the political elite as a proxy for measuring the civil-military gap over time. Relying on a composite measure of military experience across the executive and legislative branches of government, we correlate these data with a yearly database on U.S. relations with other countries around the world from 1816 to 1992. Specifically, we identify whether the United States initiated the use of force, called a militarized interstate dispute (MID), against each possible target country for every year, called a dyad-year.[1] We

---

[1] The method is explained in greater detail in chapter 3 and in Bennett and Stam (2000). For a dispute to qualify as a MID, the initiating state must use military force, threaten to

find that as the percentage of veterans serving in the executive branch and the legislature increases, the probability that the United States will initiate militarized disputes declines by nearly 90 percent. At the same time, however, once an MID has been initiated, the higher the proportion of veterans in the government, the greater the level of force the United States will use in the dispute.

With regard to the critical issue of casualty sensitivity, our findings are just as striking: the belief, widely accepted by policymakers, civilian elites, and military officers, that the U.S. public is especially casualty phobic (meaning that public support for a mission will evaporate at the first sign of casualties) is a myth. Our survey indicates that the public will accept casualties if they are necessary to accomplish a declared mission, a finding consistent with other research that suggests the public will support casualties if the mission is being actively pushed by the nation's leadership (Larson 1996; Kull and Destler 1999). On realpolitik missions such as the defense of South Korea and Taiwan, there is a broad consensus that these goals are worthy priorities for U.S. foreign policy and worth the loss of substantial American lives, at least on the order of another Desert Storm (which had 383 combat deaths). No such consensus exists, however, with regard to interventionist missions such as nation building in Congo or protection against genocide in Kosovo, precisely the missions that dominated American foreign policymaking in the decade between the 1991 Gulf War and the terrorist attacks of September 11, 2001. Here there is confusion over what the American public really thinks, and important divisions emerge between civilian elites who are influencing policy, on the one hand, and military elites who are implementing policy, on the other.

Casualty sensitivity appears to be a function of what might be called rational calculations. People who think the national interest is not engaged by certain missions do not support casualties in those missions. People who think that force is not very effective have a lower acceptance for casualties across the board. Yet even when these "rational effects" are accounted for, the military showed a significantly lower tolerance for casualties than its civilian counterparts on interventionist missions. Moreover, this effect remains prominent despite the disproportionately low number of women in the military relative both to the civilian elite and to the mass public. As a group, women offer substantially lower numbers for "acceptable casualties." Thus the gap between male military officers

---

use force, or move its military forces so as to communicate a threat. Thus the U.S. initiation of hostilities with Spain in the Spanish-American War is an example of one MID for the year 1898. By contrast, in 1897 the United States did not initiate any MIDs with any other country. From 1816 to 1992, there are 8,780 dyad-years representing the universe of U.S. relations with foreign states. Over the same period, the United States was involved in 243 MIDs, of which it initiated only 111.

and their civilian male counterparts is even larger than is first apparent. Within the military we find that attitudes on casualties appear to be associated with both age and service. Most important, we find that younger officers and those in the Marine Corps and Air Force are the most willing to tolerate casualties in nontraditional missions. Since these officers are the most likely members of our sample to see combat in such missions, this result undermines the claim that military casualty sensitivity is a function of self-preservation.

Scope and Approach

This book operates at the intersection of a variety of different literatures. It is, first and foremost, a book about civil-military relations and the use of force. Scholars have long recognized that civil-military relations are partly an end to themselves and partly a means to other ends (Feaver 1996; 1999). Civil-military relations are an end to themselves because one of the defining features of a democracy is civilian control of the military. The vast majority of the literature on U.S. civil-military relations (or indeed, civil-military relations elsewhere) addresses the problem of maintaining civilian control, regardless of what civilian control might mean for other desiderata.[2] As Samuel Huntington (1957) argued, however, civil-military relations are also a means to other ends, most importantly the security of a nation from external threat and internal subversion. Huntington claimed that some patterns of civilian control would be disastrous for a nation's defense because they would undermine military effectiveness (1957, 96–97), but remarkably few scholars have taken up this line of analysis.[3] The one relatively rich area of research using civil-military relations as an explanatory variable concerns decisions for the use of force. The existing literature here is either theoretical or historical case study.[4] Our contribution lies not on the theoretical end, nor in adding

[2] This is especially true of the work that is part of the recent renaissance in U.S. civil-military relations research: Weigley (1993); Kohn (1994, 2002); Avant (1994); Desch (1999); and Feaver (2003).

[3] The only works looking systematically at how different patterns of civil-military relations affect military effectiveness are Millett and Murray (1988), Biddle and Zirkle (1996), and Brooks (2000).

[4] The classics of the theoretical literature include Vagts (1937), L. Smith (1951), Huntington (1957), Janowitz (1960), and Finer (1962); for a more recent theoretically oriented analysis see Feaver (2003). The general empirical literature covers a wide range of cases, but focuses on great power behavior: J. Snyder (1984), Van Evera (1984), Posen (1984), Lee (1991), Sagan (1994), and Cohen (2001, 2002a). The most important works focusing on U.S. civil-military relations and the use of force include Betts (1991), Petraeus (1987, 1989), Weigley (1993, 2001), Gacek (1994), Kohn (1994), and Weigley (2001).

more detail to an already rich case study literature, but rather in bringing large-*n* analysis (including surveys of civilian and military groups and comprehensive datasets of U.S. conflict behavior) to bear on a topic that has hitherto only been addressed with deductive or case study analysis.

The second major literature our book engages concerns the determinants of the use of force more generally. The literature here is large, mostly looking at the role of power politics variables. Over the past four decades, many volumes have been written about the impact of systemic variables such as the distribution of military capabilities or alliance ties.[5] In addition, Thomas Schelling's (1960, 1966) tremendous impact on the field led to a burgeoning literature on crisis-bargaining strategies and crisis escalation.[6] In recent years, scholars of international conflict began to shift their attention to the impact of aggregate unit-level variables such as regime type—most notably in the literature on the so-called democratic peace.[7] Within this literature, domestic political considerations, such as the link to elections and the link to partisan politics, have received by far the most attention.[8]

Despite the many studies and the great progress that has been made in understanding the sources of militarized conflict, a number of substantial lacunae remain in this literature. As we discuss below, numerous studies have documented variations in both elite and mass opinions about the use of force and military operations. But these changes in opinions have not heretofore been connected to actual changes in international military behavior. We hope our linkage of the literature on the civil-military gap to the quantitative literature on militarized disputes will open a new avenue into the study of international conflict. At the very least, our work incorporates a new level of analysis and a new set of arguments into the study of militarized disputes.

The third literature our book engages concerns U.S. public opinion and foreign policy, especially concerning the use of force. Again the literature

---

[5] The literature is much too extensive to recite here, but the ideas were rooted in Morgenthau (1985), Waltz (1958, 1979), and Blainey (1973), among others. A few examples of the evolution of quantitative work in these areas are Singer, Bremer, and Stuckey (1972), Organski and Kugler (1980), Bueno de Mesquita (1981), Huth, Gelpi, and Bennett (1993), and Mansfield (1994).

[6] Once again, the literature here is very extensive, but some of the prominent works are Schelling (1960, 1966), George and Smoke (1974), Snyder and Diesing (1977), Mearsheimer (1983), Axelrod (1984), Huth (1988), Leng (1993), and Pape (1996).

[7] See, for example, Doyle (1986), Maoz and Russett (1993), Ray (1995), Rousseau et al. (1996), and Maoz (1997).

[8] See, for example, Ostrom and Job (1986), Russett (1990), Gowa (1999), Gaubatz (1999), Goemans (2000), and all the articles by Bueno de Mesquita et al. (1981, 1992, 1995, 1999, 2000a, b, and 2002). There is also an extensive literature on internal unrest and the diversionary use of force, but like the democratic peace literature, these studies focus on highly aggregated unit level data. For a review of this literature, see Levy (1989).

is vast, although it tends to specialize either in elite or mass opinion but not both at the same time.[9] Our contribution is partly in providing more extensive analysis of new data that have been only summarily analyzed elsewhere.[10] We are the first to analyze in any fashion the data presented in chapters 4 and 5.[11] Moreover, this book integrates survey responses across mass and elite samples, and across civilian, military, and veteran samples, and then explicitly links opinion data to behavioral data. No other study of public opinion and the use of force approaches the topic in this fashion.

Throughout the book, we use a two-stage approach. First, we analyze the causal logic underlying competing claims in the public debate and deduce a set of testable hypotheses therefrom. One of the most striking features of public discussions about U.S. civil-military relations is the large number of contradictory claims and hypotheses advanced. We impose some analytical order onto the cacophony, identify the basis for each set of claims, and along the way, we build a logical model of how civilian and military opinions in theory might affect the use of force. Second, we test the hypotheses against appropriate data. Some of the claims in the literature are inherently untestable and others may be testable in principle but the data for doing so do not yet exist in a usable form. A major contribution of this book, however, is that it makes use of new data to provide a more systematic empirical evaluation than hitherto existed. We test as many of the competing claims as we can, therefore, and in the concluding chapter identify where future research and analysis could profitably be directed to advance the understanding of these issues.

This study is focused on the United States, looking at civilian and military opinions there and how those opinions affect U.S. uses of force. Obviously, our findings have implications for other countries, not only for how they might interact with the United States but more profoundly for how similar dynamics may be at work in their own civil-military policymaking milieu. But we note these implications in passing, and since we have only U.S. data, we can only speculate about how applicable our analysis might be to other countries.

---

[9] See J. Mueller (1973, 1994), Jentleson (1992), Lian and Oneal (1993), Oneal and Bryan (1995), Peffley, Langley, and Goidel (1995), Holsti (1996), Jentleson (1998), and Sobel (2001). There are important exceptions that do explicitly compare elite and mass attitudes but these do not consider the added dimension of civilian versus military. See Wittkopf (1990); Kull and Destler (1999); Reilly (1999).

[10] Some analyses of these data have been reported in Holsti (2001), Davis (2001), Gronke and Feaver (2001). An overall summary of the project that generated these data is found in Feaver and Kohn (2001b).

[11] Early results of our analysis were presented at public conferences in Feaver and Gelpi (1999a,b) and published in Feaver and Gelpi (1999c).

This book also addresses the effect of the civil-military gap on the use of force. Our purpose is to evaluate whether or not, and how, civil-military issues shape the use of force. Civil-military considerations are only one set of issues related to the use of force and may not even be the primary ones. We will control for factors that we know affect the use of force, but in order to isolate the effects of civil-military variables we may have to bracket other issues that we know are important.

Perhaps the chief consequence of this focus is that we adopt a decision theoretic approach instead of a game theoretic approach; that is, we look at U.S. uses of force as if they were a decision problem for U.S. policymakers, not a result of strategic interaction between the United States and foreign competitors. Of course, U.S. decision makers are not deciding whether to use force in a vacuum. They are responding to or anticipating challenges in the international system, and those challenges are coming from states who are themselves anticipating and responding to actions by the United States. It is even possible that these external actors may be factoring into their strategic calculus estimates of U.S. civil-military relations and how those civil-military issues affect the way the United States uses force as a tool of statecraft. For instance, if conditions make civilian leaders more willing to use force, then foreign states might compensate by being more cautious and appeasing the United States. If this effect were strong, we might actually observe a reduction in the American use of force, but this would be due to an increased propensity on the part of the United States to use force.[12] In the jargon of political science, by treating our problem as if it is a decision theory problem when it may be a game theory problem, we introduce the potential for selection effects that might lead us to over- or underestimate the importance of the factors we are studying.[13] When discussing our research design in chapter 3, we explain the steps we have taken to address this issue.

The advantage of the approach we are taking is that it best captures the intermediate stages along the causal path from civil-military issues to

---

[12] The opposite logic likewise holds. If the configuration of civil-military relations makes the United States more cautious about using force, opponents might seize on this and press their advantage, ultimately provoking the United States into initiating military force despite its greater reluctance to do so.

[13] If such a selection mechanism were operating, it would likely not be due to other actors making judgments about U.S. civil-military relations. Except in the most extreme cases—possibly the more dramatic episodes in Clinton's stormy relationship with the military—it is doubtful that American civil-military dynamics reach the level of salience needed to be a major factor in other leaders' strategic calculi. It is possible, however, that other actors are responding to an observable implication of our civil-military dynamic, namely, the fact that some leaders are more interventionist than others. As we discuss in the text, we cannot rule this possibility out, but omitting it from our analysis, which we do, has the effect of biasing our analyses against finding the civil-military effect we uncover in chapter 3.

the use of force. We would not be able to include all of these beginning and intermediate steps postulated as important by the literature if we also tried to include the reactions of other states in our model. A fully specified model would be intractable, which may be one reason why analysts who do capture the interstate strategic interaction have opted for relatively impoverished civil-military dynamics (Bueno de Mesquita and Lalman 1992; Bueno de Mesquita, Siverson, and Woller, 1992; Bueno de Mesquita and Siverson 1995). Better to bracket off strategic interactions with other states than to bracket off civil-military issues of direct interest to our study. Our approach therefore makes best use of the new data the Triangle Institute for Security Studies (TISS) examination of the gap has generated, specifically the survey data on civilian and military attitudes to military missions and to the human costs likely to be associated with those missions.[14]

Framed this way, the issue is how civil-military relations affect decisions on the use of force. The use of force can be disaggregated into two separate decisions: the decision whether to use force and the decision on the amount of force to use. As we discuss in more detail in chapter 2, these decisions are logically linked. A positive decision to escalate from diplomatic negotiations to the use of military force implies a decision on what kind of force to use. Likewise, constraints on the level or kinds of force used probably affect the prior decision of whether to use force in the first place. A decision maker may be willing to use force if and only if it is of a certain kind. Colin Powell famously advised that if the president is unwilling to use massive force, then it is better not to use force at all, implying one set of logical links between the two decisions (Powell 1992); the fact that he had to press civilians on this point implies that other decision makers held the opposite but (in theory) no less logical combination of preferences. Because of the linkage, it makes analytical sense to separate the decisions into discrete points so as to capture both independent and interdependent effects.

Decisions on the use of force are cost-benefit calculations. Do the benefits of bombing Serbia outweigh the costs of doing so? One way civil-military relations might affect the use of force is if civilians and the military differ on their estimations of these benefits and costs. The benefits involve estimations of the national interest and estimations of the utility of force, that is, whether force can achieve the goals implied by the mission. The costs involve not only crude financial costs—the dollars spent

---

[14] Note that since we lack survey data over time, we are limited in the kind of time-series analyses we can do. Where survey data is lacking, we are forced to use proxies of the "civil-military gap" to get a first-order approximation of the effects we are studying.

on jet fuel, exploded ordinance, military rations, and so on—but also more abstract costs like potential damage to other interests and values such as relations with allies. Importantly, there are also human costs: the dead and wounded that result from a use of force.

Estimations of the human costs of the use of force are what is meant by the term "casualty sensitivity" (Larson 1996). Some of the most important claims in the literature on U.S. civil-military relations are that civilians and the military are differentially casualty sensitive and that other changes in the gap contribute to changes in the sensitivity of civilians and the military to casualties. A related claim is that over time the American public has become so sensitive to casualties that it is essentially casualty phobic: even very low casualties are considered intolerable (Luttwak 1994). Casualty sensitivity feeds directly into both components of the force decision: if the casualties are thought to be prohibitive, decision makers may refuse to use force in the first place; and the effort to control casualties is an important, some have argued overwhelming, consideration on how force is used. Accordingly, in chapters 4 and 5, we focus on the casualty question, analyzing the only systematic data extant that compare civilian and military attitudes on casualty sensitivity.

The foregoing suggests yet another framing issue: how we are treating the role of public opinion in decisions to use force and what we mean by "public," that is, whose opinion is considered relevant.

We adopt several conventions that are now standard in the general literature on public opinion and the use of force (Holsti 1996, Kull and Destler 1999). First, we distinguish between three levels of civilians: the civilian policymakers, who are closeted in the corridors of power with military leaders deciding on national security issues and making the final determination on whether and how to use force; the elite public, sometimes called the attentive public or opinion leaders, the subset of the general population that is most involved in the public debate on these matters; and the largest group, the mass public, or more particularly the mass voting public, the *demos* that makes up the citizenry of the United States of America. A similar division can be found on the military side of the civil-military divide: senior Pentagon leaders as decision makers; the up-and-coming officers as "elite"; and the rest of the rank-and-file officers and enlisted as the military analog to the mass public. Of course, each group can be broken down further by gender, race, age, occupation or service specialty, and so on.

To make the analysis tractable, we must simplify this admittedly stylized model even further. As is standard in the literature, we assume that civilian policymakers are taking their cues from both the elite and the mass public (Kull and Destler 1999). Thus, since we have data on what decision makers do (that is, uses of force) but no systematic data on what decision makers think, we focus on elite and mass opinion as surrogates and influences on decision makers' opinions. Civilian policymakers are most attuned to elite public opinion, since this represents by definition the views of the people most active in public debates over policy and since the policymakers are themselves a part of the elite. But decision makers are also sensitive to what the mass voter thinks since that may determine whether they hold on to their positions of power. At the same time, policymakers seek to shape the opinion of elites who themselves seek to shape mass opinion so as to influence policymakers. As for the military, we will focus on "elite" opinion, the officer corps and especially those officers who have been identified by the military as likely candidates for promotion to higher ranks. This convention is standard in the civil-military relations literature ever since Huntington (1957) and is appropriate when the dependent variable of interest is policy outputs; officers have clear influence over policy while the influence of enlisted opinion is fairly negligible. And given the hierarchical nature of the military, this influence is greater the more senior the officer becomes (and the more likely the officer is to gain seniority).

Even distinctions as stylized as these are often lost in the current literature on civil-military relations and the use of force. Only rarely is "civilian" disaggregated into mass versus elite, and further breakdowns are even more rare. The infamous debate over whether African Americans were (or should have been) less willing to support the Persian Gulf War force because they were the ones supposedly more likely to die in combat is a prominent exception (Puddington 1991). There is also some debate over whether gender is a significant factor in foreign policy opinion (Holsti 1996, 166–68) Therefore we explore whether race and gender are important confounding factors in linking civil-military relations to the use of force. Likewise, Thomas Ricks (1997) claims that there is a generational shift in officer opinion, and so we look at age effects as well. On the whole, however, most of the public debate treats the players at very high levels of aggregation and we begin our discussion there; we add complexity to the discussion as logic and evidence demand.

A final word on the scope of this project. This book uses appropriate statistical techniques to analyze aggregate survey data and aggregate behavior data. We use these data to test hypotheses that have currency in the literature, either because the hypotheses derive from conclusions of other historical case study analyses of civil-military relations or because they are logical deductions from plausible models of how civil-military relations function in the United States. Our findings are remarkably robust in statistical terms, showing that, for instance, civil-military differences that are discernible in survey data are strongly correlated with the propensity of the United States to use force over time, even after controlling for the other factors that affect so complex a behavior as the initiation of force in an international conflict. What we have not done, however, is trace every step in the logic train posited by our argument through a series of intensive case studies of actual decisions to use force. Such an additional task would render an already formidable project intractable. We recognize that case studies exploring the causal mechanisms posited in our argument would be a fruitful next step for research, and in the conclusion we suggest ways of extending the work in this fashion. Yet since the existing literature is already strong in case study analysis but weak in the methods we employ here, it is appropriate to limit our scope as we have done. Our book, in other words, is neither the first nor the last word on the subject—but our findings are sufficiently conclusive and provocative to merit standing alone as the *next* word in an evolving debate.

The TISS Data

While the perception of basic civil-military differences of opinion on foreign policy and the use of force has wide currency, there are few systematic studies of those differences.[15] Systematic analysis is rare because systematic data on civilian and military opinions are rare. Members of the uniformed military are not regularly captured in the extensive polling done of the American public. Even polling done on American foreign policy and explicitly including foreign policy "leaders," such as the quadrennial American Public Opinion and Foreign Policy surveys by the Chicago Council on Foreign Relations, is of limited utility because military respondents are not included in the sample (Reilly 1999). The centerpiece of this book, therefore, is original survey data collected explicitly to explore the civil-military dimension. The survey data were collected in 1998 to 99 as part of a larger project sponsored by the Triangle Institute for Security Studies, a consortium of faculty at Duke University, the University of North Carolina at Chapel Hill, and North Carolina State University interested in national and international security.

To explore attitudes across a wide segment of civilian and military elites and the mass public, the TISS project completed a broad, in-depth survey

---

[15] Although there are few systematic studies of this perception, Ole Holsti's seminal 1999 article evaluating some twenty years of survey data from the Foreign Policy Leadership Project is an important exception. The larger TISS project on the civil-military gap, from which this book stems, is another. The following section is adapted from Feaver and Kohn

of some 4,891 respondents representing three key groups: the general public, influential civilian leaders, and up-and-coming military officers.[16] The survey sought responses to some 250 questions covering a range of issues: from the respondent's social and religious values to views on national security policy, and from military professionalism to the civil-military relationship itself. (The survey instrument is presented in Feaver and Kohn 2001b.) Between fall 1998 and spring 1999, the survey instrument was mailed to civilian leaders and administered to military officers.

To reach the group that we refer to as "civilian elite," we followed procedures developed by Ole Holsti and James Rosenau in the Foreign Policy Leadership Project (FPLP) (Holsti 1996, 129–90). To achieve a broad, comprehensive sample, eight subsamples were chosen to receive the survey. The eight subsamples were drawn from lists such as *Who's Who in America* and other directories of prominent Americans in the categories of "Clergy," "Women," "American Politics," "State Department," "Media," "Foreign Affairs," and "Labor." Our elite civilian sample generated 989 responses out of 3,435 requested.

We sought to reach a comparable group of military officers, which we refer to as "military elite" or "up-and-coming military officers." We defined this group as "officers whose promise for advancement has been recognized by assignment to attend in-residence the professional military education course appropriate for their rank." Thus the full military sample of 2,901 respondents (out of 5,889 surveys sent out) is not meant to be a sample of the entire military, which would include both officers and enlisted, nor even of the entire officer corps. The elite military sample is drawn just from among officers who are likely to emerge as leaders and are likely to be promoted. These officers come from the pool of those military leaders that shape the military profession in America and function as the custodians of military culture over time.

The military sample covers the active and reserve officer corps of the Army, Navy, Air Force, and Marines, at four stages of advancement.[17]

(2001b, 5–8) and is used with the permission of the copyright holder, the Belfer Center for Science and International Affairs.

[16] The methods employed in conducting these surveys as well as reports on subsample response and subsample characteristics are described in greater detail in Newcity (1999) and are available at the project website, *www.poli.duke.edu/civmil*.

[17] The TISS sample is somewhat skewed compared with the distribution among the four principal services of the officer corps as a whole. The TISS sample is slightly overrepresented with Navy (34 percent of the TISS sample versus 25 percent of the officer corps) and Army officers (39 percent of the TISS sample versus 35 percent of the officer corps), and underrepresented with Air Force officers (17 percent of the TISS sample versus 32 percent of the officer corps). This underrepresentation is due to the fact that the Air Force did not allow us to survey Air University students. Nor were we allowed to survey Marine Corps University

For the first category, that of officer candidates before commissioning, we administered the survey at the U.S. Military Academy, the Naval Academy, the Air Force Academy, and at a sample of Army and Navy ROTC units across the country. To reach the staff college level (officers roughly a decade into their careers), we surveyed students in the resident courses at the U.S. Army Command and General Staff College and the Naval War College (junior class). For the war college level (officers roughly seventeen years into their career), we surveyed students in the resident courses at the Army War College, the Naval War College, the National War College, and the Industrial College of the Armed Forces. For generals, the so-called baby flags, or officers at roughly the twenty-five-year mark who have been selected for promotion to brigadier general or rear admiral, we surveyed current attendees and the most recent graduates of the Capstone course at the National Defense University. Capstone is an orientation course of several weeks for new active duty flag officers and is conducted under the auspices of the National Defense University in Washington, D.C. We also surveyed Army, Navy, Air Force, and Marine reservists who were at comparable stages of their military careers and who took courses by correspondence from the Army War College, the Naval War College, and the National Defense University.

Our central focus, however, is on the distinction between active duty military and the civilian elite. We exclude the precommissioned sample from our analyses because they are quite distinct in terms of their development and stage of life from the civilian and military elites. We are interested in the impact of the civil-military gap on American foreign policy, and the link between precommissioned officers and American foreign policy decisions is rather oblique. Moreover, we have no civilian sample that represents a comparable group to the precommissioned officers. The tremendous differences in age, socialization, and so on would make a comparison between precommissioned officers and the civilian elite rather like one of apples and oranges. We do include the military reservists as a comparison group that stands somewhere between the civilian elite and the active duty military. We do not, however, theorize extensively about the impact of reservist status. As noted in the conclusion, one fruitful avenue for further research would be to extend the analysis in these other subsamples. Restricting the data this way means that we are analyzing a military

---

students; however, our sample of Marine officers corresponds to their numbers in the military establishment (9 percent of the TISS sample, 8 percent of the officer corps). Our Marine and Air Force samples were drawn, instead, from students attending either Army and Navy Staff and War Colleges or the National Defense University. We have no reason to believe that this feature of the TISS military sample influenced our findings.

sample of some 1,011 returned questionnaires out of 2,515 sent. Of the military respondents, 623 were active duty military and the remaining 388 were from the reserves.

A shortened version of the survey instrument was also administered by telephone to a representative random national sample of 1,001 members of the general public during September and October 1998. There was a 63 percent response rate for this survey. We refer to this sample as the "mass public" or "general public."

Organization of the Book

The book proceeds as follows. Chapter 2 explores civil-military differences on when and how force should be used. It begins with a brief review of the existing literature, which consists primarily of case studies of U.S. decision making during the cold war, and identifies areas of consensus and disagreement. The chapter uses the findings of the existing literature to inform analyses of the results of the TISS series of surveys. The chapter explores answers respondents gave to a series of foreign policy questions about the use of force—when it should be used, for what purposes, and in what fashion—and compares the TISS data with other survey data as appropriate. The analyses lead to the conclusion that civilian and military opinions on the use of force do differ in predictable ways, and that veteran opinions track more or less with military opinions. The analyses also lead to the conclusion that elite and mass opinions differ in predictable ways and that these differences show up in different responses by elite veterans and mass veterans.

Chapter 3 explores whether these survey results matter for the actual conduct of American foreign policy. We derive hypotheses concerning how different levels of veteran representation in the political elite (referring to the policymaking community, as distinct from the broader civilian elite public) might in theory affect the propensity of the United States to use force in international diplomacy. The chapter next details the results of a series of statistical tests of these hypotheses against data collected on all U.S. relations with foreign countries from 1816–1992. The findings are remarkably robust through different sensitivity tests and statistical controls. Consistent with the expectations of one strand of the civil-military relations literature, we find that the more veterans there are in the political elite, the less likely the United States is to initiate the use of force. At the same time, we also find that if the United States does initiate the use of force, the more veterans in the political elite, the greater the likelihood that the use of force will be on a large scale.

Chapter 4 evaluates a claim that has wide currency in conventional wisdom: that the American public is so casualty phobic that policymakers are constrained from putting U.S. forces at risk around the world. The chapter compares the responses of the civilian mass, civilian elite, and military elite samples in the TISS survey to a series of hypothetical questions asking how many casualties would be acceptable to achieve a range of different plausible military missions, from stabilizing a democratic government in Congo to defending Taiwan against invasion by China. The analyses show that there is little empirical support for the conventional wisdom that the general public is reflexively casualty phobic. On the contrary, the controversial missions that characterized the first post–cold war decade of American foreign policy—for example, intervening in civil wars—the public is considerably less casualty sensitive than either the civilian or the military elite. The conventional wisdom, based on a misreading of key events like Somalia and Vietnam, is mistaken. In reality, policymakers can count on sizable public support for military operations, provided that the leaders will carry them through to victory.

Chapter 5 explores the determinants of the civilian and military responses to the casualty question in greater detail. The TISS data permit the testing of various hypotheses for why there is a noticeable civil-military difference on the casualty question, that is, whether it is a result of other demographic differences between our civilian and military samples or whether it is a function of other attitudes the respondents hold on foreign policy. The data also permit the exploration of whether military casualty sensitivity is a function of rank, combat orientation, or even general service orientation of the respondent. Our results indicate that the civil-military gap regarding casualty sensitivity is not a simple spurious result of demographic or other factors. A substantial opinion gap exists even after we account for the impact of numerous demographic and attitudinal factors. Civilian and military attitudes reflect basic rational calculations about the costs each respondent is willing to see the United States pay to pursue what that respondent considers to be priority missions. Moreover, elite respondents' beliefs about the willingness of the American public to tolerate casualties were powerfully associated with their own aversion to casualties. Social contact with the military is also a powerful factor in explaining respondents' attitudes toward casualties; people who reported higher social contact with the military reported greater casualty sensitivity, and this factor appears to account for much of the difference between civilian and military groups. Within the military, casualty sensitivity is not a function of self-preservation or of careerism but rather appears to be related to doubts about the quality of political leadership and support undergirding the missions. Casualty phobia may well be a proverbial closed circle of logic: military officers express casualty shyness because they are taking cues from political leaders who express casualty shyness because they buy into the myth that the general public is casualty phobic—which it is not.

The book concludes with a summary of our findings and a discussion of the significance of our argument, both for the academic literature and for policymakers in government. We suggest that our findings raise interesting questions that constitute a rich research agenda for the field.

Chapter Two

THE CIVIL-MILITARY OPINION GAP

OVER THE USE OF FORCE

I T IS conventional wisdom that military experience colors people's attitudes about America's role in the world, as we noted in chapter 1. In this chapter, we use the TISS survey data of elite civilian and elite military opinion to explore the extent to which this conventional wisdom is correct. We focus specifically on civilian and military opinion on three broad foreign policy considerations. First, we assess the kinds of foreign policy goals that military and civilian elites believe are important for American foreign policy. Second, we examine the extent to which elite civilian and military respondents believe that military instruments are important for achieving those goals. And third, we investigate the extent to which respondents believe that the implementation of military missions should be influenced by political and diplomatic constraints.

We focus primarily on the civil-military gap at the elite level because we believe that civilian and military elites are most likely to be able to influence American foreign policy. In addition, the TISS survey provides a uniquely rich source of data for exploring these attitudes. Nevertheless, within the limits of available data we also examine whether the patterns of opinion we observe are restricted to elites or whether they are also reflected in the general population.

Our findings indicate that civilian and military elites differ significantly in terms of their foreign policy priorities and the extent to which they are willing to place constraints on the implementation of military operations. We find little civil-military gap, however, with regard to the importance of military tools to achieve various foreign policy goals. Interestingly, the civil-military opinion gap regarding the use of force appears to differ at the elite and mass levels.

We begin by describing the dimensions of foreign policy opinion that are central to the use of force. Second, we briefly review the literature on American civil-military relations with an eye toward developing expectations about how civilian and military opinion may vary across these dimensions. Third, we describe the methods used in collecting and analyzing our opinion data, with a focus on the way we operationalized the concepts of interest to our study. Fourth, we analyze civil-military differences in foreign policy opinions along the three central dimensions we identify in the first section. Fifth, we compare the elite findings with data collected in other (that is, non-TISS) surveys of mass public opinion. The chapter concludes with a brief summary of our major findings.

Dimensions of Opinion Regarding the Use of Force

There are three key dimensions to the decisions whether and how to use military force, and civilians and military might differ along any or all three: (1) foreign policy priorities, (2) the appropriateness and effectiveness of military force, and (3) the appropriateness of political constraints on the use of force. Although the range of possible variation is in principle infinite, most studies of opinion on American foreign policy cluster attitudes on these issues along several basic spectrums—left/right, hawk/dove, optimistic/pessimistic, and so on—and we adopt a similar approach.

First, individuals' preferences may vary in terms of the range of issues which they believe are important for American national security. Some may have a relatively restrictive set of issues that meet this criterion. Traditionally, conservative thinkers are likely to conceive of national security in terms of interstate issues that represent a substantial threat to sovereignty. These issues—such as control of territory, the maintenance of geostrategic access and position, and the defense of allies—represent what might be called the "realpolitik" bases of national security as they have been construed more or less for the past 350 years.

Others, however, may believe that American security interests extend to issues that do not fit within this inter-state security paradigm. Human rights abuses, the internal collapse of governance, or the alteration of a state's domestic regime are all issues that some may believe impinge upon American security interests. These issues may require intervention inside the boundaries of an allegedly sovereign state and may challenge the claims of sovereignty made by the ruling group within that state. We call this cluster of opinion "interventionist." It is important to note that individuals with interventionist preferences will generally also accept that military force should be used to address the issues preferred by the realpolitik thinkers. Thus interventionists will generally have a wider set of issues across which they will support the use of force, while realpolitik thinkers will only support force over a narrower range of issues.[1]

---

[1] The realpolitik versus interventionist typology represents a compromise. Earlier drafts of this study distinguished between traditional and nontraditional, terms that had broader intuitive appeal in the popular literature, perhaps, but which raised problematic and unintentional value judgments—after all, as more than one reviewer observed, the United States military has a long tradition of undertaking so-called nontraditional missions. Although

Second, regardless of what kinds of issues people believe are relevant to American security, they may differ in their beliefs about the appropriateness of military tools for addressing those issues. It would be quite possible, for example, for one to believe that the spread of democracy is an extremely important issue for American security, but also to believe that America's military can do little to achieve this goal. Thus we examine respondents' views about the appropriateness and effectiveness of using military tools to address both interventionist and realpolitik goals.

Third, independent of what kinds of issues people believe are important or the appropriateness of the military for addressing those issues, opinions may differ over *how* military force should be used. Although there is almost an infinite array of options for the use of force, it makes sense to simplify the "how" decision into a single continuum of restraint, ranging from thoroughly constrained (for example, pin-prick bombings, such as those used against Bosnian Serb positions before the summer of 1995) to thoroughly unconstrained (for example, the total ground, air, and sea war of World War II). Those on the "constrained" end of the spectrum tend to view force as a coercive bargaining tool for use in the negotiated resolution of disputes; those on the "unconstrained" end of this continuum tend to view military force as exercising a strategy for victory in a zero-sum confrontation.

The Civil-Military Opinion Gap over the Use of Force

The literature on elite opinions and foreign policy has long sought to examine preferences regarding the use of force (Wittkopf 1990; Peffley, Langley, and Goidel 1995; Holsti 1996). One of the central divisions

---

the terms "realpolitik" and "interventionist" are somewhat artificial, we believe that the audience can gain a working understanding of what we mean by them. In any case, as the analysis of the survey data shows, civilian and military elites draw such a dichotomy, regardless of how it is described. In his analyses of public opinion and foreign policy, Bruce Jentleson (1992, 1998) makes a further empirical distinction between interventions designed to alter the regimes of other states and those designed to prevent human rights abuses. We do not make this distinction in our conceptual framework for two reasons. First, our survey analyses did not reveal such a distinction in opinion at the elite level. In one of several sensitivity analyses, we grouped questions according to the principal policy objective typology outlined by Jentleson and conducted a cluster analysis. The results were fairly dispositive with an alpha of 0.78; in our survey elite opinion clustered around two dimensions, which we call realpolitik and interventionist, and not around the more differentiated three dimensions proposed by Jentleson. Second, our measures of conflict behavior used in chapter 3 cannot capture the distinction between a humanitarian and a state-building intervention, so the Jentleson typology, even if used in this chapter, would have to be collapsed in the next anyway.

among elites that may relate to the use of force is the distinction between civilian and military leadership (Huntington 1957; Janowitz 1960; Posen 1984; J. Snyder, 1984; Van Evera 1984; Betts 1991). In general, there have been two schools of thought regarding civilian and military opinions and the use of force. For many years, the traditional view held that militaries are susceptible to militarism, defined as an exaltation of the martial way of life and an excessive faith in military solutions to political problems. Militarism made militaries war-prone and therefore a threat to the polity they are supposed to protect (Vagts 1937; Ekirch 1956). In particular, militarism might lead military elites to have rather expansive foreign policy goals. American history is replete with concerns over the growth of militarism among military elites. Indeed, the framers of the Constitution worried about militarism and feared that the mere existence of a standing army might be a catalyst for involving the fledgling Republic in foreign conflicts. The belief that military influence would make the government more bellicose was one impetus behind the framers' decision to make civilian control of the military so central a feature of the Constitution and a point of emphasis in the early days of the Republic (Kohn 1975).

Despite this long-standing concern—or perhaps because of it—a second school of thought contends that militarism is not a substantial concern—at least not within the American military elite. The consensus in the literature on U.S. cold war and post–cold war civil-military relations is that civilian policymakers tends to have more expansive foreign policy goals and tend to have greater faith in military solutions to political problems.[2] The military, according to this view, tends to be more conservative in its estimation of what goals are important for American security. Moreover, these observers contend that military elites are more circumspect about the effectiveness of military tools for addressing problems that range beyond traditional missions of national security (Huntington 1957; Janowitz 1960; Betts 1991).[3] Case studies of cold war crises have found some

---

[2] The evidence on countries other than the United States is more ambiguous. On the one hand, there is some evidence that militaries in other countries are more bellicose; see, for example, Brecher (1996), or the literature on the cult of the offensive (J. Snyder 1984; Van Evera 1984), or recent analysis of the conflict in South Asia (Schofield 2000). On the other hand, there is also evidence supporting the opposite view; see Andreski (1980), Sagan (1986), and Maoz and Abdolali (1989).

[3] Huntington is not entirely consistent on this point, however. On the one hand, Huntington claims that the conservative military favors preparedness but rarely favors war—that the military officer is a reluctant warrior and only favors war when a victorious outcome can be a near certainty—whereas the liberal civilian favors an adventuresome foreign policy while restraining military preparedness (Huntington 1957, 69–70). On the other hand, Huntington appears to draw the opposite picture when he contrasts two views of peace and war. The first view is the desire for a sharp distinction between peace and war, the desire to put off the use of force as much as possible, and then to implement a massive use of force

evidence that civilian decision makers were more willing to use force than were the most senior military advisors, albeit with many exceptions and nuances (Petraeus 1987, 1989; Betts 1991).[4] This effect is likely to be more pronounced on so-called interventionist missions, assignments that would distract the military from its central mission of deterring attacks on the homeland and winning high-intensity wars over vital national interest, such as World War II. Civilians, by contrast, are more willing to see these other missions as appropriate uses of the military and so are willing to advocate the use of force to accomplish them. Thus the civil-military divide has grown more pronounced in the post–cold war era, leading to concern about the so-called reluctant warriors, military advisors who are actively resisting civilian-led initiatives to use force abroad (Weigley 1993; Kohn 1994; Avant 1996/97; Feaver 1998; Desch 1999; Rizer 2000).

Although these schools of thought differ in their expectations regarding the civil-military gap over foreign policy priorities and the effectiveness of military force, they have reached a fairly strong consensus regarding civilian and military differences over how to use force. The literature on U.S. civil-military relations theory and practice (Huntington 1957; Janowitz 1960; Halperin 1972; Petraeus 1987; Betts 1991; Gacek 1994) contends that while civilians may be more inclined than the military to use force in pursuit of less-than-vital national interests, they are only willing to use force in measured amounts. The classic exemplar of this view is Secretary of State Madeleine Albright's comment on *The News Hour with Jim Lehrer* television show (January 9, 2001): "[The use of force] doesn't have to be all or nothing. We should be able to use limited force in limited areas." The literature does not explore in any detail why civilians hold this preference, except to suggest that civilians are more sensitive to the political costs of war and especially to the human costs of war. Another possibility may be that civilians are more willing to "think outside the box," and propose unconventional uses of the military; certainly,

---

when you do. Observers familiar with American defense policy since 1990 would confidently code that as a military viewpoint, encapsulated in the Powell Doctrine. The opposite view, which permits the gradual application of force, measured for the case in hand, is clearly the civilian viewpoint espoused by Les Aspin in his famous debate with Powell, and owes much to the great civilian strategists of the 1950s (Kissinger, Schelling, Osgood, Kaufmann, and Huntington). But Huntington appears to code these views exactly oppositely. Huntington dismisses sharp distinctions and the massive use of force as the pre–World War II liberal view of war (Huntington 1957, 317). He later worries that the Vietnam debacle may have falsely invalidated the theories of limited war and so left the United States with unpalatable all-or-nothing choices. Indeed, one of the things Huntington worries about as threatening U.S. national security is precisely the rise of what later became known as the Powell Doctrine. See Goodpaster and Huntington (1977), 17–22.

[4] The empirical literature is largely confined to the U.S. case, although there is at least one study that has applied the argument to other countries (Lee 1991).

this was behind Deputy Secretary of Defense Paul Wolfowitz's frustration with the military options on Iraq presented to him in the summer of 2002 (O'Hanlon 2002).

The military is more reluctant to intervene with force in a given situation but, if compelled to do so, argues strenuously that the force should be overwhelming and decisive.[5] The military position is encapsulated in what has come to be known as the Powell Doctrine of overwhelming force (unattributed 1992; Stevenson 1996; Dauber 1998), which rejects the incremental use of force and instead calls for using force only in circumstances where the political will is present to use force essentially without restrictions. The Powell Doctrine explicitly links the decision whether to use force to the decision how to use force. If political leaders are unwilling to use force in the way the military recommends, then force should not be used. The story of the use of force during and after the cold war is a story of civil-military disagreements over the how question, with civilians seeking limited uses and gradual escalation and the military seeking fewer restrictions on how force is used (Betts 1991; Gacek 1994; Feaver 1995).

In sum, the older traditional view of military elites was that they tend to be more expansive in their foreign policy goals, tend to have greater faith in the importance of the military in achieving those goals, and tend to believe that the military should be left unconstrained in accomplishing those missions. More recent studies of American civil-military relations, however, suggest that civilian elites will have a broader foreign policy agenda and a greater faith in the ability of the military to achieve those goals. At the same time, civilian elites should also be more eager to put restrictions on the level of force used by the United States. In particular, civilian elites should show less support than military elites for the Powell Doctrine, which calls for the use of massive or decisive force and recommends delegating to the military sufficient autonomy to perform the mission with a minimum of political micromanagement.

---

[5] Arguably, this is the proper way to fit within our framework the "cult of the offensive" literature, which views the military as favoring the offensive for parochial organizational and bureaucratic reasons. The "cult of the offensive" is less a preference for going to war (that is, a preference on the "whether" dimension) and more a preference for how to fight if you are in a conflict (that is, offensive operations trump defensive ones). Of course, in the extreme (as in the "cult" claim), the belief that offensive operations will always win over defensive ones can lead states to initiate wars when they otherwise might not wish to. The cult of the offensive literature claims, for instance, that precisely this happened prior to World War I; Continental militaries, convinced that offensive operations would prevail on the battlefield, dictated the pace of crisis negotiations and forced civilians into a war they did not necessarily want. The cult of the offensive school largely derives from a particular reading of the Continental powers prior to World Wars I and II (Posen 1984; J. Snyder 1984; Van Evera 1984), although it has also been extended to analyses of U.S. and Soviet nuclear strategy (Sagan 1986).

Observing Elite Civilian and Military Opinion

We tested these expectations about elite civilian and military opinion using survey data collected by the Triangle Institute for Security Studies. This section contains a technical discussion of our methods; the next section reports the results of the analysis. As described in greater detail in the previous chapter, the TISS series of surveys was implemented between September 1998 and May 1999. The surveys targeted two distinct populations of respondents: American civilian elites and American military elites. A third survey conducted at the same time targeted the mass civilian public with a national telephone survey. Since that instrument was shorter, most of the relevant "use-of-force" questions were not asked. Thus our analysis here is limited to the elite samples, except where noted in the text. The civilian elite population was reached via a mail survey sent to a sample of *Who's Who in American Politics* as well as additional targeted subsamples. Military elites were reached either via mail or via distribution of the survey at military institutions.

To assess the gap between civilian and military elite opinion, we distinguish between fire levels of military status:

1. Elite civilians who have never served in the military (*civilian elite nonveterans*)

2. Elite civilians who report prior service in the military (*civilian elite veterans*)

3. Elite civilians currently enrolled in a professional military education program (*civilian elite PME*)

4. Officers currently active in the reserves or National Guard and taking correspondence or on-site courses at professional military education institutions (*elite reserve and guard*)

5. Officers currently on active duty taking courses at professional military education institutions (*elite active duty military*)

We began our analysis of the civil-military opinion gap with simple comparisons across the groups using histograms and cross-tabulations. These analyses give us the absolute difference of opinion across these five groups. Differences of opinion are important, of course, but there are many other ways in which our military sample could differ from the civilian sample, and some of these differences might be just as fundamental as or even more fundamental than any attitudinal differences we observe. For instance, there are more males and more highly educated individuals in the elite military sample than in the civilian elite sample (and, of course, more than in the general population as a whole). It is at least plausible that some civil-military attitudinal differences may be a function of these other demographic differences. To see whether civil-military differences persist (or emerge) once we have controlled for these demographic effects, we used multivariate regression and logit analysis.

Put another way, the absolute differences of opinion are important in determining the overall size of the civil-military opinion gap. Regression analysis, in contrast, allows us greater precision in assessing whether military experience is the *cause* of these differences of opinion or whether the civil-military gap is really a function of demographic differences between the military and civilian society. Of course, finding out that a particular difference of opinion between civilian and military elites is really a function of, say, the gender distribution of the military does not erase the actual gaps in opinion between those inside the military and those outside it; but it would indicate that those opinions were not a result of military experience per se, and it would suggest tailored policies for closing the gap (in our hypothetical example, if the civil-military difference is really a gender difference, then closing the civil-military gap will require involving more women in the military). Unfortunately, the research and sampling design of the larger TISS project does not allow a definitive answer to whether any civil-military differences are a function of socialization (that is, military experience changed the attitudes of respondents) or selection (that is, only people with a certain attitude profile are attracted to military service in the first place). At best, the data make suggestive indications of whether socialization or selection or both are at work, and, where appropriate, we point out those indications in the analyses below.

Attitudes about a complex concept like the use of force are not likely to be captured in a single question or two. Therefore we break down the use-of-force concept into several subsidiary components—in the jargon of political science, several different "dependent variables"—and then use a battery of questions from the TISS survey to capture as much of each underlying concept as possible. We used the following coding rules to operationalize our key dependent and independent variables.

Dependent Variable (1): Importance of Human Rights as a Foreign Policy Goal

Our first dependent variable captures the extent to which the respondent believes that the promotion of human rights around the globe is an important foreign policy priority for the United States. We rely on this measure as our principal indicator of respondents' support for interventionist foreign policy goals because of its prominence in public debates over the use of force after the cold war, especially concerning Kosovo, Somalia, and Rwanda.

Our scale measure is constructed as a mean of the respondents' support for questions about possible goals for American foreign policy: (1) "helping to improve the standard of living in less-developed countries"; (2) "combating world hunger"; (3) "fostering international cooperation to solve common problems such as food, inflation, and energy"; and (4) "promoting and defending human rights in other countries."[6] Note that by itself, this scale does not tap directly into attitudes about using the military to promote this interventionist agenda; for that concept, we use another scale, described below.

For each of these questions the respondents' answers were coded as follows: very important = 4, somewhat important = 3, no opinion = 2, not important = 1. We identify respondents' mean response as their level of support for the interventionist agenda of international human rights.

Dependent Variable (2): Importance of Realpolitik Goals

Our second dependent variable measures the extent to which respondents support what might be considered "traditional" geopolitical or realpolitik goals for American foreign policy. Once again, issues were selected on the basis of their prominence in American debates over intervention abroad. The scale is created from respondents' level of agreement with the following statements: (1) the United States should contain communism; (2) the United States should maintain superior military power worldwide; (3) there is considerable validity in the "domino theory"; (4) Russia is generally expansionist; (5) there is nothing wrong with using the CIA to undermine hostile governments; (6) the United States should take all steps to prevent aggression by any expansionist power; (7) any Chinese victory is a defeat for America's national interest; and (8) the emergence of China as a military power is a threat to the United States.[7]

---

[6] These items scaled together reasonably well (alpha = .71). Specific items from the questionnaire were worded as follows: Question 1: "Here is a list of possible foreign policy goals that the United States might have. Please indicate how much importance you think should be attached to each goal." q01a: "Helping to improve the standard of living in less-developed countries." q01c: "Combating world hunger." q01e: "Fostering international cooperation to solve common problems such as food, inflation, and energy." q01h: "Promoting and defending human rights in other countries."

[7] Specific question wording from the TISS survey questionnaire was as follows. Question 1: "Here is a list of possible foreign policy goals that the United States might have. Please indicate how much importance you think should be attached to each goal." q01f: "Containing communism." q01j: "Maintaining superior military power worldwide: (1) very important, (2) somewhat important, (3) not important, (4) no opinion." Question 2: "This question asks you to indicate your position on certain propositions that are sometimes described as lessons that the United States should have learned from past experiences abroad." q02a: "There is considerable validity in the 'domino theory' that when one nation falls to aggressor nations, others nearby will soon follow a similar path." q02c: "Russia is generally expansionist rather than defensive in its foreign policy goals." q02d: "There is nothing wrong with using the CIA to try to undermine hostile governments." q02e: "The U.S. should

For each question, responses were coded as follows: agree strongly = 5, agree somewhat = 4, no opinion = 3, disagree somewhat = 2, disagree strongly = 1. We identify the respondents' mean answer to these eight items as their level of concern for traditional realpolitik goals.

Dependent Variable (3): Role of Military Instruments in Foreign Policy

In addition to considering the extent to which civilian and military elites view different foreign policy issues as important, we must also capture the extent to which they believe that military tools are appropriate for coping with those issues—our third dependent variable. The TISS survey listed a variety of potential tasks for the military and asked respondents to "please indicate how important you consider each potential role for the military." To gauge respondents' attitudes regarding the appropriateness of military tools for interventionist missions, we analyze the importance they placed on the military's role in "address[ing] humanitarian needs abroad" and the importance of the military "as an instrument of foreign policy, even if that means engaging in operations other than war."[8]

With regard to realpolitik missions, we analyze the importance that respondents place on the military's ability "to fight and win our country's wars."[9] For each of these questions the respondents answers were coded as follows: very important = 4, somewhat important = 3, no opinion = 2, not important = 1. We also asked respondents to rate the effectiveness of military force relative to other foreign policy tools in coping with "the emergence of China as a great military power."[10] Respondents were asked to rank military tools as much more effective = 5, somewhat more effective = 4, equally effective = 3, somewhat less effective = 2, or much less effective = 1.[11]

---

take all steps including the use of force to prevent aggression by any expansionist power." q02g: "Any Chinese victory is a defeat for America's national interest." Question 3: "This question asks you to evaluate the seriousness of the following as threats to American national security." q03a: "The emergence of China as a great military power." Alpha = 0.71.

[8] Question 7: "The following are some possible uses of the military. Please indicate how important you consider each potential role for the military." q07a: "As an instrument of foreign policy, even if that means engaging in operations other than war." q07e: "To address humanitarian needs abroad."

[9] TISS survey questionnaire q07b: "To fight and win our country's wars."

[10] TISS survey questionnaire, question 4: "Reviewing some of the earlier list of possible threats to national security, how effective is the use of military tools compared to non-military tools for coping with them?" q04a: "The emergence of China as a great military power."

[11] "No opinion" responses were recoded as "equally effective."

Dependent Variable (4): Effectiveness of Military Force

The TISS survey allows for analysis of yet another closely related concept and our fourth dependent variable: civil-military attitudes on how effective military force is. This variable captures the extent to which respondents believe that military force is an effective tool in combating a variety of potential threats to national security. It explicitly does not seek to differentiate by mission, and instead seeks to determine whether respondents differ in their overall views regarding the effectiveness of force. Respondents were asked to compare the effectiveness of military and nonmilitary tools to address the following potential threats: (1) Chinese military power; (2) the proliferation of weapons of mass destruction; (3) the flow of immigrants and refugees to the United States; (4) international terrorism; (5) drug trafficking; (6) Islamic fundamentalism; and (7) attacks on computer networks. For each item the respondents could rank military tools as much more effective = 5, somewhat more effective = 4, equally effective = 3, somewhat less effective = 2, or much less effective = 1.[12]

Dependent Variable (5): Powell Doctrine

Finally, our fifth dependent variable compares elite civilian and military attitudes on how force should be used, specifically the appropriateness of what has come to be known as the Powell Doctrine. The TISS survey included questions concerning two key assertions of the Powell Doctrine: (1) military force should be used in pursuit of total victory; and (2) military force should be used quickly and massively rather than gradually. We code respondents' level of support for the Powell Doctrine as their mean level of support for these two statements.[13] As was the case with the realpolitik variable, responses were coded as follows: agree strongly = 5, agree somewhat = 4, no opinion = 3, disagree somewhat = 2, disagree strongly = 1.

---

[12] "No opinion" responses were recoded as "equally effective." The specific question wording from TISS survey questionnaire for questions q04a–q04g is as follows: q04a: "The emergence of China as a great military power." q04b: "The proliferation of weapons of mass destruction to less-developed countries." q04c: "Large number of immigrants and refugees coming to the U.S." q04d: "International terrorism." q04e: "International drug trafficking." q04f: "Expansion of Islamic fundamentalism." q04g: "Attacks on American computer networks." Scale for questions q04a–q04g: (1) Much more, (2) somewhat more, (3) equally, (4) somewhat less, (5) much less, (6) no opinion. Surprisingly, responses to these seven disparate items correlated very highly (alpha = 0.83)

[13] Specific question wording from TISS survey questionnaire: q02i: "Military force should be used only in pursuit of the goal of total victory." q02j: "Use of force in foreign interventions should be applied quickly and massively rather than by gradual escalation." The correlation between these two responses is 0.43.

Key Explanatory Variable: Military Status of Respondent. Military status is our central explanatory variable. As noted above, we are interested in whether elite respondents are in the military or not. However, we are further interested in knowing whether elite civilians had any military experience (elite veterans) or not (elite nonveterans); and, if not, whether the elite civilians were in the special subsample of civilians enrolled in one of the military graduate schools.[14] These categories range across a continuum of exposure to and participation in the military. Thus we will refer to a respondent's position among these categories as his or her military status.

Civilian Elite, Nonveterans. These respondents were drawn from our sample of the civilian elite and stated on their survey that they had never served on active duty in the military or in the military reserves. This group represents the elite respondents with the lowest level of direct exposure to and experience in the military.

Civilian Elite Veterans. These respondents were drawn from our sample of the civilian elite and stated on their survey that they had at one time served in the active duty military or the military reserves. We distinguish them from the nonmilitary civilian elite in order to determine whether previous military experience moderates the distance between civilian and military preferences on the use of force.

Civilian Elite, Professional Military Education (PME). These respondents were drawn from our military sample, but the respondents stated that they had never served in the active duty military or in the military reserves. These respondents came into our sample because they were civilian elites (often civil service employees from the State Department or the Pentagon) who had been selected to attend one of the professional military institutes, such as the National Defense University or the Naval War College. Once again, we distinguish these respondents from the nonmilitary civilian elite in order to determine whether exposure to military values and instruction serves to bridge the civil-military divide.

Elite Reserve and Guard. These respondents were drawn from our military sample and indicated that they were currently serving in the military reserves or National Guard. We distinguish reserves from active duty military in order to determine whether the higher level of exposure to civilian society and institutions that reservists experience makes their attitudes more like those of civilian elites.

---

[14] Recall that we are not including the precommissioned military subsample (cadets, midshipmen, and ROTC students) in our analyses, even though they were included in the overall TISS military sample.

Elite Active Duty Military.   These respondents were drawn from our military sample and indicated that they were currently serving as active duty military personnel.

The variables for recording the respondent's military status were coded in the following manner. We began by creating a dummy variable that takes on a value of 1 for *all* respondents drawn from the civilian elite sample who report no prior military service, and for respondents who were reached at military educational institutions and stated that they had never served in the military (the civilian PMEs). It takes on a value of 0 otherwise. This is the variable identifying the civilian elite as a whole. Then the variable for civilian elite PMEs takes on a value of 1 *only* for those respondents reached at military institutions who reported no military experience, and it is coded 0 otherwise. The civilian elite veterans variable takes on a value of 1 for all respondents in the civilian elite sample who reported that they had previously served in the military and takes on a value of 0 otherwise. Next, we created a dummy variable identifying the respondents in the reserves. The military reserves variable takes on a value of 1 for respondents reached through the military sample who reported that they were currently serving with the reserves or National Guard and is coded 0 otherwise. Finally, the variable identifying the active duty military elite is omitted from the analysis so that these respondents can serve as the comparison group.

Interpretation of these coefficients is made somewhat more complex because the civilian veterans and civilian PME variables are coded as *interaction* effects with the civilian elite variable. That is, the civilian veterans and PME dummy variables test whether there are significant differences *within* the civilian elite population. As a result, the coefficients in the regression analyses should be interpreted as follows. The coefficient for the civilian elite represents the average difference of opinion between the active duty military respondents and the civilian elite *nonveterans*. Since the civilian PME variable is an interaction term (that is, it is coded 1 only if the civilian elite nonveterans variable *and* the civilian PME variable are equal to 1), its coefficient represents the average difference between the civilian PMEs and the civilian elite *nonveterans*. The difference between the civilian PMEs and the active duty military can be calculated by adding the coefficient for the civilan elite nonveterans and the civilian elite PMEs. The mechanics of this interpretation may be clarified through an example. Imagine that the coefficient for the civilian elite was 0.5 and the coefficient for the civilian PMEs was −0.4. This set of coefficients would indicate that the average response of civilian elite nonveterans was 0.5 units *higher* than that of the active duty military elite. In addition, the average response for the civilian PMEs was 0.4 units *lower* than that of the civilian elite nonveterans, which would also make it 0.1 (0.5 − 0.4) units higher than the average for the active duty military.

The coefficient for civilian elite veterans should be interpreted in the same manner as the civilian PME variable—with the obvious exception that the effects refer to veterans rather than to PMEs. The coefficient for the military reserves simply refers to the average difference in responses between the active duty military and the National Guard and reserves.

Demographic Control Variables

Our central focus is on the impact of military status, but we recognize that demographic features of respondents are important factors in shaping attitudes. Many of these demographic factors are correlated with military status (for example, the elite military has a higher proportion of males than does the civilian elite) and so it is useful to distinguish whether any observed differences (or similarities) are a function of demographics rather than military experience. Therefore we control for the respondents' age and gender (female respondents are assigned a value of 1, males 0). In addition, we control for minority status (African American and Hispanic respondents are assigned a value of 1, others 0) and political party identification.

Potentially Confounding Variable: Social Contact

We also introduce another control variable that is closely associated with military status, namely the extent of social contact with the military. Theoretically, social contact is an ambiguous control variable for attitudes on the use of force. For some issues, such as the question of casualty sensitivity we address in chapters 4 and 5, the theoretical link is obvious; people who have friends in the military may be more sensitive about the prospect of seeing those friends die in combat. For the more general attitudes about the use of force analyzed in this chapter, it is less obvious why social contact should have a posited causal connection; any observed statistical association may be as much a selection effect as a socialization effect. In other words, it is plausible that people who regularly associate with military officers do so because they have attitudes similar to the military, whether or not they have served in the military themselves; it is also plausible that regularly socializing with the military may serve to bring the attitudes of civilian elite nonveterans in line with those of active duty military elites. However, the possibility that it might be socialization rather than selection makes social contact an especially interesting control variable for understanding the civil-military gap. Finding that social contact "accounts" for otherwise statistically significant civil-military gaps suggests that efforts to promote civil-military interactions may well shape the de facto civil-military gaps over time. Of course, as emphasized above, finding that military status is not a statistically significant variable in multivariate regression models is not evidence that there is no civil-military gap on that issue—it is only evidence that the civil-military differences may be a function of other differences in civilian and military institutions. We measure social contact though responses to several TISS questions about the number of people serving in the military whom they interact with in social and community groups, at work, and among their personal friends.[15]

An important criticism of earlier TISS analyses (Szanya and McCarthy 2002) recommended the inclusion of yet additional control variables: closeness with which the respondent followed military affairs in the news, respondents' confidence in the military, and general attitudes on domestic and foreign policy. We do not use these control variables in the models presented here, although we did do sensitivity analyses to explore their impact. There is not a good theoretical or policy reason for controlling for respondents' self-reporting on how closely they follow military affairs; military buffs who might be expected to have a attitude profile similar to the military would score just as high on these as antimilitary activists who would have the opposite profile. Similarly, there is no sound theoretical reason to separately control for confidence in the military as an institution when measuring attitudes about the use of force. On some questions, such as those concerning military effectiveness, this may even be tapping into the same underlying concept—confidence in the military qua military—thus making it illegitimate as a control variable. At the same time, given the nature of our sample, both of these variables should be closely correlated with military status and social contact, thus making it problematic to include them all in a single model. In sensitivity analyses, these variables do not follow any systematic pattern, thus supporting our reluctance to include them; sometimes they were statistically significant and appeared to erase civil-military differences and sometimes they did not.

There is, however, a strong theoretical reason *not* to follow Szanya and McCarthy's (2002) approach of controlling for general attitudes on domestic and foreign policy when examining specific attitudes about domestic or foreign policy. To begin with, to do so is tantamount to controlling for the very thing you are measuring. Moreover, while it is possible that attitudes toward foreign policy are causally prior to military service (the selection effect), it is also possible that military service is causally prior to foreign policy (the socialization effect). Since we cannot know

---

[15] Specifically, we rely on questions 28–30 on the TISS survey.

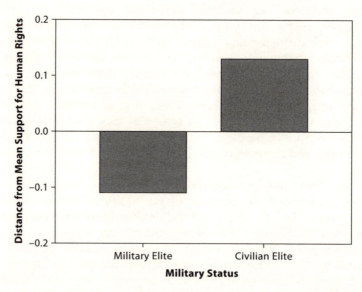

Figure 2.1. The elite civil-military gap regarding human rights abroad.

for certain which effect is at work, controlling for those attitudes in the same model produces incoherent results. It amounts to controlling for intervening variables; one cannot conclude that the antecedent factor (military service) has no impact if the coefficient is statistically insignificant while controlling for the intervening factor (attitudes on foreign policy). If foreign policy attitudes are causally related to each other and are dependent on military status, then we would *expect* military status to become insignificant when controlling for foreign policy attitudes.

Civil-Military Differences over Foreign Policy Priorities

We begin by examining the question of foreign policy priorities as captured by our two attitudinal scales: (1) support for the interventionist foreign policy agenda of international human rights, (2) support for traditional realpolitik goals. We present differences of opinion on these scales in a series of figures. Each figure compares the mean response for the principal subgroups to the mean response of all survey respondents. The wider the spread between the groups, the greater the civil-military elite gap. As a first cut, we grouped our respondents into two broad categories: active duty military and civilian elites (including veterans and nonveterans); the results are displayed in figure 2.1.

Here we can clearly see a difference of opinion between civilian and military elites. The average civilian elite score on the human rights scale

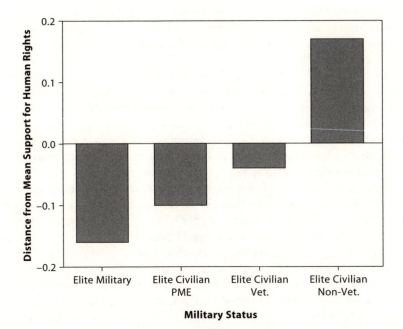

Figure 2.2. The elite civil-military gap regarding the importance of human rights abroad: Distinguishing among civilian elite nonveterans, veterans, and PMEs.

is significantly above the mean level for the entire sample, while military officers—on average—score below the mean. A difference of means tests indicates that the civil-military gap is statistically significant at well below the .01 level. We should be careful, however, not to exaggerate the size of this difference. The average score for an active duty military respondent was −0.24 lower than for a member of the civilian elite. Given the distribution on the scale for the entire TISS sample, this means that the average active duty military respondent ranked in about the 35th percentile in his support for human rights, while the average civilian elite ranked in about the 55th percentile.

Presenting the data in this way, however, obscures much of the civil-military distinction, because the civilian elite sample includes wide variation in level of connection to the military. That is, some of the civilian elite respondents have previously served in the military, some are currently attending military educational institutions, and some have no formal exposure to the military at all. When we distinguish between the civilian elite veterans and nonveterans and the civilian PMEs, as seen in figure 2.2, a sharper civil-military difference emerges.

These results indicate that civilian and military elites do differ in terms of their interventionist foreign policy priorities. As figure 2.2 indicates, elite civilians without military experience are the most supportive of the United States' adopting an international human rights agenda. The gap between civilian elite nonveterans and the active duty military is 50 percent larger than the gap between the military and the civilian elite as a whole. Thus while the average level of civilian elite support for human rights is in about the 55th percentile, the average level of civilian elite *nonveteran* support for human rights is nearly in the 70th percentile. Support for international human rights declines as respondents have a greater connection to the military. Civilian veterans and PMEs, for example, are moderately supportive of human rights as a foreign policy goal, while active duty military officers are the least supportive group.

These differences of opinion are both substantively and statistically significant. For example, more than 35 percent of civilian elite nonveterans rated "the promotion of human rights" as a "very important" foreign policy goal for the United States. Only 21 percent of civilian elite veterans rated this as a "very important" goal, while less than 14 percent of active duty military officers made this same assessment ($p < .01$). Table 2.1 displays a regression analysis of our human rights scale while controlling for other demographic factors in our samples; the same pattern emerges. The coefficient for civilian elite nonveterans is positive and statistically significant, indicating that this group expresses stronger support for international human rights than do elite military officers. The coefficients for civilian elite veterans and civilian elite PMEs are both negative and statistically significant, indicating that these groups give responses that are significantly closer to those of active duty military officers than do civilians with no such ties to the military. Finally, military reservists are not more supportive of human rights than are those on active duty.

These results indicate that the civil-military gap over interventionist foreign policy priorities persists even after we account for the significant demographic differences between the civilian and military samples. Specifically, civilian elite nonveterans remain more supportive of international human rights than elite military officers even after we account for the gender, age, race, and party identification of these respondents. These results suggest that the civil-military opinion gap over the importance of human rights is a function of the military experience of these individuals, and not simply a function of gender, race, age, or political differences. With regard to the control variables themselves, the results generally reflect one's intuitions about this issue. Women, minorities, and those who identify with the Democratic Party tend to be more supportive of an international human rights agenda. Republicans, in contrast, are substantially less supportive. Interestingly, older respondents tend to be slightly more supportive of making international human rights a top priority for U.S. foreign policy.

TABLE 2.1
Military Status and Support for Interventionist and Realpolitik Goals

	Interventionist Goals		Realpolitik Goals	
Respondent's Military Status				
Civilian Elite Nonveteran	0.11***	0.08	−0.18***	−0.06
	(0.04)	(0.06)	(0.05)	(0.06)
Civilian Elite Military Education	−0.12*	−0.11*	0.17**	0.13*
	(0.06)	(0.07)	(0.07)	(0.07)
Civilian Elite Veteran	−0.10**	−0.09*	0.17***	0.15***
	(0.05)	(0.05)	(0.05)	(0.05)
Military Reserve	0.01	0.01	0.12***	0.19***
	(0.04)	(0.05)	(0.04)	(0.04)
Control Variables				
Gender	0.19***	0.19***	0.13***	0.12***
	(0.06)	(0.04)	(0.04)	(0.04)
Age	0.01***	0.01***	−0.002	−0.002
	(0.002)	(0.002)	(0.002)	(0.002)
Minority	0.19***	0.20***	0.13**	0.12*
	(0.06)	(0.06)	(0.06)	(0.06)
Education	−0.002	−0.002	−0.16***	−0.15***
	(0.03)	(0.03)	(0.03)	(0.03)
Democrat	0.15***	0.14***	−0.25***	−0.24***
	(0.04)	(0.04)	(0.04)	(0.04)
Republican	−0.08**	−0.07**	0.27***	0.27***
	(0.03)	(0.03)	(0.03)	(0.03)
Military Social Contact		−0.02		0.06***
		(0.02)		(0.02)
Constant Term	2.76***	2.84***	3.80***	3.57***
	(0.18)	(0.19)	(0.19)	(0.21)
Number of Observations	1,950	1,938	1,950	1,938
R = squared	0.10	0.10	0.15	0.15
Std. Error of the Estimate	0.57	0.57	0.63	0.63
F = Statistic	21.27***	18.27***	34.65***	32.02***

Note: Standard errors for coefficients in parentheses. All tests for statistical significance are two-tailed.
* = $p < .10$. ** = $p < .05$. *** = $p < .01$.

But while the civil-military opinion gap over support for humanitarian missions is not a function of demographic differences between our civilian and military samples, it may be linked to the extent of contact that civilian nonveterans have with those in the military. The second column of table 2.1 adds the extent of military social contact as a control variable. The inclusion of this variable shrinks the substantive size of the gap between civilian nonveterans and active duty military respondents, and it makes the gap statistically insignificant. Other aspects of results remain essentially unchanged. These results suggest that the extent of contact with those who have served in the U.S. military may be one important source of the civil-military gap and may be an important pathway through which the gap can be ameliorated. This interpretation of the results is made somewhat tentative by the fact that the military social contact variable itself is not statistically significant in this analysis either. However, its impact is in the expected direction—contact with the military reduced support for humanitarian missions—and this pattern of effects is consistent with other analyses of the military contact variable elsewhere in this chapter and in chapters 4 and 5. This pattern of foreign policy priorities is directly reversed when we turn our attention to support for "realpolitik" security issues. Again we begin with a simple dichotomous comparison of active duty military elites versus the aggregate of the civilian elite. As shown in figure 2.3, the average civilian elite score on the realpolitik scale is below the mean level for the entire sample, while military officers—on average—score above the mean. Once again, difference of means tests indicates that the civil-military gap is statistically significant at well below the .01 level, but the gap is somewhat smaller than the one we observed regarding human rights. In this case, the average civilian elite response is −0.22 lower than for a member of the military. This difference places the average civilian elite respondent in about the 45th percentile in terms of his or her support for human rights, while the average active duty military respondent is in about the 57th percentile.

When we distinguish between veterans and nonveterans in the civilian elite sample, as shown in figure 2.4, sharper divergences emerge. In this case, elite military officers are the most supportive of realpolitik goals for American foreign policy. Civilian elite veterans and civilian PMEs are once again moderate on these issues, although they tend to be closer to the active duty military. Civilian elite nonveterans, in contrast, are the least supportive of these traditional security priorities. Specifically, the average civilian elite *nonveteran* scored in about the 36th percentile in terms of support for realpolitik goals, as compared with the 45th percentile for the civilian elite overall.

Table 2.1 also displays a regression analysis of our realpolitik scale that mirrors this same pattern. The coefficient for civilian elite nonveterans is negative and statistically significant, indicating that this group expresses less support for realpolitik goals than do elite military officers. The coefficients for civilian elite veterans and civilian elite PMEs are both positive and statistically significant, indicating that these groups give responses that are significantly closer to those of active duty military officers than do civilians with no such ties to the military. Finally, in this case we do observe a significant difference between the active duty military and the reserves. Reservists are even more supportive of realpolitik goals than are those on active duty.

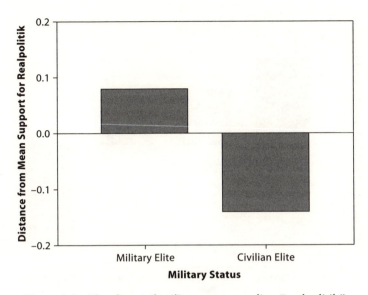

Figure 2.3. The elite civil-military gap regarding "realpolitik"
foreign policy goals.

As was the case with the interventionist attitudes, the civil-military differences of opinion on realpolitik questions are substantively and statistically significant. For example, more than 82 percent of active duty military officers stated that the emergence of China as a great military power represented a "moderately serious" or "very serious" threat to American national security. In contrast, only 66 percent of civilian elite nonveterans made this same assessment ($p < .01$). Of course, 66 percent represents fairly strong support for the realpolitik agenda in absolute terms, but it represents noticeably weaker support compared with the military profile. Table 2.1 also indicates that these differences persist even after we account for other demographic influences. Some of the control variables continue to operate as expected. For example, Republicans are more supportive of realpolitik goals; Democrats are significantly less so. Interestingly, however, women and minorities tend to be more supportive of realpolitik goals—just as they were more supportive of human rights. Thus women and minorities would appear to be more generally internationalist in their views. Age had no impact on support for realpolitik foreign policy goals.

Interestingly, the introduction of military social contact has an even stronger impact on support for realpolitik goals than it did with regard to humanitarian ones. As the final column in table 2.1 indicates, the inclusion of the military social contact variable as a control substantially shrinks the opinion gap between civilian nonveterans and active duty mili-

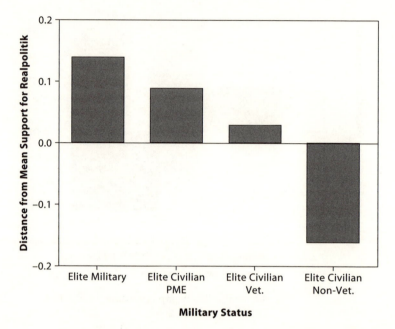

Figure 2.4. The elite civil-military gap regarding "realpolitik" foreign policy
goals: Distinguishing among civilian elite nonveterans, veterans, and PMEs.

tary and renders the gap statistically insignificant. Instead, the military
contact variable has a substantial positive impact on respondents' support
of realpolitik goals. That is, respondents who reported more contact with
members of the U.S. military expressed significantly more support for
realpolitik foreign polity objectives. Once again, this pattern of results
indicates that the extent of contact between civilian nonveterans and the
military may be an important source of the civil-military opinion gap. In
sum, a noticeable difference appears between the foreign policy priorities
of active duty military elites and civilian nonveteran elites. Moreover,
these differences conform to the expectations of the recent case studies
of elite foreign policy debates (Petraeus 1987, 1989; Betts 1991). The
differences should not be exaggerated, but neither should they be dismissed. Civilian elites appear more sympathetic to arguments that the
United States should expand its foreign policy goals to include nontraditional missions related to human rights. Military elites are more supportive of a traditional cold war foreign policy agenda. Notably, civilians with
military experience share preferences much closer to those of the active
duty military elite than do their nonmilitary counterparts. As we noted
above, these differences in opinion appear to be a direct result of military
experience and connection to those in the military, not a result of demo-

graphic differences between the civilians and those serving in the military. In the investigations that follow, unless otherwise explicitly noted, we will move directly to the level of analysis that allows us to distinguish between the veterans and nonveterans in our civilian samples.

A Civil-Military Gap Regarding the Utility of Force and the Role of the Military?

Attitudes on foreign policy priorities are only part of the story. It is one thing to think that promoting human rights is an important goal of foreign policy; it is another thing to advocate military tools for reaching that goal. Here the TISS data are more ambiguous on whether a meaningful civil-military gap exists. There appears to be a statistically significant civil-military gap and it is generally consistent with the hypothesis that civilians are more interventionist than the military, but the gap is substantively very small on these issues. On balance, this pattern does not contradict the basic gap thesis but neither is it very strong confirmation of it.

Two sets of questions on the TISS survey plumbed attitudes on this general topic: one asking respondents to evaluate the relative importance ("very," "somewhat," "not," or "no opinion") of different potential roles for the military; the other asking respondents to evaluate the relative effectiveness of military tools compared with nonmilitary tools ("much more," "somewhat more," "equally," "somewhat less," "much less," or "no opinion"). Both sets asked respondents to consider a range of scenarios that fall along the continuum we have called "interventionist" and "realpolitik" uses of the military. We begin with the realpolitik issues for both sets of questions and then turn to the interventionist responses.

Table 2.2 displays the importance that respondents placed on the role of the American military in fighting and winning wars. These results are consistent with the pattern we found regarding foreign policy priorities. Active duty military officers place the greatest importance on this realpolitik role, with 99 percent of them rating it as "very important." Civilian elite nonveterans are not as supportive, with only 89 percent of these respondents rating "fighting and winning wars" as a very important role for the military. As noted in the table, this difference is statistically significant. Its substantive significance, however, remains somewhat open to interpretation. Is the gap between 89 percent and 99 percent big or small? It is true that this goal receives nearly unanimous support from the active duty military and something less than that from civilian elite nonveterans. Nonetheless, it is difficult to claim that nonveterans are unsupportive of the military's role in fighting and winning wars.

TABLE 2.2
Military Status and the Importance of Fighting and Winning Wars

	Military Elite	Active Reserves	Civilian PMEs	Civilian Veterans	Civilian Elite Nonveterans	Total
Not Important	2	1	0	1	15	19
	0.3%	0.3%	0.0%	0.3%	2.2%	
No Opinion	1	0	0	0	5	6
	0.2%	0.0%	0.0%	0.0%	0.7%	
Somewhat	3	2	1	10	52	68
Important	0.5%	0.5%	0.9%	3.3%	7.8%	
Very	617	384	108	292	598	1,999
Important	99.0%	99.2%	99.1%	96.4%	89.3%	
Total	623	387	109	303	670	2,092

Chi-squared (12 d.f.) = 98.54 (p < .01).
Note: Percentages calculated within each column.

Regression analyses revealed that the civil-military gap observed in table 2.2 is not a function of demographic differences across the samples. These results are robust and statistically significant. Thus the civil-military gap we observe is consistent with the pattern observed in previous case studies (Petraeus 1987, 1989; Betts 1991) as well as in our survey results regarding foreign policy priorities. In other words, while the difference between nonveterans and those with military experience on this question is relatively small in absolute terms, it is more generally noteworthy because it fits a systematic civil-military opinion pattern. We remain, however, cautious about the substantive size of this gap. On the one hand, large majorities of all the groups rate "fighting and winning wars" as a "very important" role for the military. On the other hand, it is somewhat remarkable that more than 10 percent of civilian elite nonveterans would actually report that this role is *not* very important for the military. This is not necessarily evidence of an interventionist mindset, because, as discussed earlier, we theorize that the interventionist profile would support the interventionist missions *and* the realpolitik missions. We hesitate to press this data too far, however, because the difference is very slight and may be an artifact of pre-September 11th views about the absence of any direct threat to the United States. Nevertheless, future research might explore whether there is a core viewpoint among civilian elite nonveterans that would support replacing the realpolitik military role with a purely interventionist role.

For the second set of questions, assessing the relative effectiveness of military and nonmilitary tools, table 2.3 displays respondents' views regarding the effectiveness of military force in coping with the emergence of China as a great power. Once again, the differences are in the direction

TABLE 2.3
Military Status and the Effectiveness of Force in Coping with China

	Military Elite	Active Reserves	Civilian PMEs	Civilian Veterans	Civilian Elite Nonveterans	Total
Much Less Effective	72	34	13	56	159	334
	11.7%	8.8%	11.9%	19.1%	23.8%	
Somewhat Less Effective	138	73	21	54	112	398
	22.4%	18.8%	19.3%	18.4%	16.8%	
Equally Effective	205	159	41	90	216	711
	33.3%	41.0%	37.6%	30.7%	32.4%	
Somewhat More Effective	129	80	16	58	101	384
	20.9%	20.6%	14.7%	19.8%	15.1%	
Much More Effective	72	42	18	35	79	246
	11.7%	10.8%	16.5%	11.9%	11.8%	
Total	616	388	109	293	667	2,073

Chi-squared (16 d.f.) = 71.31 (p < .01).

Note: Percentages calculated within each column.

anticipated by our analyses of foreign policy priorities. Nearly 24 percent of civilian elite nonveterans view military force as "much less effective" than other means of coping with China, while only 12 percent of active duty military officers made this same judgment. This difference is statistically significant, but the substantive size of the difference remains tentative. Moreover, as indicated by table 2.6, all of the differences in opinion displayed in table 2.3 can be accounted for by demographic differences across the civilian and military samples. None of the categories of military status differs significantly from one another once we account for the impact of gender, age, race, and party identification. In fact, the only coefficients that are significant at the .05 level in the logit analysis of this question are those for gender and party identification. Women and Republicans are more likely to view force as an effective tool against China, while Democrats are not. Thus differences of opinion over the effectiveness of military force in containing China appear to be almost entirely gender and partisan divisions rather than an explicitly civil-military one. Of course, a civil-military gap that can be "explained away" by demographic factors is still a civil-military gap if those demographics are skewed in either the civilian or the military world; since our military sample is disproportionately Republican and disproportionately male, these demographics have a cross-cutting influence on shaping the de facto gap on this issue.

The picture becomes still more murky when we analyze the interventionist scenarios. Table 2.4 displays the importance that respondents placed on the military in an interventionist role, namely "as an instrument of foreign policy, even if that means engaging in operations other than war." Here the pattern of responses is directly opposite to the pattern we observed regarding foreign policy priorities. That is, the active duty military are the most supportive of this interventionist role, while civilian elite nonveterans are less enthusiastic. Specifically, nearly 53 percent of elite active duty officers rated this role as "very important" while only 30 percent of civilian elite nonveterans agreed with this assessment. However, it is possible that the wording of this question may have generated this anomalous result by setting up very different contexts for the civilian and military samples' views of this question. The phrases "an instrument of foreign policy" and "operations other than war" were specific terms that had received official endorsement as a part of the Clinton administration's foreign policy at the time of these surveys. Active duty military officers, reservists, and civilian PMEs were probably aware of the specific policy meanings of these phrases as well as the political implications of supporting or opposing them. To say that this role was not important would have been to call White House policy explicitly into question. It is possible that larger proportions of civilian elite veterans and nonveterans, in contrast, were not aware of the charged political atmosphere surrounding those phrases. Consistent with this explanation, table 2.4 indicates that virtually the only differences across the categories of military status occur between those whom we reached at military installations and those whom we did not. That is, active duty military, reservists, and civilian PMEs are nearly indistinguishable from one another, as were civilian veterans and civilian nonveterans. The two samples, therefore, may well have interpreted this question in rather different contexts. Obviously, if we are correct about this question-wording problem, our ability to draw conclusions from these responses is undermined.

Table 2.5 displays the importance that respondents placed on using the military to "meet humanitarian needs abroad." Here we see a return to the pattern that we saw with regard to foreign policy priorities. Less than 5 percent of active duty military elites rated this as a "very important" role for the American military. Among civilian elite nonveterans, in contrast, nearly 20 percent of respondents judged this role to be "very important." Civilian veterans and PMEs are in between these two groups—though somewhat closer to the views of the active duty military elite. This opinion gap is statistically significant ($p < .01$), but it is not overwhelmingly large. Nevertheless, even this degree of civil-military opinion gap could have at least modest substantive importance. For example, if one thinks about a military intervention for humanitarian needs, it is difficult to say whether those who rate this role as "somewhat important" would actually support the operation in practice. Some probably would; others

TABLE 2.4

Military Status and the Importance of the Military as a Tool of Foreign Policy

	Military Elite	Active Reserves	Civilian PMEs	Civilian Veterans	Civilian Elite Nonveterans	Total
Not Important	26	18	7	45	95	191
	4.2%	4.7%	6.5%	14.9%	14.2%	
No Opinion	3	0	1	6	20	30
	0.5%	0.0%	0.9%	2.0%	3.0%	
Somewhat Important	264	154	37	160	352	967
	42.4%	39.9%	34.3%	53.0%	52.8%	
Very Important	329	214	63	91	200	897
	52.9%	55.4%	58.3%	30.1%	30.0%	
Total	622	386	108	302	667	2,073

Chi-squared (12 d.f.) = 167.03 ($p < .01$).

Note: Percentages calculated within each column.

TABLE 2.5

Military Status and the Importance of the Military for Humanitarian Needs Abroad

	Military Elite	Active Reserves	Civilian PMEs	Civilian Veterans	Civilian Elite Nonveterans	Total
Not Important	177	126	28	128	193	652
	28.5%	32.6%	25.7%	42.4%	28.8%	
No Opinion	4	2	0	1	7	14
	0.7%	0.5%	0.0%	0.3%	1.0%	
Somewhat Important	410	236	71	143	342	1,202
	66.0%	61.2%	65.1%	47.2%	51.1%	
Very Important	30	22	10	31	128	221
	4.8%	5.7%	9.2%	10.2%	19.1%	
Total	621	386	109	303	670	2,089

Chi-squared (12 d.f.) = 113.26 ($p < .01$).

Note: Percentages calculated within each column.

would not. Those who view military's role as a defender of human rights as "very important," however, on the other hand, will almost certainly support the operation. Thus. there is a solid core (one fifth) of support for humanitarian intervention among civilian elite nonveterans, but the core of support among the active duty military is trivial (one twentieth).

In table 2.6 we can see that the civil-military gap over the appropriateness of using the military to address humanitarian needs appears to be a function of demographic differences between our civilian and military samples. Once we control for the influence of gender, age, race, and party identification, the gap between the civilian and military elite is no longer significant. Here we find that older respondents are less supportive of this role for the military, while women, minorities, and Democrats are more supportive. Republicans are not significantly different from Independents on the issue. Thus as was the case regarding the appropriateness of force in containing China, we find that the civil-military gap with regard to military interventions to defend human rights is actually a function of gender, age, race, and political identification. Of course, this statistical result does not erase the existence of the gap, but it suggests that the gap is not a function of military experience per se.

Thus at best we find modest support for the hypothesis that elite civilians and active duty military officers differ in their views of the appropriateness of military force to address interventionist and realpolitik issues. Elite civilians without military experience placed somewhat greater importance on the use of military tools to address nontraditional areas of security policy—such as meeting humanitarian needs abroad. At the same time, nonmilitary civilians placed slightly less importance on the use of military tools to address the most traditional role for the military—winning wars. Throughout, civilian veterans consistently held attitudes much closer to those of active duty military elites.

As one final look at this issue, consider whether civilian and military elites differ in terms of their overall perception of the effectiveness of military tools relative to other possible strategies. To assess this, we use the effectiveness of force scale described earlier in this chapter. The two principal differences between this scale and the questions described in tables 2.2 through 2.5 are that this scale does not distinguish between realpolitik and interventionist missions, and it explicitly asks respondents to compare the effectiveness of military tools with whatever other nonmilitary options they can think of. The results of this analysis are also presented in table 2.6.

At first, the analysis of this fuller scale does not appear to yield any more promising results. As the third column in table 2.6 indicates, once we control for the demographic differences across samples, we find little evidence of a link between military service and attitudes toward the effectiveness of force. The gap between civilian nonveterans and active duty military attitudes is neither substantively nor statistically significant. Once again, however, including a measure of the respondents' contact with the military can shed light on the analysis. In the final column of table 2.6 we add military contact as a control. As the coefficient for this variable indicates, the greater a respondent's contact with members of the military, the greater his or her confidence in the effectiveness of the members of the military, the greater his or her confidence in the effectiveness of force.

Moreover, the inclusion of this control variable doubles the size of the civil-military gap and makes it statistically significant. How can the inclusion of a control variable have such an effect? What these results indicate is that civilian elites tend to be fairly confident in the effectiveness of military force despite the fact that their lack of contact with the military would lead us to expect a lower level of confidence. Thus we would interpret this result as providing at least modest support for the assertion that lower levels of knowledge about the military may lead to greater expectations for the effectiveness of military operations.

We should not exaggerate the importance of this effect, however, since the absolute size of these gaps is quite small. The coefficient for civilian elite nonveterans is 0.16, indicating that these respondents score an average of 0.16 points higher on the military effectiveness scale than do the active duty military. This gap corresponds to roughly a 5 percentile increase in the perceived effectiveness of force. The total effect civilian elite veterans was 0.25 (0.16 + 0.09), resulting in about a 10 percentile increase. These differences are less than half the size of what we observed with regard to foreign policy priorities.

Thus we find some civil-military differences regarding the effectiveness and appropriateness of military force, but they are not dramatic and they are counterbalanced by a consensus that emerges if one looks only at absolute numbers. Very strong majorities of both elite military and elite nonveteran civilians support the traditional role of the military (99 percent and 89 percent, respectively). Likewise, the difference between elite military and elite civilian nonveterans on the humanitarian role for the military is primarily one of emphasis; the same percentage agreed that it was very important or somewhat important, but far more civilian elites (20 percent) than military elites (5 percent) were willing to rank it as very important. What makes differences like this substantively significant, as we shall see, is that they interact with and reinforce other attitudes regarding the use of force to produce a consistent profile of viewpoints varying directly with military experience.

Intriguingly, on one use-of-force issue elite opinions did *not* conform to this view. We had expected that the elite military would be less supportive than elite civilians (especially elite civilians without military experience) of the traditional State Department preferred role for the military "as an instrument of foreign policy, even if that means engaging in operations other than war." Instead, elite military are more supportive than elite civilian nonveterans. As we noted above, however, this may well be a problem with the wording of the question, which matched official policy phrases and thus was considered in a different political context by our military respondents.

TABLE 2.6
Civilian and Military Views of the Appropriateness of Military Force

	Humanitarian Needs Abroad	Cope with Chinese Power	Overall Effectiveness of Force	
Respondent's Military Status				
Civilian Elite Nonveteran	0.03	−0.22	0.08	0.16**
	(0.15)	(0.14)	(0.06)	(0.08)
Civilian Elite Military Education	0.14	0.23	0.01	−0.02
	(0.22)	(0.20)	(0.08)	(0.09)
Civilian Elite Veteran	0.16	0.24	0.10	0.09
	(0.16)	(0.15)	(0.06)	(0.06)
Military Reserve	0.01	0.20	0.21***	0.26***
	(0.14)	(0.19)	(0.05)	(0.06)
Control Variables				
Gender	0.72***	0.54***	0.19***	0.19***
	(0.14)	(0.19)	(0.05)	(0.05)
Age	−0.02***	−0.002	0.001	0.001
	(0.006)	(0.006)	(0.002)	(0.002)
Minority	0.25	0.21	0.15**	0.14*
	(0.20)	(0.19)	(0.08)	(0.07)
Education	0.08	−0.28***	−0.30***	−0.3***
	(0.10)	(0.10)	(0.04)	(0.04)
Democrat	0.60***	−0.49***	−0.28***	−0.27***
	(0.14)	(0.12)	(0.05)	(0.05)
Republican	−0.15	0.36***	0.20***	0.20***
	(0.11)	(0.10)	(0.04)	(0.04)
Military Social Contact				0.05*
				(0.03)
Constant			3.99***	3.79***
			(0.24)	(0.26)
Number of Observations	1,936	1,919	1,924	1,912
Likelihood Ratio	104.16***	97.51***		
F = statistic			19.02**	17.62***

Note: Standard errors for coefficients in parentheses. All tests for statistical significance are two-tailed.
* = $p < .10$.   ** = $p < .05$.   *** = $p < .01$.

The Elite Civil-Military Gap Regarding How to Use Force

The civil-military gap becomes once again more pronounced and substantial when we look at civilian and military elite support for the Powell Doctrine, which we operationalize as support for the idea that military force should not be used incrementally but should be used decisively so as best to achieve total victory. Figure 2.5 shows that the civil-military elite gap reappears here as well.

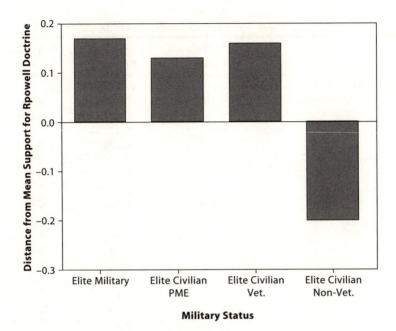

Figure 2.5. The elite civil-military gap in support for the Powell Doctrine.

As expected, elite civilian nonveterans are substantially less supportive of the Powell Doctrine and are therefore more supportive of placing constraints on the use of force. Once again, the views of elite civilian veterans match much more closely with those of active duty military elites.

This gap is both statistically significant and substantively large. For example, nearly 45 percent of elite military officers agree strongly with the statement that "military force should be used quickly and massively." In contrast, less than 25 percent of civilian elite nonveterans agree strongly with that statement. Following the now-familiar pattern, civilian veterans are substantially closer to the active duty military, with nearly 42 percent of civilian elite veterans agreeing strongly. It is worth noting that the differences on the other Powell Doctrine question are smaller, but in the same direction. The regression analyses in table 2.7 demonstrate that each of these differences is statistically significant. In particular, note that the coefficients for civilian elite veterans and civilian elite nonveterans are of nearly identical size but in opposite directions. This result indicates that the opinions of civilian veterans are virtually indistinguishable from those of the active duty military elite.

The second column of table 2.7 indicates that the civil-military gap over the Powell Doctrine may be in part a function of partisan differences over the use of force. In particular, Democrats are much less supportive of the

TABLE 2.7
Military Status and Support for the Powell Doctrine

	Without Control Variables	Demographic Controls	Military Social Contact
Respondent's Military Status			
Civilian Elite Nonveteran	−0.36***	−0.15*	0.03
	(0.07)	(0.09)	(0.03)
Civilian Elite Military Education	0.06	−0.11	−0.17
	(0.12)	(0.13)	(0.13)
Civilian Elite Veteran	0.35***	0.22**	0.18*
	(0.08)	(0.09)	(0.09)
Military Reserve	0.28***	0.27***	0.38***
	(0.08)	(0.08)	(0.09)
Control Variables			
Gender		−0.10	−0.11
		(0.08)	(0.08)
Age		0.001	0.001
		(0.004)	(0.004)
Minority		0.11	0.09
		(0.13)	(0.13)
Education		−0.32***	−0.31***
		(0.06)	(0.06)
Democrat		−0.57***	−0.5***
		(0.08)	(0.08)
Republican		0.21***	0.21***
		(0.06)	(0.06)
Military Social Contact			0.09**
			(0.04)
Constant	3.49***	4.83***	4.48***
	(0.05)	(0.35)	(0.38)
Number of Observations	2,020	1,930	1,918
R = squared	0.04	0.11	0.11
Std. Error of the Estimate	1.19	1.14	1.14
F = statistic	19.35***	24.26***	22.06***

* = $p < .10$.   ** = $p < .05$.   *** = $p < .01$.
Note: Standard errors for coefficients in parentheses. All tests for statistical significance are two-tailed.

principles of the Powell Doctrine than are either Republicans or Independents; Republicans are significantly more supportive than the other two groups. Once we account for these differences the gap between civilian nonveterans and active duty military respondents is cut approximately in half, but the gap remains statistically significant. In light of Colin Powell's prominence in the political arena as a Republican, it may not be surprising to find such a partisan effect.

Finally, the addition of social contact with the military continues to act as an important source of the civil-military gap. The final column of table 2.7 adds this as a control variable, and as expected, contact with the military increases respondents' support for the Powell Doctrine. Moreover, the inclusion of this variable reduces the expected gap between civilian nonveterans and active duty military attitudes toward the Powell Doctrine to nearly zero. Thus civilian nonveterans who have contact with members of the military express levels of support for the Powell Doctrine that are very similar to that of active duty military officers. Civilian nonveterans who do not have contact with members of the military, however, are significantly less supportive of this view.

Getting the Big Picture:
The Overall Opinion Gap on the Use of Force

In sum, our analysis of civilian and military elite attitudes provides qualified support for the argument that elite civilians tend to have a more interventionist foreign policy agenda, and that they are willing to use the military to achieve those foreign policy goals. In addition, we find support for the claim that elite civilians, while more willing to use the military, are also more willing to place constraints on how it is used. Our study has thus been able to replicate and extend with systematic data on elite opinion what others have found through careful case studies of elite decision making. First, we find that civilian elites without military experience are somewhat more hawkish in comparison to the military elite with regard to interventionist military missions such as the promotion of human rights across the globe. In particular, civilians tend to weight interventionist foreign policy goals as more important. We also found some modest evidence that civilians view military force as more effective and more appropriate for interventionist missions than do military officers. Consistent with the consensus in the literature, we also find that elite civilians are more willing to place limits and constraints on the manner in which force will be used. Interestingly, our analyses also indicate that these gaps may be explained by the level of contact that nonveterans have with the U.S. military.

Finally, we find that elite civilian veterans consistently hold views that are substantially closer to those of active duty military elite officers than do elite civilian nonveterans. Since opinions vary with veteran status, the survey results provide strong support for using the level of military experience in the political elite as a measure of the civil-military gap in our analysis of whether opinion gaps can influence actual American conflict behavior, which we address in chapter 3.

The Civil-Military Gap at Elite and Mass Levels

Our central aim in this book is to connect civil-military preferences regarding the use of force to actual American conflict behavior and the willingness of American civilian and military policymakers to accept casualties on various kinds of military missions. Our contention is that civil-military differences of opinion at the elite level are important for understanding American conflict behavior and the willingness to accept casualties. Nonetheless, the TISS data also speak to other important issues, including whether patterns that show up in elite attitudes are also present in mass public opinion. Others have compared elite and mass opinion (Wittkopf 1990; Holsti 1996; Kull and Destler 1999; Reilly 1999), but none of these has focused on civil-military differences across elite and mass samples (with the obvious exception of the previously published TISS studies, Feaver and Kohn 2001a, b).

Unfortunately, the TISS data are richest with respect to elite opinion and much more scant with respect to mass opinion. The TISS study did include a survey of American public opinion, but because of the costs and time constraints involved in conducting a telephone survey, it included a much more limited battery of questions. In fact, of all the questions we analyzed above, the only one asked on the mass public survey was how serious a threat the emergence of China as a great military power constituted for American national security. Obviously, the answer to this question alone cannot determine whether the civil-military gap looks the same at the mass and elite levels. One thing that these responses do reveal, however, is that veterans among the American public are strongly supportive of realpolitik security goals. Specifically, more than 42 percent of veterans among the mass public rated the emergence of China as a "very serious" threat, compared with 33 percent among the active duty military elite.

Given the paucity of available evidence from the TISS data, we searched for other surveys of the American public that might give us some insight on the mass-elite angle of the civil-military opinion gap regarding the use of force. Surprisingly, very few of the numerous surveys of the American public actually ask respondents whether they have ever served in the military. For example, despite the massive battery of demographic information collected by the National Election Study, the surveys do not record whether the respondent ever served in the military. The General Social Survey has occasionally asked whether respondents are veterans, but these surveys did not include questions about the use of military force. The only surveys that we were able to find that asked respondents both about their military experience and about American decisions to use force were a series of surveys conducted by CBS News and the *New York Times*. These surveys were conducted in August 1990, December 1992, January

1993, May 1993, and September 2000.[16] The 1990 survey asked respondents a number of questions about the American intervention in the Gulf immediately following Saddam Hussein's invasion of Kuwait. The December 1992 survey asked respondents about President George H. W. Bush's recent decision to intervene in Somalia, and the January 1993 survey asked about both Somalia and the intervention in Bosnia. Finally, the September 2000 survey asked respondents to look back at the Vietnam War and draw some lessons on how best to use military force.

These surveys provide a good test of the impact of military experience on the views of the American public regarding the use of force, because they cover both interventionist and realpolitik conflicts. Both Bosnia and Somalia constitute interventionist conflicts; the Gulf War is more appropriately viewed as a realpolitik conflict. The central issues at stake in the Gulf were the traditional issues of national security such as sovereignty, the defense of allies, access to vital natural resources, and the maintenance of the balance of power. The Vietnam War does not fit neatly into the interventionist-realpolitik cognitive map, but this does not matter for our purposes since the Vietnam questions we consider here only relate to the constraints placed on the use of force.

We operationalized the dependent, explanatory, and control variables for the mass opinion analyses as follows.

Dependent Variable (1): Gulf War, August 1990

Respondents were asked whether they approved of the deployment of U.S. troops to the Gulf War region in Operation Desert Shield. Those who said "yes" were coded as a 3, and those who said "no" were coded as a 1. "Don't know" and "no opinion" responses were coded as a 2.

Dependent Variable (2): Somalia/Bosnia, December 1992

We analyzed a scale of support for intervention in these two conflicts. Our scale consisted of the mean response to several items.

1. "Do you think the United States should be sending U.S. troops to Somalia to try and [sic] make sure shipments of food get through to the people there, or should U.S. troops stay out?"[17]

---

[16] These surveys used the standard random digit dialing survey methodology used in commercial polling and in many academic studies. Specifically, these surveys used random digit dialing with primary sampling units (PSUs). Blocks of one hundred phone numbers were stratified by region, area code, and size of metropolitan area. Respondents within a household were selected according to Backstrom and Hursh-César (1963).

[17] Responses of "should stay out" were given a value of 1, "no opinion" and "don't know" were given a value of 2, and "should be sending troops" was given a value of 3.

2. "Do you think U.S. troops should stay in Somalia only as long as it takes to get supply lines to make sure people don't starve, or do you think troops should stay there as long as it takes to make sure Somalia will remain peaceful?"[18]

3. "Given the possible loss of American lives and the other costs involved, do you think sending U.S. troops to make sure food gets to the people of Somalia is worth the cost, or not?"[19]

4. "These days, do you think the United States has a responsibility to give military assistance in trouble spots around the world *when it is asked to by its allies*, or don't you think the United States has that responsibility?" (Emphasis added.)[20]

5. "Do you think the United States has a special responsibility to provide humanitarian assistance *when people in other countries need help*, or don't you think the U.S. has that responsibility?" (Emphasis added.)

6. "What should the United States do about the situation in what used to be Yugoslavia? In order to help stop the fighting in what used to be Yugoslavia, would you favor or oppose the United States using its military to keep Serbia from violating the United Nations ban on Serbian flights over Bosnia?"

Dependent Variable (3): Bosnia, January 1992

As with the December 1992 survey, we measured support for the intervention in Bosnia through a series of questions. The responses to each question were coded in the same manner as questions with similar wording on the December 1992 survey. Our measure of support for intervention in Bosnia in January 1993 was calculated as the mean response to the following items.

1. "Do you think the United States has a responsibility to do something about the fighting between Serbs and Bosnians in what used to be Yugoslavia, or doesn't the United States have this responsibility?"

2. "What should the United States do about the fighting between Serbs and Bosnians in what used to be Yugoslavia? Would you favor or oppose the United States using its military to enforce the United Nations ban on Serbian flights over Bosnia?"

---

[18] Those who said "we should not be there" were given a value of 1, those who said "until supply lines are set up" were given a value of 2, and those who said "until Somalia will remain peaceful," were given a value of 3.

[19] Answers of "no" were given a value of 1, "don't know" and "no opinion" were coded as 2, and "yes" answers were given a value of 3.

[20] Responses of "does not" were coded 1, "it depends" was coded 2, and "has responsibility" was coded 3. This same scale was used for measuring the subsequent question about responsibility for humanitarian assistance.

3. "Would you favor or oppose the U.S. sending troops to help get food and medicine through to civilians trapped by the fighting in what used to be Yugoslavia?"

Dependent Variable (4): Vietnam, September 2000

We could not find a good measure of the general public's tolerance for constraints on the use of force—as far as we can tell, this is not a topic on which there is ample survey data. However, we did find a question regarding the lessons of the Vietnam conflict that provides at least some purchase on the underlying concept of tolerance for constraints on the use of force. Respondents were asked, "What do you think is the most important lesson the U.S. learned from the Vietnam war?" Respondents who chose the option "don't get involved if we are not prepared to win or fight to a finish" were given a value of 1. All other responses were given a value of 0.

Explanatory Variables for the Mass Opinion Analyses

RESPONDENT IS A VETERAN

Each of the respondents was asked, "Have you yourself ever served in the U.S. armed forces or the U.S. reserves?" We identified anyone who responded with a "yes" as a veteran, and "no" and "don't know" answers were coded as nonveterans.

DEMOGRAPHIC CONTROL VARIABLES FOR THE MASS OPINION ANALYSES

Interviewers identified the respondents' gender and asked for their year of birth as well. Any respondent that identified him- or herself as "black" or "Hispanic" we coded as a "minority" (value of 1). All other respondents were coded as not part of a minority group (value of 0). Respondents were also asked, "Do you think of yourself as closer to the Republican Party or to the Democratic Party?" Those who said Republican were coded 1, those who said Democratic were coded 3. Neither, both, or "don't know" answers were coded 2.

The Veteran's Effect among the American Public

As we noted above, within our civilian elite sample, those with military experience consistently hold views that are closer to those of the military elite than are the views of nonveterans. Analyzing the CBS/NYT surveys, we can determine whether veteran opinion in the general public follows a similar pattern. We cannot compare the opinions of the mass public with the opinions of the mass military, that is, to enlisted personnel; unfortunately, we do not have a sample of enlisted personnel to compare to the CBS/NYT samples of the American public. Nevertheless, we *can* compare any veteran-versus-nonveteran patterns within the mass public to the pattern we observed within the civilian elite. If the civil-military gap has the same effects at the mass level that we observed among elites, then we would expect the veterans within the American public to offer somewhat greater support for the Gulf War than do nonveterans. Conversely, we would expect nonveterans within the American public to be somewhat more supportive of the Somalia and Bosnia operations. Finally, we would expect veterans to express greater opposition to the constraints that were placed on American military strategy in Vietnam.

The results of our analyses of the civil-military gap in American public opinion are displayed in table 2.8. The coefficient for veteran status is positive and statistically significant in each case, indicating that veterans within the American public are more supportive of all military interventions than are those with no military experience. Moreover, this veteran's effect at the mass level remains significant even when we control for the influence of gender, age, minority status, and political identification. The negative coefficients for gender indicate that women in the general public tend to be less supportive of the American military interventions in the Gulf, Somalia and Bosnia. Interestingly, the gender gap is much larger for the realpolitik mission in the Gulf, relative to the interventions in Bosnia and Somalia. Older respondents are less supportive of all three military operations, while minorities are less supportive of military interventions in Kuwait and Bosnia. Minorities are not less supportive of intervention in Somalia. The negative coefficient for the Political Party Lean variable indicates that Democrats tend to be less supportive of the Gulf War operation. Interestingly, the partisan gap disappears for the interventions in Bosnia and Somalia. This suggests that Democrats tend to be relatively more supportive of interventionist missions than they are of realpolitik operations.

This veteran's effect at the mass level is not overwhelmingly large. For example, in August of 1990 slightly more than 75 percent of nonveterans among the mass public stated that they supported the Desert Shield deployment in the Gulf. Among veterans, however, more than 88 percent of the respondents stated that they approved of this deployment. Clearly both veterans and nonveterans were supportive of President Bush's decision, but support among veterans bordered on unanimous, while there remained substantially more room for debate among nonveterans. In the case of Somalia, in December 1992 slightly less than 65 percent of nonvet-

TABLE 2.8
Veteran Status and American Public Support for Recent Military Interventions

Independent Variables	Desert Shield (8/90)	Bosnia and Somalia (12/92)	Bosia (1/93)	Should Have Fought to Win in Vietnam (9/00)
Respondent Is a Veteran	0.59***	0.13***	0.10***	1.03***
	(0.23)	(0.05)	(0.04)	(0.21)
Gender	−0.53***	−0.05	−0.09***	0.01
	(0.17)	(0.04)	(0.03)	(0.15)
Age	−0.01***	−0.004***	−0.004***	−0.001
	(0.004)	(0.001)	(0.001)	(0.005)
Minority	−0.51***	0.08	−0.08**	−0.61**
	(0.17)	(0.05)	(0.03)	(0.30)
Political Party Lean	−0.70***	−0.03	−0.27	−0.76***
	(0.14)	(0.04)	(0.25)	(0.18)
Threshold 1	−4.11***			0.83*
	(0.39)			(0.43)
Threshold 2	−3.77***			
	(0.39)			
Constant Term		2.62***	3.16***	
		(0.10)	(0.07)	
Number of Observations	1,393	824	1,167	1,119
F = statistic/Chi-squared	91.00***	6.24***	12.41***	53.97***

Note: Standard errors for coefficients in parentheses. All tests for statistical significance are two-tailed.
* = $p < .10$.   ** = $p < .05$.   *** = $p < .01$.

erans stated that the operation was "worth the cost." The support among mass level veterans, however, was over 75 percent. Veterans also exhibited a greater willingness to remain in Somalia, with nearly 55 percent of veterans stating that U.S. forces should remain there until the situation became politically stable. Only 45 percent of nonveterans supported this "state-building" goal for the U.S. military. In May of 1993 nearly 52 percent of veterans in the American public supported sending American troops to Bosnia. Only 43 percent of nonveterans supported this deployment.

As for mass attitudes on whether to put constraints on the use of force, the results are as expected, although the only available question is of dubious value. When asked what lesson the United States should have learned from the Vietnam experience, more than 26 percent of veterans stated that America "should not get involved if it is not prepared to fight to win." Only 10 percent of nonveterans listed this as the primary lesson of Vietnam. This, at least, is consistent with our expectation that people with military experience will be more likely to oppose constraints on the use of force than would nonveterans.

Thus the civil-military gap within the mass public does not follow the same pattern as the civil-military gap within the elites. Elite opinion appears to track the civilian-interventionist, military-realpolitik pattern predicted by the standard case study treatments of American civil-military relations. Mass opinion, by contrast, appears to follow the pattern expected by the "militarist" school. That is, mass-level veterans are more supportive of the use of force across a broader range of circumstances. Mass-level veterans, like their elite veteran counterparts, however, are also more opposed to constraints placed on how military force is used; since this latter prediction is made by both the case study literature and the militarism hypothesis, this finding is not dispositive between the two schools.

We were surprised by this finding and can only speculate as to why military experience appears to have a differing effect on the elite and mass samples. It is not, for instance, anticipated by other studies comparing mass and elite opinion. A staple of other mass-elite comparisons is the finding that at least since the 1980s, the general public tends to be more reluctant than the elite to consider the use of U.S. troops overseas (Wittkopf 1990, 153–56; Reilly 1999, 100–102), although the public is *more* supportive than elites for using force to counter terrorism. It is hard to see how this general finding would lead to the expectation that mass veterans would be *more* interventionist than elite veterans.

It is important to note that the reverse veteran's effect in the mass public does not appear to be a function of demographic differences between the mass and the elite samples. Most of the opinion gaps at both the mass and the elite level remain significant even when we account for these factors. One possible source of this difference might be the type of military service experienced by members the American public and the civilian elite respondents. For example, perhaps the civilian elites mostly served as officers while the veterans among the mass public were mostly enlisted personnel. The experience of military service might differ substantially for officers and enlisted personnel, and thus respondents might have drawn differing lessons from that experience with regard to the use of force. The responses do not, however, fit the pattern we would expect from an enlisted-officer distinction. Enlisted personnel are more likely to be in front-line units and thus bear directly the risks of combat; one would therefore expect that revulsion at the horrors of war would be most acutely felt at the enlisted (and therefore at the mass public) level. The greater support for military operations among mass veterans is therefore something of a surprise.

If the nature of the military experience matters greatly, our analyses in the next chapter face a larger hurdle, for we are obliged by data limitations not to distinguish between many types of service in our measure of military experience in the political elite. We were, however, able to distinguish between enlisted and officer for part of our analysis in the next chapter and determined that this distinction had no statistical effect on our results. We cannot be certain whether other variations in military experience matter. In the book's conclusion, we flag this concern as a priority for future research.

Presently, the best test we can do is an admittedly modest one. The CBS/ NYT surveys did not ask respondents whether they served as officer or enlisted personnel, but the TISS survey did ask civilian elites to give the highest rank they attained during military service. We can, therefore, test whether the type of military experience (enlisted or officers) that civilian elites enjoyed affected their answers to the battery of questions we analyzed above. We found that it did not. Although veteran status had a significant impact on support for human rights, realpolitik goals, the Powell Doctrine, and so on, the actual rank that the respondents achieved had no impact at all on these views. The coefficient for highest rank never approached significance when it was included in any of the regression or logit analyses discussed above.

But while the cause of the differing veteran's effect among elite and mass respondents remains a matter of speculation, it is important to note that this distinction does appear to be consistent and robust. Veterans among the American public do appear to be more supportive of all types of intervention, regardless of the specifics of question phrasing or the precise mission. Likewise, the views of elite veterans and elite military officers showed discernible differences between interventionist and realpolitik issues.

Foreign Policy Priorities within the Military

Thus far we have discussed the gap between civilians and the military regarding foreign policy priorities. The TISS data also allow for explorations of differences *within* the military. For considerations of space, we do not present all the analyses here and simply summarize the most important findings. Respondents serving in the Navy, Air Force, and Marines are all statistically more supportive of international human rights as a foreign policy goal than are respondents from the Army. Officers from the Air Force and Marines are also more supportive of the military's taking a role in defending human rights. Moreover, respondents from the Marines are substantially (though perhaps not surprisingly) more supportive of using the military for "operations other than war."[21] These

---

[21] Note that the TISS military sample has a smaller number of Air Force officers relative to their true representation in the population of military officers. The greater support within the Air Force for interventionist goals raised the concern that our finding of a civil-military

interservice differences are important, because officers from the services most likely to engage in interventionist missions also appear to be the most supportive of these types of operations.

Another factor that has an important influence on foreign policy priorities within the military is the level of confidence that military officers express in political leaders and governmental institutions. Military elites who express greater confidence in civilian policymakers and political institutions are significantly more supportive of an international human rights agenda, more supportive of a military role in defending human rights, more supportive of military engagement in operations other than war, and less supportive of the Powell Doctrine. This suggests that building up the confidence and trust that military leaders have for their civilian counterparts represents an important tool for bridging the civil-military gap—a conclusion that is reinforced by the analysis of casualty aversion presented in chapters 4 and 5.[22]

Finally, one significant "nonfinding" that emerged is that the reasons that military respondents gave for joining the military had virtually no impact on their foreign policy priorities. Those who stated that they joined the military because they were drafted did not differ significantly from those who said they joined in order to "serve their country" or those who said they joined to "have a career in the military." This "nonresult" is important, because it suggests that the experience of being in the military appears to have a consistent effect on respondents' views, regardless of why they decided to join the military. Of course, without being able to observe people's attitudes before and after they join the military, we cannot definitively determine whether military experience causes these attitudes, or whether people who already have these attitudes select themselves in the military. Nonetheless, the fact that respondents who joined the military for such disparate reasons should end up with so few significant differences of opinion at least suggests that the experience of being in the military is shaping respondents' attitudes.

---

gap regarding foreign policy priorities might be due to our underrepresentation of Air Force officers. To guard against this possibility, we reanalyzed the data and compared the civilian elite specifically with Air Force officers. The civil-military gap remained substantial and statistically significant. Thus, even if the entire military had views identical to those of our Air Force sample, we would still find a significant civil-military gap.

[22] Since our poll was conducted under the tenure of President Clinton and at the height of the Lewinsky scandals, this finding is almost certainly contaminated in part by the "Clinton effect"—the military's distinctive distrust of Clinton for idiosyncratic reasons. Given that Clinton was an interventionist president, the causal arrow for military elites may run in the opposite direction—military elites who support the interventionist mission are more likely to have confidence in an interventionist president. Analysis of military attitudes under different kinds of political leaders is needed to sort out these nuances.

Conclusion

In this chapter we have examined the elite civil-military opinion gap regarding whether and how to use military force. Our analysis of TISS survey data supports and extends with systematic data the results of several previous case studies of American elite decision making (Petraeus 1987, 1989; Betts 1991). Recall that we divided our analysis of the opinion gap on whether and how to use force into three stages: (1) foreign policy priorities; (2) the appropriateness and effectiveness of military force; and (3) tolerance of political constraints on how military force is used. With regard to foreign policy priorities, we found a consistent albeit not dramatic pattern in the civilian and military responses. Elite military officers and civilian veterans are more supportive of realpolitik goals—such as defending against a rising China. Elite civilians without military experience, in contrast, were more supportive of interventionist goals, the human rights agenda featured prominently in foreign policy debates in the 1990s. It is important to note, of course, that in absolute terms all respondents rank the realpolitik goals as more important than the interventionist ones. In relative terms, however, the gaps are noticeable. The elite civil-military gap regarding the appropriateness of force to achieve foreign policy goals is also relatively consistent with this pattern—although the civil-military differences were not as substantively large or as robust. Finally, elite military officers and civilian veterans are substantially less supportive of placing constraints on how military force is used than were civilian nonveterans. Reservists consistently give responses that match up with their active duty counterparts.

All of these findings run contrary to the traditional "militarism" school of thought regarding the elite civil-military gap. Our examination of opinion gaps between veterans and nonveterans in the American public, however, supported the militarist view. In the CBS/NYT surveys of the general public, veterans are more supportive of using military force across both realpolitik and interventionist missions.

The elite civil-military opinion gap regarding the use of force is not large, but it fits into a systematic pattern. The pattern is sufficiently robust, and matches findings from the case study literature. It begs the obvious question, does the gap matter? In the next chapter, we examine the impact that these differing views might have had on actual decisions to use military force over the past 177 years.

CHAPTER THREE

THE IMPACT OF ELITE VETERANS ON AMERICAN
DECISIONS TO USE FORCE

> My feeling is that [National Security Advisor Anthony
> Lake] must always be conscious when it comes to making
> military decisions on the use of military power that the
> president has not served and that he has not served.
> —GENERAL JOHN SHALIKASHVILI,
> *Chairman of the Joint Chiefs of Staff*

IN CHAPTER 1, we recounted the difficulties Colin Powell had in dealing with the Clinton foreign policy team. His dilemma was well expressed in his memorable exchange with Madeleine Albright, who asked him, "What is the point of having this superb military that you're always talking about if we can't use it?" Powell reported that he thought he would have an aneurysm; his soldiers were not pieces on a global game board to be moved around at will (Powell 1995, 576–77).

In this chapter we examine the extent to which such disputes are a function of an enduring civil-military gap. Chapter 2 established that military experience "matters" in the sense that civilians and military personnel tend to give different responses on surveys asking about the appropriate criteria for when and how to use force. Moreover, civilians who are military veterans give responses that are more similar to those of military officers than to those of civilians who have never served. This finding from the survey data is consistent with other research that has shown how differing civilian and military opinions shaped policy debates at the highest decision-making levels within the United States during the cold war (for example, Petraeus 1989; Betts 1991; Gacek 1994). Here we assess whether this opinion gap "matters" in terms of the actual conduct of American foreign policy.

Specifically, we examine whether the prevalence of military experience among the policy-making elite affects the propensity of the United States to use military force. Because veteran opinion corresponds with military opinion, we use veteran presence in the political elite as a proxy for measuring the civil-military gap over time. Relying on a composite measure of military experience across the executive and legislative branches of government, we examine the impact of elite military experience on the U.S. propensity to initiate and to escalate militarized interstate disputes between 1816 and 1992.

The results of these analyses are striking. We find that as the percentage of veterans serving in the executive branch and the legislature increases, the probability that the United States will initiate militarized disputes declines. At the same time, however, once a dispute has been initiated, the higher the proportion of veterans, the greater the level of force the United States will use in the dispute. These results are statistically robust and are not spurious; they hold even when we control for other factors that are known to affect the propensity to use force. The civil-military gap matters, at least insofar as the use of force goes.

We begin by first analyzing the causal logic underlying competing claims in the public debate over the civil-military gap. We deduce several expectations from this discussion regarding the nature of the civil-military gap and its impact on the use of force. Second, we describe the research design and measurements we use to test our hypotheses. Third, we examine the link between elite military experience and the American use of force through a systematic analysis of over 175 years of U.S. conflict behavior, from 1816 to 1992. We conclude with a discussion of the implications of our results.

From Beliefs to Behavior:
The Civil-Military Gap and Interstate Conflict

Although civilian and military preferences regarding the use of force may differ, civilians have had the final say regarding both when and how military force will be used throughout U.S. history. The American military has never openly challenged the fundamental principle of civilian control, and we do not anticipate that it will do so. Nonetheless, even under the basic rubric of civilian control, one can imagine varying levels of military influence (Feaver 2003).

Military preferences shape U.S. foreign policy to a greater or lesser extent through at least two significant mechanisms. First, while the military may not determine American policy, its advisory role is well respected and established. Given their obvious expertise regarding the use of force, military advisors will have the opportunity to persuade civilian policymakers to adopt views that reflect the beliefs and preferences of the military. Second, even if military advisors are unable to alter the views of policymakers, their preferences may constrain them because of the leverage that the military can give to competing civilian elites (that is, elite members of a competing political party or faction). The norms of civilian control may inhibit military leaders from openly and publicly challenging civilian decisions regarding the use of force, but competing civilian elites are under no such constraint. Research indicates that one of the keys to maintaining public support for the use of force is the existence of an elite consensus in support of the issue (Larson 1996). Should civilian leaders select policies that are contrary to military advice, however, competing civilian elites will be ready and willing to attack the leadership for ignoring such expert advice if the policy is eventually judged a failure.[1] Thus military preferences may influence the civilian elite, despite the strong American norm of civilian control, to the extent that these views can either persuade or coerce civilian policymakers to alter their choices.[2]

The linkage between military preferences and American conflict behavior may be further complicated by the fact that individuals' preferences over when and how to use military force are likely to be related to each other. That is, an individual's preferences regarding one dimension may be contingent on the policy outcome on the other dimension (Hinich and Munger 1997).[3] For example, it would be entirely consistent for a realpolitik policymaker to oppose intervention in response to human rights abuses abroad, but also to argue that if the United States does intervene in such conflicts it should do so with a high level of force. There are a variety of ways to represent social choice problems in this context, but perhaps the simplest here is to collapse the two choices on a single policy dimension and allow preferences to be non-single peaked (Hinich and Munger 1997).[4]

First, state leaders must decide whether or not to use force. If they choose not to initiate, then no force is used and the status quo prevails. If the decision is made to initiate, however, then a second decision must be made regarding how much military force will be used. This decision tree has three end-nodes: (1) no force is used and the status quo prevails, (2) limited use of force, and (3) large-scale use of force. Our contention is that civilian and military elites have different preference rankings across these three outcomes. Moreover, preference rankings within each of these

[1] This mechanism has been developed into a formal model of democratic government, domestic constraints, and the use of force. See Schultz (1999).

[2] It is a happy fact that for over two hundred years of U.S. history there has never been a coup or even a threat of a coup. But it would be a mistake to infer from this that civilian control over any given policy has never been challenged or subverted. On the contrary, civil-military relations in the United States are a game of strategic interaction between civilian leaders and military leaders, and the military has on occasion thwarted civilian leaders from doing what they wanted to do. This theme is developed at length in Feaver (2003).

[3] We would like to thank Michael Munger and Emerson Niou for clarifying for us the implications of this issue for our hypotheses.

[4] This approach is most appropriate in this case because decisions regarding the second dimension (*how* to use force) disappear if a prior decision has been made *not* to use force.

groups may vary depending upon the nature of the goal for which force is being contemplated.

The specific preferences of the relevant actors can be deduced from what is known about their views in general. Both previous case study research and our own survey research suggests that civilian elite nonveterans would most prefer a limited intervention. This preference for limited involvement appears to hold regardless of whether the goals of the military operation are realpolitik issues such as the defense of Kuwait or South Korea, or interventionist issues such as the civil war in Somalia or human rights abuses in Kosovo. However, nonveteran civilian rankings of the other two outcomes—do nothing and use large-scale force—appear to switch depending on the nature of the issue. That is, faced with realpolitik threats, nonveteran civilians seem likely to prefer large-scale force to doing nothing (for example, Kuwait and Korea). With regard to interventionist issues, however, it is arguable that nonveteran civilians would prefer doing nothing to escalating to the large-scale use of force (for example, in Kosovo and Somalia).

While nonveteran civilians' preferences are defined by their focus on limited force as the most attractive option, the military elite consistently ranks this as its least-preferred outcome. This preference against limited military action is consistent across policy issues. The military's relative ranking of large-scale force and doing nothing, however, changes depending upon the nature of the issue at stake. With regard to realpolitik issues, the military's most preferred option is the large-scale use of force. It is important to note that some members of the military may have a rather restrictive conception of a realpolitik threat. Given that the military views an issue as a threat to American national security, however, its most preferred outcome is to use force on a large scale, while doing nothing ranks in between large scale and limited force. With regard to interventionist issues, however, the military's most preferred outcome is to do nothing, while large-scale force remains preferable to limited force.

Given these preference rankings, what kind of advice is the military likely to offer to civilian leaders? With regard to realpolitik issues, the military would like to counsel civilians to use force on a large scale. However, it will be wary of advising civilians to do so because of the fear that once the United States becomes involved in the conflict, civilians will place constraints on how force will be used. This subsequent choice would, of course, present the military with its least preferred outcome. The cautious and restrained nature of the military advice prior to the Gulf War may serve as an example of this pattern. Many in the military saw a threat to American security, but advised caution regarding the use of force partly out of fear that civilians would constrain the nature of the operation (Betts 1991).

With regard to interventionist issues, however, military advice is likely to be adamantly opposed to using force rather than merely cautious. In this case, the military's most preferred option is to do nothing, and it will attempt to persuade civilian elites to stay out. Military advisors should be particularly adamant in this regard because they are aware that while limited intervention is civilians' most preferred outcome, a large-scale use of force is their least-favorite option. Thus a decision to use force on an interventionist issue such as Kosovo or Somalia will most likely present the military with its least-preferred outcome: the limited use of force.

Not surprisingly, we expect that military preferences will have a greater influence on civilian policy choices when civilian leaders share preferences that are similar to those of the military. Moreover, our findings in chapter 2 indicate that civilians who have served in the military have preferences that are closer to those of the military than are the views of civilian non-veterans. Thus we expect that American conflict behavior will tend to reflect "military views" as the proportion of civilian policymakers with military experience increases.

Once the decision has been made to use military force, the nature of the military's advice to civilian policymakers becomes more straightforward. The military always prefers the large-scale use of force to the limited use of force. Indeed, the limited use of force is always the military's least-preferred outcome. Thus once civilian policymakers have decided to use force (and the "do nothing" option disappears), military advisors will always counsel strongly for using force on a large scale. Once again, we expect this advice to be more influential when the civil-military gap is small.

Of course, the decision to use force is influenced by many factors, of which civil-military relations may not be the most important. The presence of these other factors presents a challenge for testing the influence of the civil-military opinion gap over time. Even so, it should be possible to isolate the impact of civil-military relations relative to other contributing factors that shape the use of force. The hypotheses that follow, then, are all subject to the ceteris paribus condition; controlling for all the other factors that affect the decision to use force, we expect that:

Hypothesis 1: As the proportion of civilian policymakers with military experience increases, the probability that the United States will initiate militarized disputes will decrease.

Hypothesis 2: The impact of policymakers' military experience on American decisions to initiate militarized disputes will be more pronounced with regard to interventionist threats rather than realpolitik threats.

Hypothesis 3: As the proportion of civilian policymakers with military experience increases, the level of force the United States uses in disputes it initiates will increase.

Measuring the Impact of the Civil-Military Gap
on American Conflict Behavior

To test these hypotheses, we relate the civil-military gap to U.S. conflict behavior over the nineteenth and twentieth centuries while controlling, as far as possible, for other factors that are known to shape the use of force. We discuss the results of our analyses in the next section. We encourage skeptical readers to read this section, a technical discussion of the methods involved, closely, as it explains how we addressed most of the counterarguments our findings generated. Most important, we address our reasons for, first, remaining confident in our findings despite inherent limitations in the historical data and, second, remaining confident that our finding of a strong statistical correlation is not spurious.

Scope

We test for the impact of the elite civil-military gap on American decisions to use force with a cross-sectional time-series dataset composed of interstate dyads of which the United States was a member between 1816 and 1992.[5] State membership is determined by the Correlates of War dataset's definition of membership in the international system. One difficulty in using such dyadic pooled time-series data is determining which states were capable of interacting. During the latter part of the twentieth century, this issue seems less salient because of the frequent opportunities for interaction among states. As we move back in time through the nineteenth century, however, it becomes less plausible to assume that all states were capable of fighting with one another. Following a number of prominent analyses of the use of force, we address this problem by analyzing only "politically relevant" dyads (Maoz and Russett 1993; Oneal and Russett 1997), which are defined as: (1) any pair of states in which at least one of the states is a major power; or (2) any pair of states that share a border or are divided by less than 250 miles of water.[6]

---

[5] This dataset was defined through the use of EUGene, a data generation program produced by D. Scott Bennett and Allan C. Stam (Bennett and Stam 1998). The analysis of binary pooled time-series data has recently come under considerable methodological criticism. We approach the problem of temporal dependence in the manner advocated by Beck, Katz, and Tucker (1998). In addition, we rely on Huber-White robust standard errors that allow for clustering on each dyad in order to deal with spatial autocorrelation and heteroskedasticity. Because of the skewed distribution of the dependent variable, we also tested Gary King and Langche Zeng's (2001) rare-event logit estimator. It produced identical results, so we retained the traditional logit specification.

[6] The analysis of "politically relevant" dyad-years versus all dyad-years has been a source of some debate. In general, the effect of analyzing politically relevant dyads should be to

Since the United States became a major power (according to the Corre-lates of War Capabilities Dataset) in 1898, this rule implies that we ana-lyze all interstate dyads including the United States from 1898 onward. Prior to 1898, the rule implies that we analyze American relations with all of the major powers during that period as well as American interac-tions with Mexico.[7] For the entire 177 years under study, there are 8,780 dyad-years involving the United States.

Dependent Variable (1): Initiation of Force by the United States

Our argument made specific predictions about how civil-military factors might affect two different aspects of the use of force. The first aspect is the *propensity* to initiate the use of force, and thus our first dependent variable is the propensity of the United States to initiate the use of force.[8] We code American initiations of force on the basis of the Correlates of War (COW) Militarized Interstate Disputes (MIDs) dataset, which defines the initiation of militarized disputes as explicit threats to use force, dis-plays of force, mobilizations of force, or actual uses of force (Jones, Bremer, and Singer 1996). This variable is coded on an annual basis for each dyad, set at one for each year that the United States initiated a milita-rized dispute against the other state in the dyad, and otherwise at zero.[9] For the entire 177 years studied, there were 111 militarized disputes initi-

---

increase the size of estimated coefficients by reducing the problems associated with analyz-ing rare events (King and Zeng 2001). Because the United States became a major power in 1898, our analysis does look at all dyads in the twentieth century. The impact of veterans remained consistent across the nineteenth and twentieth centuries, suggesting that the selec-tion of politically relevant versus all dyads is not an issue for this analysis.

[7] This excludes U.S. conflicts with Native American tribes, because the Correlates of War datasets do not identify these groups as nation-states.

[8] We also investigated the possibility that the presence of veterans might be associated with the probability that the United States would become a target in a militarized dispute. No such hypothesis emerges from our data on civilian and military preferences, but we investigated the possibility that other states might anticipate levels of U.S. "intervention-ism" and alter their behavior on the basis of the perceived preferences of U.S. leaders. We found no support for this hypothesis. Thus—as expected by our argument—the initiation of U.S. MIDs is related to the presence of veterans but the targeting of MIDs against the United States is not. This pattern increases our confidence that we are identifying a causal relationship rather than a spurious correlation between veterans and the overall frequency of disputes.

[9] As is the case with all analyses of dispute initiation, the distribution on this dependent variable is quite skewed. The United States was a member of 8,790 politically relevant dyad-years from 1816 to 1992, and it initiated disputes in 111 of those cases. U.S. dispute initia-tions were relatively rare (1.26 percent of the cases), but did differ substantially from the frequency of dispute initiations in a random sample of politically relevant dyad-years. As can be seen above in note 5, King and Zeng's (2001) rare-events logit estimator yielded identical results to those presented here.

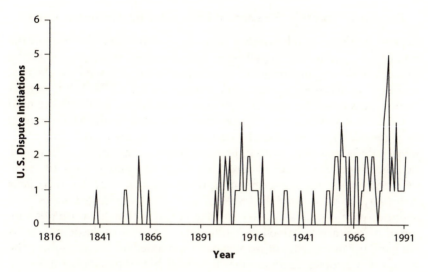

Figure 3.1. Annual dispute initiations by the United States.

ated by the United States. Over the same period, the United States was also involved in 132 other militarized disputes that were initiated by other states. But since our theory only addresses disputes initiated by the United States, we do not include them in our analysis.

Several types of actions by the United States can constitute the initiation of a MID. Using military force to attack another country obviously constitutes the initiation of a militarized dispute. In addition, instances in which the United States either explicitly threatened to use military force against another state, or instances in which the United States mobilized or moved its military forces in a manner that threatened another state are also identified as U.S. initiations of a MID. Fordham and Sarver (2001) have argued that the MIDs database is inappropriate for studies like ours that focus on uses of force by the United States. Fordham and Sarver generously shared their data with us, and we also constructed a measure of U.S. dispute initiation based on their data.[10] Results for our analyses were similar to our findings regarding MIDs, and so we retained the more commonly used specification of militarized disputes. To give readers a sense of what the MID data we use look like, we display the annual number of dispute initiations by the United States in figure 3.1.

[10] The Fordham and Sarver (2001) dataset is on American "uses of force." Thus it includes cases that were not initiated by the United States and it includes uses of force against nonstate actors. In order to merge these data with ours we applied COW coding rules to the Fordham and Sarver data to create a measure of U.S. initiations against other states.

Dependent Variable (2): Level of Force Used by the United States

We also predicted a relationship between civil-military factors and the *level* of force used (that is, whether unconstrained in keeping with the classical "military" preference or constrained in keeping with the classical "civilian" preference). Once again, we rely on the COW MIDs dataset for our measure of the second dependent variable, the level of force used by the United States in the disputes that it initiated. In the MIDs dataset the highest level of force used by each side in a dispute is coded on a five-point scale as follows: 1 = no militarized response to a MID initiation by the other state, 2 = threat of force, 3 = show of force, 4 = use of force, 5 = war. For our purposes, of course, the first category of this variable is irrelevant, for we analyze the level of force only if the United States initiated a dispute. Threats of force involve verbal actions that are not supported by militarized behavior. A show of force involves the actual movement and use of troops, but stops short of extended or direct combat. The use of force involves direct military hostilities but stops short of full-scale war. Wars are defined as military engagements in which the combatants suffer at least 1,000 battle deaths. Thus the dataset would code the 1998 U.S. air strikes against Saddam Hussein in response to his refusal to cooperate with UNSCOM inspectors as a level 4 initiation by the United States. The American launching of the Gulf War in 1990, on the other hand, is a level 5 initiation by the United States.[11]

Key Explanatory Variable: The Elite Civil-Military Gap

We have no way of directly measuring the preferences of policymakers regarding the use of force across the span of American history. However, we can measure the military *experience* of American policymakers. That is, we can determine whether each of these policymakers ever served in the military. As we discussed above, this measure acts as a surrogate indicator for the presence of "military views" within the civilian policymaking elite.

Focusing on military experience as a measure of the gap fits nicely within the causal chain with which we link the civil-military gap to the use of force. We view the impact of the gap as a two-stage process. First,

[11] The MIDs database codes the United States as the initiator against Iraq in the Gulf War because the initial Iraqi attack was directed at Kuwait, not at the United States. Note that this coding is not a moral judgment about who is to blame for the war. Conceptually, this coding is analogous to viewing the Gulf War as two separate wars: one involving Iraq and Kuwait, which began with the Iraqi invasion and ended with the annexation of Kuwait, and the other involving the United States and Iraq, which began with the U.S. air strikes and ended with the Iraqi cease-fire.

military experience shapes individuals' attitudes and preferences regarding the use of force.[12] Second, these differing preferences, in turn, alter American conflict behavior. That is, although our aggregate analysis of American conflict behavior draws a direct linkage between military experience and dispute behavior, we view attitudes as an intervening variable between military experience and American foreign policy.

Our approach requires us to assume that the link between opinions about the use of force and military/veteran status has been more or less constant over the time. We are not arguing that all elite civilians have always thought exactly the same way or that all elite military have always thought exactly the same way. Rather, we are assuming that the general structure of opinion has been relatively constant over time, and we believe that this assumption is both modest and plausible. Although there have certainly been changes at the margins, it is striking that the broad contours of our results in chapter 2 are consistent with the findings of several studies of U.S. civil-military relations during the cold war (Petraeus 1987, 1989; Betts 1991), with Huntington's (1957) canonical text that considered the sweep of U.S. civil-military relations since the founding of the Republic, and with Emory Upton's (1917) classic critique of nineteenth century American civil-military relations. Compared with military officers, American civilian leaders have tended to be more willing to use force as a foreign policy tool and more willing to limit how that force is used. As Albright said, "limited force in limited areas." Of course, one can always think of prominent counterexamples, of military hawks like General Curtis LeMay and of civilian doves like Senator Paul Wellstone, but the findings of the larger literature are rather consistent on this point.[13] Importantly, if our assumption is invalid and veteran status is not associated with foreign policy preferences in a consistent manner, then our esti-

---

[12] Of course when military service is voluntary (or avoidable), our analysis cannot determine whether military experience causes individuals to alter their foreign policy preferences or whether those who already have views compatible with the military are simply more likely to signup. Examining this causal link would require panel survey data that allowed us to track individuals' opinions over time, data that are obviously unavailable. For our purposes here, however, this distinction is not central. Our focus is on determining whether or not the presence of "military views" among the policymaking elite has an influence on American conflict behavior—regardless of why those views are held.

[13] Readers should note that the "policy" elite we reference here is not exactly the same group as the "civilian elite" described in the survey data reported in chapter 2. Here we are concerned with the most senior political leaders in the executive and legislative branches. Survey analyses examined a broader group that included leading Americans from the worlds of business, academia, the media, and so on. One might expect that the policy elite would be drawn from the broader civilian elite and so might share its general distributional features. In any case, since we cannot obtain data on the military experience of the civilian elite over the period of this study, we cannot include them in this analysis.

mates will generally tend to be dampened toward zero and we will thus be less likely to uncover any statistically significant relationships.

Our analyses in this chapter also treat all forms of military experience as the same. This assumption is perhaps more problematic, because intuitively there would seem to be a difference in perspective between a draftee who served his minimum tour and a career officer who rose to the highest military ranks before pursuing a political career. Likewise, it is plausible that there is a difference in perspective between serving during combat versus serving during peacetime, or serving in a combat unit versus serving as a cook, or serving in the reserves versus active duty. As reported below in the section describing tests of robustness, we were able to assess the impact of one likely source of variation, whether the veteran in the political elite had been an officer or in the enlisted ranks, and this distinction did not have a statistically discernible effect. As reported in chapter 2, however, there is at least some evidence of a difference in perspective between veterans in the mass public and veterans in the elite—in some polls. Recall that in chapter 2 veterans in the mass public were more supportive of all military missions, even ones that were the kind of interventionist missions that military officers viewed with greater skepticism. The mass versus elite distinction is less worrying for us in this chapter since we can and do independently control for the presence of veterans in the mass public (and so will be able to capture any countervailing effects in the data). Moreover, our focus on political leaders means that we are, by definition, looking at elite effects; as reported in the previous chapter, we found no enlisted versus officer distinction in the elite data. Nevertheless, the possibility that other variations in military experience may have shaped opinion differentially in the past is at least plausible. Given the limits of the data, we are unable to account for all variations in these analyses and so in the final chapter we flag this as a priority for future research.

For our present purposes, this limitation in the data biases our analysis *against* finding any effect. If variations in military experience matters in ways we are not able to capture, then it will show up as more noisy variation in the data, driving coefficients toward zero and lowering the likelihood of finding any statistically significant relationship. Put another way, our assumptions increase the likelihood that we will falsely reject a veteran's effect when there really is one, and decrease the likelihood that we will falsely accept a veteran's effect when there really is none.

The next issue is the determination of whose military experience might be relevant for predicting the use of force. The president's military experience should be an important aspect of this process, but should by no means be the only factor. The president inevitably relies on advice from members of his cabinet and his national security team, so surely their military experience will shape the views and the information they convey to him. In addition, the president must also be concerned about how other policymakers will respond to his decisions regarding whether and how to use force. Congress has often publicly debated American decisions to use force, and as we noted earlier, public support for a military operation may depend critically on the existence of an elite consensus in support of the operation (Larson 1996). Thus the president must be concerned with whether legislators will hold hearings or make public statements that question the administration's policy. Congress also retains an important budgetary and constitutional link to American uses of force, and the president may consult directly with prominent members of Congress who have expertise in foreign affairs.

Consequently, our measure of the military experience of policymakers encompasses the executive and legislative branches. We do not include the military experience of the Supreme Court or other aspects of the judiciary, because judges have not historically played a role in American decisions to use force or debated such decisions publicly. For the executive branch, we recorded the percentage of veterans serving in the cabinet for each year. Thus we include the military experience of the president, the vice president, and any other cabinet officers serving during that year. Data for this variable are from the *Biographical Directory of the United States Executive Branch, 1774–1989* (Sobel 1990).[14] For Congress, we use the percentage of veterans serving in the House of Representatives for each year.[15]

To convey a sense of what these data look like, we display both of our measures of military experience in figure 3.2. The proportion of veterans in the House ranged between 13 percent and 72 percent, while the percentage of veterans in the cabinet ranged from 0 percent all the way to 92 percent. Both measures were low in the early nineteenth and early twentieth centuries, and both rose after the conclusion of the Civil War, World War I, and World War II.

The two variables are closely related to one another, correlating at 0.85 ($p < .01$). Thus we combine these two indicators into a single composite measure of elite military experience by simply taking their average.[16]

---

[14] Data for 1990 to 1992 were taken from the biographies of cabinet secretaries available on the websites of each cabinet department.

[15] We thank William T. Bianco for generously sharing these data with us (Bianco and Markham, 2001).

[16] Because the two variables correlate so highly, however, differing functional forms had little impact on the results. For example, weighting the military experience of cabinet members twice as heavily as that of the House members had no impact on our results. Below we demonstrate that our findings are robust across several other variations in these coding rules.

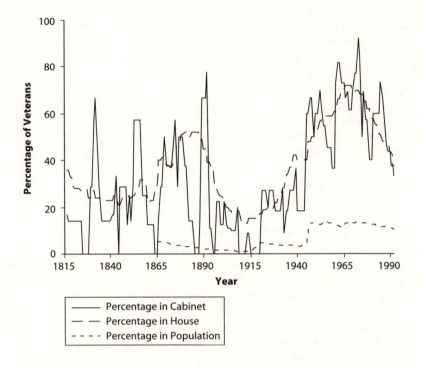

Figure 3.2. Percentage of veterans in Cabinet, House of Representatives,
and U.S. Population.

Secondary Explanatory Variable: Interventionist versus
Realpolitik Uses of Force

One important aspect of our argument is that civilians differ from those
with military experience in terms of their willingness to use military force
to address issues that are outside the realpolitik scope of American security policy—especially those that involve intervention inside other states.
To test this hypothesis, we divided dyads into two categories: states whose
actions could represent a threat to the core bases of American security,
and states whose actions could not represent such a threat. The former
category we labeled "realpolitik" targets and the latter we labeled "interventionist." We defined interventionist targets as any state that: (1) faced
worse than a 99:1 disadvantage against the United States in terms of relative military capabilities, and (2) was not allied with a competing major
power. Such small, nonaligned states clearly do not have the capability to
threaten American security in a realpolitik manner. Instead, disputes with
such states were likely to involve U.S. intervention inside the minor state

because of domestic turmoil or because the United States was dissatisfied with the policies or behaviors of the ruling government of such states. States that enjoyed less than a 99:1 disadvantage against the United States or were allied with a rival major power were coded as realpolitik targets. This coding rule results in approximately 51 percent of the dyad-years in our dataset being coded as interventionist.

This division is crude, but it captures the essence of what we mean by U.S. interventionism. Moreover, this division makes a variety of coding assignments that would match with our intuitive understanding of realpolitik and interventionist threats and our distinction between interstate and intrastate intervention. For example, Cuba is coded as an interventionist threat until the Castro revolution. Castro, however, develops Cuban military capabilities sufficiently that, beginning in 1960, Cuba becomes a realpolitik threat. Similarly, Haiti, the Dominican Republic, and the Central American countries are interventionist threats (that is, interventionist conflicts), while Mexico is a realpolitik threat (especially in the nineteenth century). Our measure of interventionism is intended to identify states against which the United States was likely to be using force for reasons other than the defense of traditional national security goals. To the extent that the United States initiated militarized disputes against interventionist states, it was targeting extremely weak states that were not allied with rival external powers. In such cases the United States was likely to be intervening in the domestic politics of such states to alter their governments or their government's internal policies. Our hypothesis is that policymakers with military experience would be more reluctant to engage in such interventions.

Control Variables

Because decisions to use force are multifaceted and complex, even if we did find a relationship between our measures of the civil-military gap and the propensity to use force, we would not expect it to be the only (or even the most important) factor influencing the use of force. A large body of literature on international conflict has already identified numerous factors that affect the use of force, including distance, military capabilities, and democracy, for example. To the extent that the elite military experience is correlated with any of these factors, the failure to include that factor in our analysis might bias our estimate of the impact of elite veterans. Control variables thus allow us to address many of the critiques we have encountered, most of which take the form of conceding a statistical correlation but denying a causal relationship on the grounds that some other factor is the true causal agent. As far as possible, we have controlled for every plausible alternative argument in our empirical analysis.

Including additional control variables cannot artificially inflate the estimated impact of our variable of interest. It can, however, introduce problems such as multicollinearity.[17] Such problems would inflate the standard errors of the coefficients and could reduce the statistical significance of our results. Thus the inclusion of control variables can only provide a more stringent test of our hypotheses.[18] Including these variables also allows us to compare the impact of elite military experience with the influence of other prominent causes of conflict.

The variables that we utilize are clustered into three categories: variables that address likely counterarguments or potential sources of spuriousness for our results; variables that are not likely sources of spuriousness, but are known to be important determinants of the use of force and thus are useful for illustrating the comparative importance of our main explanatory variable; and variables that are needed to address other methodological concerns.

Potentially Confounding Variable (1): Log of Casualties in Previous U.S. War. Controlling for the human costs of U.S. participation in a war helps address one of the most obvious counterarguments to our finding of a relationship between elite veterans and the use of force: American war experience. The presence of veterans in the political elite is obviously a function of U.S. participation in a war, and it is reasonable to expect American conflict behavior to change after a major war. Perhaps this war memory or "war weariness" is the true causal factor and the presence of

---

[17] Multicollinearity levels do become high (auxiliary $R^2 = 0.8$) for the elite veterans variable, because of our specification of an interaction with interventionist targets. Auxiliary regressions for the balance of military capabilities also revealed relatively high collinearity levels (auxiliary $R^2 = 0.71$). Nonetheless elite veterans, its interaction term, and military capabilities all retain their statistical significance, making the issue of multicollinearity irrelevant. The dummy variables for the major power status of the United States and its partner in the dyad also suffer from some moderate collinearity problems (auxiliary R^2 are 0.5 and .71 respectively), which could account for their statistical insignificance; however, the relatively small size of their coefficients appears to be a more likely cause. Comparing their coefficients with our estimate for the impact of the cold war (also a dummy variable, making such comparisons possible), we can see that the standard error for the U.S. major power status variable is smaller than the standard error for the cold war variable. Its coefficient, however, is less than one-fourth the size of the impact of the cold war. Auxiliary regressions on all other variables revealed auxiliary R^2's of less than 0.2.

[18] One circumstance in which it could be inappropriate to include a variable as a "control" would be if that factor actually served as an intervening variable in between our antecedent variable (elite military experience) and our dependent variable (the use of force). Controlling for an intervening variable may cause the antecedent variable to "disappear" from the equation because its influence is exerted only through the intervening factor. The insertion and removal of the intervening factor could be used to demonstrate the nature of the causal linkage, but one should not infer from such an analysis that the antecedent variable has no effect.

veterans in the political elite is merely an artifact of the costs of that war. Our measure of war weariness is the natural log of the number of U.S. fatalities suffered by the United States in its most recent war.[19]

Potentially Confounding Variable (2): Percentage of Veterans in the American Public. Controlling for the percentage of veterans in the American public provides a further test of the war-weariness hypothesis. The percentages of veterans in the elite and the mass are likely to be correlated, because they are both affected by the extent of U.S. participation in major wars. Perhaps any correlation between political elite veterans and the use of force is an artifact of a deeper relationship between the general public and conflict-proneness. That is, perhaps the political elite is merely responding to the broader currents of war weariness in the general public.[20] The percentage of veterans in the American public is displayed in figure 3.2.

Potentially Confounding Variable (3): Cold War Years. As we noted above, the percentage of veterans reached its height in the years following World War II. This time period, of course, was also the period of the cold war—the most intense security competition in U.S. history. Thus we would expect the United States to have exhibited a greater propensity to initiate the use of force quite independent of any civil-military effect. The cold war broke out for reasons that were exogenous to (but correlated with) the increase in veterans among U.S. policymakers. Thus the failure to control for the cold war period would lead us to attribute changes in American behavior to other factors when they were most likely due to the new global role that the United States assumed in the wake of World War II.[21] This indicator is a dummy variable that equals 1 during the years 1946 to 1989.

---

[19] We estimated a variety of decay functions for the decline of the war-weariness effect over time. However, the simple log of U.S. casualties fit the data best. Data on U.S. war fatalities were drawn from the Directorate for Information Operations and Reports (Statistical Information Analysis Division), U.S. Department of Defense (*http://www.web1.osd.mil/mmid/casualty*).

[20] Data for the number of veterans in the U.S. public were received from the Department of Veterans Affairs, and data for the total U.S. population figures were drawn from the COW dataset on national capabilities. Data on the number of U.S. veterans were available only from 1865. Thus we estimate our equations both with and without this control variable. Missing data points after 1865 were interpolated from the time series using STATA version 6.0. Because the time series is generally smooth, the interpolated values appear to provide a good fit. We tested the interpolation process by interpolating the entire time series on the basis of only one observation per five-year period. Regressing these interpolations on the true values yielded an *r*-squared of greater than 0.96.

[21] After presenting our results, we discuss a number of sensitivity analyses that address the robustness of our findings across various historical periods—including the cold war.

Potentially Confounding Variable (4): U.S. Involvement in Other Disputes. Both presidents and the mass public may be more likely to select policymakers with military experience when they perceive the United States as facing substantial security threats. Thus if elite military experience is positively related to American involvement in disputes, this result may be an effect rather than a cause of that involvement. Our first step toward solving this problem was to define our dependent variable as American initiations of disputes. In addition, however, we also control for the number of disputes the United States was involved in each year (either as initiator or target) outside the dyad under consideration.

Potentially Confounding Variable (5): Political Party in Power. Recent evidence suggests that elite military officers increasingly identify with the Republican Party (Holsti 2001). In addition, recent Republican administrations have been perceived both as having greater military representation among their ranks and as being more sympathetic to the views of the military than have Democratic administrations. At the same time, Republican administrations have frequently been depicted as relatively hawkish on foreign policy issues. Thus we control for the political party in power in order to distinguish the impact of military views from the impact of the Republican Party.

Potential Confounding Variable (6): Balance of Military Capabilities. One robust finding in the literature on conflict propensity is that states of vastly unequal military capabilities are unlikely to engage in conflict with one another (Blainey 1973; Organski and Kugler 1980). America experienced dramatic increases in power around the turn of the twentieth century and after World War II. Shortly after each of these changes, the percentage of veterans in the policymaking elite increased as well. Thus we must control for American capabilities in order to distinguish their influence from the impact of elite military experience. We measure the balance of military capabilities within a dyad with COW data on national material capabilities. For each year, we calculate the proportion of the capabilities within each dyad that is controlled by the United States—that is, U.S. Capabilities/(U.S. + Adversary Capabilities), subtract 0.50, and take the absolute value. The resulting variable ranges from 0 (perfectly equal capabilities) to 0.50 (capabilities entirely controlled by one state in the dyad). We then rescale this variable from 0 to 1 to make it consistent with standard measures of relative capabilities.

Comparative Variable (1): Shared Alliance Ties. States that share security interests should be less likely to engage in militarized disputes with one another (Bremer 1992; Bueno de Mesquita and Lalman 1992). Accordingly, we include a tau-b measure of alliance portfolio similarity between the United States and the other dyad member in each dyad-year. In principle, the tau-b similarity score ranges from −1 to 1, with higher values representing more similar alliance patterns; in our data, similarity scores range from −0.46 to 1.[22]

Comparative Variable (2): Major Power Status. Another well-established finding is that major powers are substantially more likely to become involved in disputes (Bremer 1992). Because the United States became a major power roughly halfway through the time period we studied and because this status altered the set of "politically relevant" dyads, we control for whether both the United States and its potential adversary were major powers. Again major power status is coded on the basis of the COW dataset on national material capabilities.

Comparative Variable (3): Adversary's Level of Democracy. The extensive literature on the democratic peace has established democracy as one of the most robust and important determinants of international conflict (Bremer 1992; Maoz and Russett 1993; Ray 1995). Thus we include the level of democracy in the opposing state. Consistent with most of the literature on the democratic peace, we measure democracy on the basis of the Polity III dataset (Jaggers and Gurr 1996). We create a net democracy score for each state, defined as its democracy score minus its autocracy score. This variable ranges from −10 (autocracy) to 10 (democracy).

Comparative Variable (4): Distance between States. One of the strongest findings in the study of international conflict is that states that are near one another are more likely to engage in military conflict (Bremer 1992). Thus we control for the distance between the United States and its potential adversary in the dyad. We measure this as the log of the number of miles between capital cities, unless the two states are contiguous, in which case the distance is defined as 0. States are coded as "contiguous" if they share a land border or if they are separated by less than 250 miles of water.

Comparative Variable (5): Adversary's Level of Force. In our analysis of crisis escalation, we control for the level of force used by the opposing state, which is measured according to the same five-point scale as the challenger's level of force.[23]

---

[22] A dummy variable identifying states with which the United States shared a direct alliance tie yielded similar results.

[23] Our use of the level of force used by the opposing state as a control variable in explaining the level of force used by the United States is a rather crude specification of

Methodological Control (1): Peace Years in the Dyad.   We correct for temporal dependence in our binary time-series cross-sectional data by accounting for the number of years that have elapsed since the previous conflict within the dyad (Beck, Katz, and Tucker 1998). We model the impact of time by including dummy variables for each elapsed year of peace, because this method is both simple and flexible in dealing with any possible pattern of temporal correlation.[24] As it happens, the dummy variables are statistically significant for peace years 0 through 4; thus we retain only these five dummy variables.

Methodological Control (2): Selection Effects Parameter.   As in any analysis of crisis escalation, we must cope with the issue of selection effects. Since the United States had to initiate a dispute before it could engage in escalation, the cases in which we can observe American decisions regarding escalation are self-selected. This nonrandom selection process can bias the coefficients in the analysis of the level of force used by the United States. We account for the nonrandom selection of crises by modeling the initiation and escalation decisions as a set of simultaneous equations.[25] In the selection equation we estimate a predicted probability of dispute initiation. We then insert this predicted value as a control variable in our analysis of escalation. By accounting for the expected probability of a dispute, we correct for the self-selection process.[26]

Does the Civil-Military Gap Influence American Conflict Behavior?. We conducted a logit analysis of every politically relevant interstate dyadic relationship in which the United States was a partner from 1816 to 1992. Table 3.1 presents our analysis of the propensity of the United States to

---

crisis escalation. In fact, the United States and its adversary were likely to be interacting strategically as they escalated a militarized dispute. This strategic interaction creates a problem of censored data (Signorino 1999; A. Smith 1999). Fortunately, our results remained robust when we specified the escalation of the United States and its adversary as endogenous variables in a bivariate probit. We retained the current specification so that we could use the full range of the COW escalation variable rather than dichotomizing it for the bivariate probit.

[24] Controlling for peace years with a spline function yielded identical results.

[25] A necessary condition for the identification of a system of equations is that at least one exogenous variable be excluded from each equation. In our analysis, the hostility level of the adversary is excluded from the selection equation, because the dispute initiation by the United States is temporally (and causally) prior to the opponent's escalation decision. The impact of peace years in the dyad and the number of years since U.S. participation in a war are excluded from the escalation equation, because these temporal effects are no longer relevant once a dispute has been initiated.

[26] In addition to this two-stage selection model, we also estimated a Heckman selection model that estimates the initiation and escalation equations simultaneously. Once again our results regarding the impact of veterans remained robust across both estimations. Again we retained the current specification so as to utilize the full COW escalation scale.

initiate militarized disputes. Our results provide strong and striking support for hypotheses 1 and 2. As predicted, the negative coefficient for elite veterans is statistically significant, indicating that the more veterans there were in the political elite, the less likely the United States was to initiate the use of force. Also as predicted, the effect of veterans on the propensity to use force was even greater in interventionist cases. As indicated by column three of table 3.1, the coefficient for this variable for realpolitik dyads is only –0.19 ($p < .10$). With regard to interventionist dyads, in contrast, the coefficient is calculated by adding that value to the coefficient on the interaction between the percentage of veterans in the policy elite and an interventionist threat (–0.47, p < .01). Thus the overall effect of elite veterans for interventionist dyads is –0.66—more than three times the impact for realpolitik dyads.

Figure 3.3 displays the predicted probability that the United States would initiate a militarized dispute as the percentage of veterans in the cabinet and Congress ranged from its historical near-minimum of 10 percent to its historical near-maximum of 80 percent.[27] When only one policymaker in ten had military experience, the probability that the United States would initiate a dispute within a given dyad was approximately 3.6 percent. At first glance, this might look like a relatively small risk. But because militarized disputes are rare events, a 3 percent probability of a dispute between a given pair of states actually indicates a relatively high risk. Moreover, the effect of a 3 percent probability is magnified by the large number of dyads in which the United States was involved each year. For large portions of our dataset, the United States was engaged in over one hundred such dyads per year. Thus a 3 percent per dyad probability of a dispute yields a prediction that, holding all other factors that influence the decision to use force hypothetically constant, the United States might initiate several additional militarized disputes per year because so few policymakers had military experience.[28]

Conversely, of course, as the percentage of policymakers with military experience increases, the probability of dispute initiation drops substantially. The impact of these changes is slightly nonlinear, with the greatest decreases in the probability of a dispute occurring as the percentage of

[27] We select this range of variation because approximately 95 percent of the cases we observe are within this range. The historical minimum percentage of veterans is 6.5 percent and the maximum percentage we observe is 81.2 percent. The mean value for this variable is 46.7 percent and the standard deviation is 20.3 percent. The median percentage of veterans in office is 50 percent, while the first and third quartiles are 28 percent and 61 percent. Thus our variation from 10 percent to 80 percent represents a plausible set of hypothetical values for judging the marginal impact of this variable.

[28] An event-count model that estimated the overall number of disputes initiated by the United States each year estimated the marginal impact of moving from 10 percent veterans to 80 percent veterans as an average of 1.3 initiations per year.

TABLE 3.1
Elite Military Experience and American Militarized Dispute Initiation

Explanatory Variables	Elite Veterans Model	Elite and Mass Veterans Model	Realpolitik vs. Interventionist Threats
Percent Veteran in Cabinet and House	−0.032***	−0.031**	−0.019*
	(0.011)	(0.014)	(0.011)
Elite Vets × Interventionist			−0.047***
			(0.012)
Interventionist Threat			1.02**
			(0.46)
Ln of Previous War's Battle	−0.16***	−0.22**	−0.17***
	(0.056)	(0.092)	(0.056)
Percent Veteran in U.S. Public		−0.042	
		(0.059)	
Cold War Years	1.70***	2.17***	1.83***
	(0.50)	(0.76)	(0.52)
Republican Administration	0.44	0.41	0.45
	(0.28)	(0.31)	(0.28)
U.S. Involvement in Other	−0.070	−0.065	−0.061
	(0.060)	(0.063)	(0.06)
Balance of Military Capabilities	−1.75***	−1.84***	−1.15
	(0.61)	(0.72)	(0.74)
Alliance Similarity	−1.41**	−1.36**	−1.77**
	(0.65)	(0.70)	(0.79)
U.S. Is a Major Power	−0.39	−0.76	−0.61
	(0.38)	(0.69)	(0.40)
Adversary Is a Major Power	−0.39	−0.43	−0.29
	(0.69)	(0.86)	(0.70)
Adversary Level of Democracy	−0.045**	−0.061**	−0.037*
	(0.023)	(0.026)	(0.023)
Ln Distance between states	−0.30***	−0.30***	−0.28**
	(0.029)	(0.031)	(0.027)
Years since U.S. Initiation in [a]			
Constant	−1.29	−2.38	0.61
	(0.90)	(1.80)	(1.04)
Number of Observations	8,739	8,464	8,739
Initial Log Likelihood	−594.92	−534.37	−594.92
Log-Likelihood at Convergence	−469.72	−419.82	−456.54
Chi-squared	601.74 (17 d.f.)	727.95 (18 d.f.)*	560.77 (19 d.f.)*

* $= p < .10.$ ** $= p < .05.$ *** $= p < .01.$

Note: Huber-White robust standard errors in parentheses. Standard errors allow for clustering by dyad.

[a] For reasons of space the temporal dependence coefficients are not reported here. As expected, years since the previous U.S. initiation did have a significant and nonlinear effect on U.S. dispute initiation as predicted by Beck, Katz, and Tucker (1998).

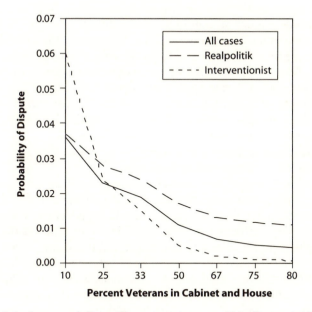

Figure 3.3. Impact of elite military experience on U.S. dispute initiations:
Realpolitik, interventionist, and all cases.

veterans ranges between 10 percent and 67 percent. By the time the rate
of military experience among policymakers reaches 67 percent, the probability that the United States would initiate a dispute within a given dyad
drops from 3.6 percent to 0.7 percent—representing more than an 80 percent decrease from its previous value, which we call a reduction in relative
risk.[29] Further increases in elite military experience up to 80 percent reduce
the probability of a dispute within a dyad to nearly 0.4 percent.

Also in figure 3.3, we compare the impact of elite veterans on the probability that the United States would initiate a crisis against realpolitik and
interventionist threats. As one would expect from the results in table 3.1,
the impact of elite veterans is much greater for interventionist cases. When
few veterans are in office, the United States is less likely to initiate a dispute against realpolitik than interventionist targets. Specifically, when
only 10 percent of policymakers are veterans, the probability of a U.S.
initiation in a realpolitik dyad is 4.7 percent and in an interventionist
dyad it is approximately 6.0 percent. As the percentage of elite veterans

[29] This relative risk is a percentage of percentages, analogous to medical research that
finds that adopting certain heart-healthy behaviors can reduce the risk of a heart attack by
50 percent—the likelihood that any individual might have a heart attack is already low, but
adopting the prescribed behavior can cut it in half.

increases, the probability of a dispute drops within both sets of dyads, but the decline is much steeper in the interventionist group. In fact, by the time the percentage of veterans reaches 50 percent, the United States is actually more than three times as likely to initiate force against a realpolitik threat. When the percentage of veterans nears its historical maximum, the probability of initiation against a realpolitik threat is 1 percent, while the probability of initiation against an interventionist threat is only .08 percent. These results are made all the more striking by the crude nature of our distinction between realpolitik and interventionist threats. More careful theorizing and empirical work on these categories would surely increase the decisiveness of this distinction.

Many of our control variables also have a significant impact on U.S. dispute initiation, but none of these effects can account for the impact of elite veterans. For example, our analysis supports the war-weariness hypothesis. The coefficient for the log of U.S. casualties in the previous war is negative and statistically significant, but it does not account for the impact of elite veterans. The percentage of veterans among the U.S. public, in contrast, has no significant effect. The fact that elite military experience matters while military experience among the public does not fits precisely with the elite-level causal mechanism that we hypothesized. The coefficient for Republican administrations was consistently positive, but did not quite achieve statistical significance ($p < .11$ for model in column 1). Thus any possible association between the U.S. military and the Republican Party cannot account for the relationship between elite military experience and American conflict behavior.[30]

Most of the other control variables perform as expected, consistent with the established literature. Not surprisingly, for example, the positive coefficient for the cold war years indicates that this period witnessed a significantly larger number of American dispute initiations than other periods of U.S. history. The negative coefficient on the opponent's democracy score indicates that the United States is significantly less likely to initiate disputes against other democratic states. The balance of military capabilities also has a significant impact on American initiation of disputes. This negative coefficient indicates that the United States is less likely to initiate disputes in dyads where military capabilities are highly unequal.

---

[30] It is also worth noting that we find little evidence of a general relationship between Republicanism and elite military experience. Since the onset of two-party competition between the Democratic and Republican parties in the mid-nineteenth century, Republican cabinets have had an average of approximately 5 percent more veterans, but this gap is not statistically significant. In the House of Representatives, however, the percentage of veterans was more than 18 percent higher under Democratic control ($p < .01$). But this gap seems more likely to be a chance result of the timing of Democratic control than a direct link between military experience and Democratic partisanship.

TABLE 3.2

Impact of Significant Variables on the Risk of American Dispute Initiation

Explanatory Variables	Change in Explanatory Variable	Change in Probability of a Dispute	Change in Relative Risk of a Dispute
Percent Veteran in Cabinet and House	10% to 80%	−3.1%	−88%
Cold War Years	Yes or No	−1.0%	−80%
Adversary's Level of Democracy	−10 to 10	−1.1%	−59%
Balance of Military Capabilities	70% to 100%	−1.0%	−49%
Alliance Similarity Score	−0.3 to 0.7	−1.4%	−72%
Previous War's Battle Deaths	383 to 400,000	−1.6%	−67%
Distance between States	0 to 9,000 miles	−0.7%	−44%

Note: Relative risk is calculated based on predicted probabilities generated from the first model in table 3.1. Predicted probabilities were generated by varying each independent variable while holding others at their means or modes.

Common security interests (as measured by alliance similarity) also had a significant dampening effect on the American initiation of disputes. And not surprisingly, distance also has a dampening effect on America's propensity to initiate disputes. American involvement in other disputes, in contrast, had no impact on decisions to initiate additional disputes. America's status as a major power also had no impact on its initiation of disputes, nor did the major power status of the adversary.

How does the substantive impact of the civil-military gap compare with the impacts of the control variables? In table 3.2, we list the statistically significant variables and the range across which we varied them in order to generate the predicted effects. In the third and fourth columns, we display the changes in the probability and in the relative risk of a dispute initiation.

The impact of elite military experience continues to be substantial, even when we compare it with other prominent and well-established sources of international conflict. Specifically, our model predicts that a change in the percentage of elite veterans from 10 percent to 80 percent—a shift from slightly less than two standard deviations below the mean to slightly less than two standard deviations above—will generate a 3.1 percent reduction in the probability of U.S. dispute initiation across all dyads. This change corresponds to an 88 percent reduction in the relative risk of a dispute.

Even the cold war, which obviously had a substantial impact on American involvement in militarized disputes, did not have as large an impact as elite military experience. The United States was at an 80 percent lower relative risk of initiating militarized disputes prior to the outbreak of the cold war, but as large as this effect is, it remains smaller than the 88 percent reduction in relative risk associated with increased veteran representation in the political elite. Other traditional "realist" variables, such as relative military power and alliance ties, also had a substantial impact on American dispute behavior, but neither of these outstrips the impact of elite military experience. These results are particularly important in light of the amount of attention that the cold war, military capabilities, alliances, and the structure of the international system have received as explanations of international conflict and American foreign policy. Our results suggest that American military behavior had been as powerfully influenced by the military experience of its leaders as it has by America's position in the international system.

Similarly, the much-touted impact of democracy is smaller than the impact of elite military experience. A shift in the democracy score of the opposing state from its minimum value of –10 (pure authoritarian state) to its maximum of 10 (pure democracy) reduced the probability that the United States will initiate a dispute by 1.1 percent—a reduction in relative risk of 59 percent.[31] This impact is undoubtedly substantial, but it remains considerably less than the 88 percent reduction in relative risk associated with moving the civil-military experience gap among the political elite from its maximum to its minimum.

Does the Civil-Military Gap Influence How America Uses Force?

Does elite military experience also have an impact on the American escalation of disputes? The answer to this question—displayed in table 3.3—appears to be an unqualified yes. Our results indicate that higher percentages of veterans in the political elite were associated with greater levels of force by the United States—if the United States did initiate the use of force. The coefficient for the percentage of veterans in the cabinet and in Congress is positive and statistically significant, and the impact of this variable is substantial.

Figure 3.4 indicates that as the percentage of veterans in the cabinet and Congress increases from 10 percent to 80 percent, the probability that the United States would engage in direct combat (use-of-force coding) increases from 2 percent to 73 percent. This same increase in the percentage of elite veterans increases the probability that the United States will escalate the dispute to the level of becoming a war from 0.06 percent to

---

[31] We use minimum and maximum values because of the bimodal distribution of this variable. Opposing states with democracy scores below –6 or above 6 made up well over half of our dataset. In fact, opposing states with democracy scores of –10 made up more than 5 percent of our dataset and opposing states with a democracy score of 10 made up more than 15 percent of the cases.

TABLE 3.3
Elite Military Experience and the Level of Military Force Used by
the United States in a Dispute

Explanatory Variables	Coefficients and Standard Errors
Percent Veteran in the Cabinet and House	0.089***
	(0.024)
Republican Administration	−0.42
	(0.47)
Cold War Years	−4.31***
	(1.24)
Balance of Military Capabilities	−1.93
	(1.45)
Alliance Similarity Score	0.89
	(1.11)
U.S. Is a Major Power	1.91**
	(0.79)
Adversary Is a Major Power	−2.73***
	(1.01)
Adversary Level of Democracy	0.066
	(0.049)
U.S. Involvement in Other Disputes	−0.10
	(0.13)
Contiguous State	−0.68
	(1.016)
Distance between States	−0.0002
	(0.0002)
Adversary's Level of Force	0.61***
	(0.16)
Selection Effects Parameter	5.17*
	(3.15)
Threshold 1	−0.61
	(1.87)
Threshold 2	2.86*
	(1.90)
Threshold 3	7.08***
	(2.04)
Number of Observations	111
Initial Log-Likelihood	−112.54
Log-Likelihood at Convergence	−92.47
Chi-squared (10 d.f.)	40.13 (12 d.f.) ***

Note: Huber-White robust standard errors for coefficients in parentheses.
* = $p < .10$.   ** = $p < .05$.   *** = $p < .01$.

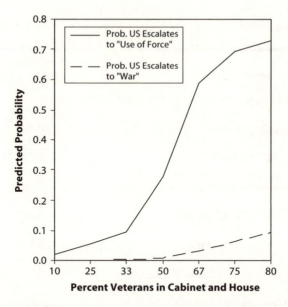

Figure 3.4. Impact of elite military experience on the level of force used in dispute.

9 percent. This latter increase is particularly substantial given the rarity of wars (0.2 percent of the dyad-years) and the gravity of escalating to such a level. Most of this impact is felt after the percentage of policymakers with military experience exceeds 33 percent. Thus policymakers with military experience may well have favored something like an informal Powell Doctrine long before any such doctrine was articulated, far back in American history.

Table 3.4 compares the marginal impact of changes in policymakers' military experience with the impact of other statistically significant variables in the model. We see that the impact of elite military experience is large in comparison with these other variables. Only the cold war, which we take to be a surrogate for nuclear deterrence, arguably has a greater impact on the level of force employed by the United States. The cold war reduced the probability that the United States would engage its forces directly by 56 percent and reduced the probability that it would escalate to war by 18 percent. The impact of major power status is dwarfed by the impact of military experience among American policymakers. America's status as a major power, for example, increases the probability that it would engage its forces directly by 12 percent. Conversely, the United States was 14 percent less likely to intervene directly against another major power. Neither of these variables, however, had any substantial impact on the probability that the dispute would escalate to war. Even the impact of the adversary's level of force is not as large as the impact

TABLE 3.4
Impact of Significant Variables on the Level of Force Used by the United States

Explanatory Variables	Change in Explanatory Variable	Change in Probability of the Use of Force	Change in Probability of War
Percent Veteran in Cabinet and House	10% to 80%	71%	9%
Cold War Years	Yes or No	−56%	18%
U.S. Is a Major Power	−10 to 10	12%	0.3%
Adversary Is a Major Power	70% to 100%	−14%	−0.4%
Adversary Level of Force	−0.3 to 0.7	39%	2%

Note: Relative risk is calculated based on predicted probabilities generated from the first model in table 3.3. Predicted probabilities were generated by varying each independent variable while holding others at their means or modes.

of elite veterans. A change in the adversary's actions from "no response" to "full-scale combat" increased the probability of an American "use of force" by only 39 percent.

Our measure of escalation is fairly crude and, as we discuss in chapter 6, developing more nuanced measures is a priority for future research. Nevertheless, it is striking that we find such statistically strong results in support of the theory's expectations, especially given the difficulties of measuring the phenomena involved. Moreover, note that the theory leads to opposite expectations from the veterans variable in these two stages of analysis: more veterans should lead to *fewer* dispute initiations but *higher* escalations. Nevertheless, the results support each apparently opposite dynamic, thus offering even stronger support for the underlying argument.

Additional Tests for Robustness

We performed a variety of checks of the robustness of our results. Because elite military experience and interventionist targets are complex concepts with no standard indicators, we reestimated our analyses of both dispute initiation and escalation with alternative measures of both concepts. For elite military experience we tested a measure that excluded the military experience of cabinet members whose positions were not relevant to national security, as well as a measure that excluded the military experience of House members and focused only on the military experience of cabinet members on the national security team (president, vice president, secretary of state, and secretary of defense/war). The impact of elite military experience remained consistent for both the initiation and the escalation of disputes and remained statistically significant across all these estimations. In fact, a dummy variable identifying when the secretary of state was a veteran was consistently significant at the .10 level. It is worth noting, however, that a simple dummy variable coding whether or not the president was a veteran was not statistically significant for either the initiation or the escalation equation. This result is consistent with the idea that the preferences of presidential advisors (and potential critics) are relevant to U.S. foreign policy behavior. With regard to interventionist targets, we conducted analyses that identified any state facing greater than a 99:1 military disadvantage as an interventionist target, regardless of its alliance ties to other major powers. We also conducted analyses that identified any minor power state that was not allied to a rival major power as an interventionist target. Our results remained robust.

Our pooled time-series analysis of dispute initiation heavily weights the post–World War II period, because of the very large number of dyads during that period. To ensure that our results are stable across the span of American history, we also analyzed a single 177-year event-count time series in which the dependent variable was the number of disputes initiated by the United States in each year. The coefficient for elite military experience remained negative and statistically significant (-0.036, $p <$ .002), and the impact of elite veterans remained substantively large. For example, the average number of dispute initiations per year over the 177-year period is 0.56, or about one dispute every other year. The model predicts that a shift in the percentage of veterans in the policymaking elite from 10 percent to 80 percent would reduce the average number of dispute initiations by 1.3 per year.

We also distinguished various historical eras and then removed each era from the analysis in order to ensure that our findings were not limited to a specific period. Specifically, we used major military conflicts (the Spanish-American War, World War I, World War II, and the cold war) to divide U.S. history into the following periods: pre-1898, 1898–1914, 1915–1945, 1945–1989, and post-1989. Our results remained consistent, even when each of these historical eras was removed from the analysis. Although the substantive size of the impact of veterans varied somewhat across these periods, elite veterans continued to have an effect across the nineteenth and twentieth centuries and across the pre– and post–World War II periods.

Finally, we investigated whether the type of military service experienced by policymakers mattered, and found that it did not. Specifically, we found no distinction between the impact of elite veterans who served as officers and those who served as enlisted personnel. These results would suggest the existence of a rather broad set of "military foreign policy preferences." Moreover, since those who served as officers generally did so by choice while those who served as enlisted may have been drafted, these results suggest that "military preferences" may remain fairly consistent regardless of whether one's service was voluntary. This result is also consistent with our findings in chapter 5 concerning the reasons respondents joined the military and their tolerance for casualties. Unfortunately, two potentially important distinctions we were not able to capture were combat experience and the timing of military experience (that is, serving in wartime or peacetime). Consistent and reliable data on combat experience and the precise timing of military experience among the policymaking elite were not available.

Conclusion

Civil-military relations at the policymaking level often seem dominated by personalities. Contrast the problems of President Clinton with those of his war-hero predecessor, President Bush; compare the rumpled tenure of Secretary Les Aspin or the academic acerbity of Secretary Madeleine Albright with the no-nonsense corporate mentality of Secretary Donald Rumsfeld; or consider the unusual charisma and political clout of General and then Secretary Colin Powell. Personalities matter and may be decisive in certain cases. Nonetheless, the findings presented here suggest that, at least when it comes to the use of force, we can identify consistent civilian and military tendencies in policymaking, irrespective of personalities.

Chapter 2 has shown that elite civilians with military experience behave like "Colin Powells" and elite civilian nonveterans are like "Madeleine Albrights"—at least where opinions on the use of force are concerned. What creates these different types? Why do civilians without military experience tend to have foreign policy views that systematically differ from the views of those who have served? We cannot definitively answer that question. We would contend, however, that service in the U.S. military is an important socialization experience that shapes individuals' attitudes. The military teaches lessons about the role of military force in American foreign policy and lessons about how military force ought to be used. These lessons do not appear to be forgotten when individuals leave the military and enter civilian life. Of course we cannot yet specify the precise mechanisms at work in this socialization process, and our data may be consistent with other explanations as well.[32] Nonetheless, our results sug-

---

[32] An important competing hypothesis, of course, is that the civil-military gap is created by self-selection rather than by socialization. That is, the civil-military differences we observe may be due to the fact that the military tends to attract individuals who already share its foreign policy views. In the absence of panel survey data looking at individuals' attitudes before, during, and after military service, we cannot definitively resolve this debate. However, several available pieces of evidence suggest that socialization is a more plausible explanation. First, our survey data indicate that the reason that military respondents gave for

gest that the relationship among military experience, foreign policy attitudes, and conflict behavior merits further attention.

Whatever the causes of this civil-military opinion gap, we have shown
that the gap had a profound effect on American military behavior from
1816 to 1992. As expected, we found that the higher the proportion of
American policymakers with military experience, the lower the probability that the United States would initiate a militarized dispute. Also as expected, we found that the impact of military experience on dispute initiation became even larger when we focused on states that represented
interventionist rather than realpolitik threats to the United States. Finally,
also as expected, we found that the veteran's effect showed up in the level
of force as well; the higher the proportion of American policymakers with
military experience, the higher the level of force used by the United States,
given that it had already initiated a use of force. Throughout these analyses, the impact of elite military experience was substantively large and
often outweighed the impact of variables that have received considerably
more attention in the study of international conflict.[33]

It may be "normal" for military personnel and civilians to develop distinctive views regarding the use of force, but when this divergence of views
begins to have an impact on American conflict behavior, one cannot simply shrug off the difference and say "Who cares?" The difference in views
between those with and without experience in the American military is a
profoundly important issue that is in need of public attention and discussion. In the wake of the cold war, the United States is faced primarily with
interventionist threats such as civil wars and the violation of human
rights. Undoubtedly, debates over what ought to be done in future Kosovos, Haitis, and Rwandas will be shaped by this pervasive civil-military
dynamic. If veteran representation in the political elite continues to decline, we can expect American involvement in many more Kosovos, Haitis, and Rwandas to come.

---

joining the military did not have a significant effect on their foreign policy views. Similarly,
as we discussed above, the presence of veteran policymakers who served as officers (self-
selected) had the same impact on U.S. behavior as the presence of veteran policymakers who
served as enlisted personnel (less likely to be self-selected).

[33] Our findings appear to contradict those of Choi and James (2002a, b), who find support for the hypothesis that as military influence increases, the propensity to engage in a
military conflict also increases. The contradiction is easily explained. Choi and James use
cross-national data, while we only look at the United States. It is entirely possible that a
different civil-military dynamic is at work in other countries. Perhaps more tellingly, Choi
and James operationalize "military influence" as military expenditures. However, military
expenditures might also be a good surrogate for "perception of the threat," for as states
perceive greater threats they are likely to increase their defense spending to meet them.
Viewed that way, the Choi and James finding might be restated thus: as perceptions of the
threat increase, the likelihood that that state gets into a military conflict also increases. This
finding is plausible, but it may not directly address civil-military issues.

CHAPTER FOUR

CASUALTY SENSITIVITY AND

CIVIL-MILITARY RELATIONS

The safest place on the modern battlefield is to be in uniform.
—ROBERT A. SEIPLE, ambassador-at-large for International
Religious Freedom at the Department of State, commenting on
the emphasis U.S. military leaders place on avoiding casualties

IN NOVEMBER 1998, as negotiations reached an impasse, NATO's
supreme commander General Wesley Clark ordered his military planners to prepare for the use of force against Serbia. The mission would
be to protect the Albanian Kosovars from ethnic cleansing, and although
NATO officially professed hope that diplomacy might avert a conflict, it
girded itself for the possibility that force might be necessary. According
to reports, Clark assumed that NATO political leaders would not authorize a ground force and so ordered his planners to prepare for an air-only
assault. But Clark reportedly imposed an additional restriction: that the
air campaign be designed in such a way as to ensure "no loss of aircraft."
The war gamers ran computer simulations over and over, changing the
packages of aircraft, ordinance, and rules of engagement, until they produced a plan that on paper promised no loss of aircraft: a war, in short,
with no NATO casualties (Drozdiak and Priest 1999; Clark 2001).

Diplomatic negotiations failed, and on March 25, 1999, NATO
launched the war Clark's planners envisioned. On June 11, after Serbian
forces agreed to withdraw from Kosovo, President Clinton declared victory. Although NATO lost three aircraft, the pilots were rescued and the
war ended with no U.S. deaths due to hostile enemy fire (although two
helicopter training accidents in Albania claimed the lives of two Army
aviators). With Slobodan Milosevic's concession, NATO enjoyed something approximating victory in combat with essentially no NATO combat
casualties. Despite this extraordinary record—and perhaps because of
it—the war raised troubling questions about civil-military relations and
the willingness of the American public and American civilian and military
elites to accept the human costs of war.[1]

---

[1] The literature and polling data regarding the willingness of the American public to
support military operations in the face of casualties are fairly well developed. The new TISS

The casualty phobia thesis—that the American public is highly averse to taking casualties and will only support a conflict if it is essentially cost free—is arguably one of the most important strategic claims in the contemporary world. It is, after all, the strategic premise behind the terrorist attacks of September 11, 2001. Osama bin Laden quite explicitly grounded his anti-American strategy in his understanding of America's Achilles heel, as demonstrated in Beirut 1983, Somalia 1993, and by extension in all the post–cold war U.S. deployments: you don't need to defeat Americans on the battlefield; if you kill enough Americans, they go home (Strobel 2001). Likewise, Saddam Hussein in 1991 and Slobodan Milsosevic also explicitly calculated that the American public would force their leaders to abandon the conflicts in the Persian Gulf and the Balkans if they killed just a few American soldiers. More recently, Hussein has appealed to this perceived casualty aversion of the American public, implying that the United States would pay a heavy price in military casualties if it attacked Iraq. In an August 8, 2002, speech that dealt mostly with the threat of war with the United States, Saddam told thousands of cheering Iraqis that "one of the lessons of recent and distant history is that all empires and bearers of the coffin of evil, whenever they mobilized their evil against the Arab nation, or against the Muslim world, they were themselves buried in their own coffin, with their sick dreams and their arrogance and greed, under Arab and Islamic soil; or they returned to die on the land from which they had proceeded to perpetrate aggression" (unattributed 2002).

Ironically, bin Laden, Milosevic, and Hussein are not that far outside the conventional wisdom, which has long held that the American public has essentially zero tolerance for casualties, especially in the post–cold war era when the stakes are perceived to be low, and especially in the kinds of interventionist missions of peace and humanitarian operations that have dominated the agenda of the decade between the end of the cold war and the terrorist attacks of September 11th. The analyses presented in this chapter show that this view is a myth. The public is not reflexively casualty phobic, and neither are elite civilians or military officers. Instead, the variation we observe in casualty sensitivity across the public, civilian

---

data expand the scope of these studies to incorporate the civilian and military elite. By contrast, relatively little has been written on casualty sensitivity in other countries. The most comprehensive comparison of casualty attitudes among U.S. and other NATO publics is Everts (2002). His conclusions about other NATO allies largely conform to our conclusions about the United States: policymakers believe NATO publics to be highly casualty phobic, but there is little polling data to support this myth. See also Dixon (2000). Comparative analysis on the related topic of force protection—the steps the military takes to minimize casualties—has received some attention in the policy literature, which contrasts the great lengths U.S. forces go to in order to minimize risk versus the relatively risk-acceptant deployments of our NATO allies. On this see Atkinson (1996) and Kretchik (1997).

elites, and military officers reflects the same civil-military gaps that we observed in chapter 2. That is, both civilian and military respondents generally appear capable of making reasoned judgments about their willingness to tolerate casualties to the extent that they view the missions as important for American foreign policy.

With regard to high-intensity realpolitik missions such as the defense of Korea or Taiwan, we find that military officers tend to be more willing to tolerate casualties than civilian elites or the mass public. Note that this finding somewhat contradicts our conclusion reported earlier that "everyone agrees that this mission is worth the sacrifice of substantial number of American lives, and all three groups gave roughly the same estimate of 'acceptable' American casualties" (Feaver and Gelpi 1999c; see also Feaver and Gelpi, 2000). As discussed below, we use a more refined measure of casualty sensitivity here that captures discernible differences between military officers, elite civilians, and the mass public. Consistent with the higher level of military support for realpolitik missions that we described in chapter 2, military officers show a markedly higher casualty tolerance for realpolitik missions. Nevertheless, we continue to find support for our earlier overall conclusion (Feaver and Gelpi 1999c): a majority of the mass public report a tolerance for casualties on a realpolitik mission on the order of those the United States suffered in Desert Storm—and within that group roughly a third expressed a tolerance for casualties considerably higher. With regard to interventionist missions, however, we find civilian elites and the U.S. public to be more willing to tolerate casualties than are military officers. This is especially true for missions of humanitarian intervention such as the 1999 conflict in Kosovo. These results are consistent with the greater support for humanitarian missions that we observed among civilian respondents in chapter 2.

To be sure, there is some evidence of casualty phobia—or, more precisely, there are pockets of opinion in all three groups (the general public, civilian elites, and military elites) that appear to express something like a zero tolerance for casualties. But casualty phobia is not the dominant feature of the general public. On the contrary, policymakers can tap into a large reservoir of support for missions, even missions that entail a fairly high human price, provided those missions are successful. The public is defeat phobic, not casualty phobic. From these results we conclude that while policymakers show great casualty aversion in the policies they pursue, they are either tying their own hands or responding to constraints imposed by the military. The general public is not demanding casualty-free uses of military force.

We develop our argument in several stages. We begin by discussing framing issues raised by the issue of casualty sensitivity. Second, we review existing arguments about casualty sensitivity and the strong consensus among popular pundits that the public is casualty phobic. Third, we analyze the Triangle Institute for Security Studies data, which contain a series of first-of-a-kind questions developed precisely to compare casualty sensitivities across civilian and military subsamples. We then show how the TISS data present a plain but profound pattern of civil-military difference on casualty sensitivity. Fourth, we show that this pattern of results is robust across a variety of measures of casualty sensitivity and across a number of statistical specifications of this relationship. Fifth, in light of these results, we return to an analysis of other empirical evidence in support of the conventional wisdom of casualty phobia. From this review we conclude that the findings of the TISS study may not be so surprising after all, because the popular belief in casualty phobia rests on a misreading of several key cases, especially Korea and Vietnam.

In this chapter we establish that there is a civil-military gap on casualty sensitivity and that the public is not as casualty phobic as popularly thought. In chapter 5 we explore the determinants of attitudes toward casualties, which begin to explain why there is such a gap. We discuss the limitations and policy implications of all of these analyses in chapter 6.

Casualty Sensitivity and the Decision to Use Force

Decisions on the use of force are cost-benefit decisions. Do the benefits of invading Iraq outweigh the costs of doing so? Civil-military relations might affect the use of force if civilians and the military differ on their estimations of these benefits and costs. The benefits involve estimations of the national interest and estimations of the utility of force, that is, whether force can achieve the goals implied by the mission. The costs involve not only crude financial costs—the dollars spent in jet fuel, exploded ordinance, military rations, and so on—but also more abstract costs like potential damage to other interests and values, such as relations with allies. Importantly, there are also human costs, the dead and wounded that result from a use of force (Nincic and Nincic 1996).

Estimations of the human costs of the use of force are what is meant by the term "casualty sensitivity," also sometimes called "casualty aversion," "casualty shyness," "casualty tolerance," and "casualty phobia." In this book we will distinguish among these various terms. Casualty sensitivity and casualty tolerance refer to the generic willingness to tolerate casualties to achieve an end. Of course, at some level virtually every rational human being has some sensitivity to casualties. Faced with the exact same outcome but with different casualties—for example, victory over Iraq with 100 U.S. combat casualties versus victory over Iraq with 1,000 U.S. combat casualties—then presumably the overwhelming majority of people would prefer the victory at a lower cost. To be sure, some might argue that low-cost victories are destabilizing because they encourage hubris and adventurism, although people rarely desire to pay higher costs as a hedge against this problem. Even more atavistic and rare is the argument that there is greater glory and honor in a fight that is bloodier. Although everyone has some level of casualty sensitivity, it is reasonable to expect that that level varies across individuals or groups. At one extreme is "casualty phobia," a reflexive opposition to any use of force that includes any risk of more than a trivial level of casualties. Pacifism, the opposition to all uses of force, is arguably the most extreme form of casualty phobia. However, it is worth distinguishing opposition to all uses of force from opposition to uses of force where the risk of casualties rises above the trivially low. A principled pacifist should equally oppose an invasion of Haiti and an invasion of Iraq; a highly casualty-phobic person might support the former if the risks were demonstrably low, but be more resistant to the latter because of greater uncertainty about the costs. Moreover, a casualty-phobic person might express support for a hypothetical question about going to war against Iraq but then reverse his position on a follow-up question asking whether he would still support it if there were "thousands of casualties." At the opposite extreme is the person who expresses a willingness for the nation to pay any price and bear any burden in order to achieve the objective; that person may still prefer to pay a lower price, but his support will not erode substantially as the costs mount. Moreover, it is reasonable to expect that the same person will express different levels of casualty sensitivity for different military contexts, perhaps because the stakes are different or the battlefield prospects are different. Finally, we will reserve the term "casualty aversion" to refer to the policies that political leaders and the military implement in order to lower casualties, perhaps in response to a strong casualty sensitivity or even casualty phobia.

By casualties, we refer to those killed in connection with a military operation, whether in combat per se or in accidents resulting from activity that is a direct result of the military operation. This, we argue, is the popular meaning given to casualties, even though the official Department of Defense definition of casualties is total dead *and* wounded.[2] In the now extensive academic literature on casualty aversion, distinctions are rarely made between fatalities and wounded, between combat and combat-related accidents, and so on—still less so in the popular press. In any case, this issue does not affect our analyses, since the TISS survey explicitly

---

[2] According to "Joint Publication 1–02, DOD Dictionary of Military and Associated Terms," a casualty is "any person who is lost to the organization by having been declared dead, duty status—whereabouts unknown, missing, ill, or injured." The dictionary is available at: *www.dtic.mil/doctrine/jel/doddict/*.

asked about "military deaths" rather than simply "military casualties."
A final definitional distinction is in order. For most of the analyses presented in this chapter and unless otherwise specified, we limit the meaning
of casualties still further to refer only to U.S. combat fatalities. In the
conclusion of this chapter, we briefly consider what our findings might
imply regarding the other human costs of war, the costs of U.S. civilians
who die in conflict and the costs represented by the other side's combatant
and noncombatant fatalities. We did not collect any data on this topic,
however, and so can only speculate.

Virtually all treatments of casualty sensitivity begin with the reasonable
assumption that the greater the number of casualties, the less support
there is for a given operation (Burk 1999). Indeed, this assumption is the
rarely specified and rarely discussed core causal mechanism behind the
so-called democratic peace. Implicit in the argument that democracies behave differently with regard to the use of force is the belief that democracies are sensitive to public opinion and public opinion is sensitive to the
human costs of war (Ray 1995; Gartner and Segura 1998). For analytical
purposes, we accept as a point of departure the idea that support for a
use of force decreases as estimates of casualties or actual casualties increase. This is what is meant by treating casualties as costs; rational actors
would always prefer getting the same benefit for less cost.

This is only a point of departure, however, for it oversimplifies a complex set of logical linkages. To begin with, a focus on the costs of an
operation without reference to the benefits is problematic. By the logic of
the conventional wisdom, there should have been less support for the
Civil War or World War II, the two most costly wars in American history,
than for the myriad smaller wars that have in fact been the most unpopular. Clearly, the American people compare the casualties (costs) to the
value of the objective (benefits) and make judgments about whether to
support the operation (net benefit) accordingly. In our subsequent analyses, we account for this important feature of casualty sensitivity in two
ways. First, in all of our questions about casualty sensitivity, we were
careful to specify the goals of the military operation, and we asked respondents to assume that the operation would be a success. In this way we are
able to set to some degree the benefits of the military engagement and
isolate respondents' views about costs. Second, in chapter 5, we begin to
examine the relationship between perceived benefits and the willingness
to suffer costs by controlling for the value that the respondent places upon
the goal of the military operation and the respondent's perception of the
effectiveness of force in achieving that goal.

It is even possible that the casualties themselves might change the value
assigned to a military operation. At least one intriguing finding challenges the idea that an increase in expected casualties translates into a

decrease in support for the operation. Using experimental survey data, Richard Herrmann, Philip Tetlock, and Penny Visser (1999) found that if the increase in casualties was due to the opponent's having nuclear weapons, then respondents were more willing to use force than in similar situations with no nuclear weapons and lower expected casualties.[3] This result suggests that what matters is not the casualties per se but how the casualties are interpreted and whether the casualties are in vain. Decision makers, especially presidents, have a great ability to shape perceptions about military events and, in so doing, to create support for an operation in a skeptical public (Brody 1984; Peffley, Langley, and Goidel 1995). In the absence of a presidential effort to justify an operation, for instance, it is reasonable to expect that a sudden increase in casualties should translate into a decrease in support for the mission. But if the president were to use the casualties to galvanize the public and to demonize the enemy, it is just as likely that the opposite causal relationship would be obtained; an increase in casualties would boost support. Presidents, in other words, may in certain circumstances be able to harness the "rally around the flag" effect to translate higher casualties into more support for the operation.

Casualty sensitivity feeds directly into decisions both about whether or not to use force and about how to do so. If the casualties are thought to be prohibitive, decision makers may refuse to use force in the first place. Moreover, if the effort to control casualties is important, this may alter the way in which the United States uses force. For instance, the most pronounced feature of the Kosovo operation was precisely the way considerations of casualties dominated decision making. An important critique of the operation is that this excessive sensitivity to casualties was itself a function of underlying civil-military issues, especially the "gap" between civilian leaders with little or no experience in combat and a military they do not understand and fear they cannot command (Hoagland 1999; Krauthammer 1999; Thurman 1999; Weiner and Perlez 1999; Wheatcroft 1999; Worthington 1999).

Finally, casualty sensitivity can be further broken down into four categories: casualties suffered by our military, casualties suffered by our civilians, casualties suffered by their military, and casualties suffered by their civilians. In this chapter we focus on the first category for two linked reasons: it is by far the dominant issue in the literature and it is therefore

---

[3] We hesitate to push this finding too far, however, since the introduction of nuclear weapons into the scenario changes the stakes of the operation dramatically and in so doing greatly raises the potential benefits of that use of force (because the opponent is that much more dangerous and that much more worth defeating). If benefits increase at the same time as costs, then Herrmann, Tetlock, and Visser cannot isolate sensitivity to casualties.

the issue on which the TISS data focused. In the conclusion of this chapter, we return to a consideration of the other categories and especially the possibility of trade-offs across them.

Sensitivity to U.S. Casualties and Support for U.S. Military Operations

Will the American public tolerate casualties? The conventional answer to this question, of course, is no.[4] As Richard Betts (1995, 76) writes, "It has become axiomatic that Americans will not tolerate many body bags in the course of an intervention where vital interests are not at stake."[5] The potential for U.S. casualties has been alleged as a major determinant of public support for a proposed use of force (Wittkopf 1990; J. Mueller 1994). Similarly, the actual number of casualties has been thought to be a major determinant for continued public support for the conflict, at least in Korea and Vietnam. The exception to this pattern is World War II, which remained relatively popular even as casualties mounted because of widespread recognition of the stakes involved (J. Mueller 1973; Gartner and Segura 1998).

Of course we would expect that any state and any society would be sensitive to casualties at some level. Moreover, it is not controversial to observe that the United States uses technology and doctrine to shift the costs of any combat from *our* troops to *their* troops (Weigley 1973; Eikenberry 1996; Sapolsky and Shapiro 1996; Huelfer 2000). At some point, it is absurd to argue the contrary, that the United States would or should choose tactics that unnecessarily raise its costs. But the conventional wisdom goes further, claiming that the willingness of the American public to accept U.S. casualties has declined from a World War II high and has dropped off precipitously since the end of the cold war.[6] The result, it is

---

[4] Although observers offer different, sometimes strongly iconoclastic, explanations for public casualty aversion, they generally agree that it exists. Exemplars of the conventional wisdom on this point include: Luttwak (1994, 1995, 1999); Eikenberry (1996); Sapolsky and Shapiro (1996); Gentry (1998); Moskos (1998); Alvis (1999); Byman and Waxman (1999); Ignatieff (2000); Klarevas (2000); Tarzi (2001); Cuningham (2000); Drozdiak and Priest (1999); Hallion (1999); Hyde (2000); Friedman (2001); M. Smith (2001); Tarzi (2001). For other, largely skeptical, reviews of the conventional wisdom, see J. Mueller (1994); Schwarz (1994); Larson (1996); Conversino (1997); Noonan (1997); Burk (1999); Erdmann (1999); Kull and Destler (1999); Record (2000); unattributed (2000); and Everts (2002).

[5] Betts himself does not buy into this view, for he goes on to point out, "There is no clear evidence for this conventional wisdom, however, and ample evidence to the contrary."

[6] James Burk (1999) distinguishes between (1) the role casualties play in the mind of the public as a factor determining whether to support the operation; and (2) the claim that the

alleged, is a public whose sensitivity to casualties is so great that it amounts to a casualty phobia that ties the hands of defense planners and paralyzes the United States on the global stage. Thus one account of the Gulf War comments: "It was well understood within the American military that holding down casualties was a political prerequisite for launching a military offensive" (Gordon and Trainor 1995, 133). The military, in particular, take public casualty phobia as an article of faith. As chairman of the Joint Chiefs of Staff, General Hugh Shelton claimed he invoked the "Dover Test" when evaluating the use of force: "Is the American public prepared for the sight of our most precious resource coming home in flag draped caskets into Dover Air Force Base, in Delaware" (Shelton 2000; see also Cuningham 2000). The implication is obvious: Americans are not.

The conventional wisdom is not clear on why the public is supposedly so casualty phobic. As discussed in the next chapter, a variety of hypotheses have been advanced—from the curse of success (we want to avoid casualties because we can) to the pernicious influence of television to changing demographics in the Western world. But regardless of the cause, the effect is allegedly profound.

Analysts also differ over the exact nature of the relationship between casualties and support. On the basis of his comparison of the Korean and Vietnam wars, John Mueller (1973, 62) claims that the public gets hardened to the costs over time; the public is "sensitive to relatively small losses in the early stages [of the conflict], but only to large losses in later stages." Benjamin Schwarz (1994) argues that casualties actually strengthen public support, at least initially, because they harden public resolve; of course, in the long run, the casualties wear down public support. Scott Gartner and Gary Segura claim that the public responds as Mueller suggests only if the war takes the form of an attrition-stalemate, with high casualties early on but then a long period of de-escalation in which there are relatively few casualties (as in Korea). If the lethality of war varies significantly over time, as was, for instance, the pattern in Vietnam, with a low number of casualties early in the conflict and a peak of casualties later on followed by a gradual de-escalation, then public support declines with marginal casualties—when casualties increase public support decreases and vice versa (Gartner and Segura 1998). Another reason that the impact of casualties may change over time is the (usually brief) upswing of support for an operation often observed during the early

United States cannot take any casualties. He says there is good empirical evidence to show that estimates of casualties do determine whether the public will support an operation. However, he questions the validity of the second claim. For our purposes, both claims are instances of casualty sensitivity, albeit differences in degree.

stages of the conflict—the so-called rally 'round the flag effect. Support then declines over time through general war weariness, regardless of the casualty rate (J. Mueller 1973; Ostrom and Job 1986; Oneal and Bryan 1995; Gartner and Segura 1998; Baker and Oneal 2001).

Whatever the actual relationship between casualties and support for military operations, policymakers believe that the U.S. public is reflexively casualty phobic.[7] This has the curious effect of becoming a self-fulfilling expectation. Because policymakers believe that public opinion does or might act this way, policymakers base their own actions on this belief. Therefore, there may be a policy effect even if the underlying public opinion is not requiring it. Thus the United States government may show casualty aversion even though the public is not casualty phobic. In chapter 6 we return to this issue and discuss further the policy implications of this view.

The existing casualty sensitivity literature has focused almost exclusively on mass public attitudes toward casualties. Remarkably little systematic attention has been paid to the attitudes of civilian and military elites. Thus it is not obvious what the existing literature leads us to expect about military attitudes toward casualties. On the one hand, the expectation of casualty phobia in the mass public implies that military officers are more casualty acceptant. There is an implicit comparison between a naive public and a "hard-nosed" view of what it takes to be a great power (or the only superpower); presumably, this more realistic view is held by the military, who understand that the exigencies of America's role in the world may dictate the use of force and that the use of force is inherently messy. On the other hand, the military's famous reluctance to engage in Bosnia and other peacekeeping missions leads to the opposite expectation that the military will be even more casualty phobic than civilians. General Powell's public debate with those arguing for a "lift and strike" option against the Bosnian Serbs in 1992 was certainly cast in those terms. The press reaction to Powell's reluctance to use force in Bosnia explicitly drew this inference, and Powell felt obliged specifically to address it (Gordon 1992). The public and private rhetoric about the use of force is dotted with claims from military officers that "it is we who will die" and with reminders from civilians that the military "volunteer for this service" (Gordon 1992; Powell 1992, 1995).

Moreover, the reaction of military officers to the extensive civilian restrictions on the use of force in recent foreign deployments also indicates the military's reluctance to suffer casualties. Many of these rules in earlier

---

[7] Kull and Destler (1999, 88–92) note that this view is prominent among elites, especially among political elites such as current and former members of the congressional staff and the executive branch.

missions like Somalia appeared designed to limit local civilian casualties and enemy casualties rather than to save the lives of American personnel. For example, some of the restrictions, like the very tight rules of engagement in Somalia, were designed to avoid "their" casualties and were criticized, especially by off-the-record military officers, as wrong-headed precisely because they increased the likelihood of "our" U.S. forces suffering casualties (Priest 1995; Korb 1997). The military has expressed opposition to deployment patterns that increase risk to U.S. forces and, understandably, prefers to deploy in ways that minimize the risks U.S. troops face. The Powell Doctrine, for instance, justifies "overwhelming force" precisely because this is thought to bring victory sooner and produce fewer total U.S. casualties than the gradual-escalation alternative.[8] When the military was given a freer hand in setting rules of engagement, they were written in ways that minimized U.S. casualties.[9]

In sum, it is generally believed, especially among policymakers, that the public is casualty phobic. Much less attention has been paid to the attitudes of civilian elites and military officers, and there is no settled view on whether elites will be more or less acceptant of casualties.

The TISS Data on Casualty Attitudes: Explaining Our Method

The TISS data are uniquely suited for exploring in greater depth the determinants of civilian and military attitudes toward casualties. But the data are not without limitations. On the one hand, they allow us to distinguish between seven levels of military status: elite civilians who have never served in the military (elite civilian nonveterans); elite civilians who report at least some prior service in the military (elite civilian veterans); elite civilians who have never served in the military but who are currently matriculated in a professional military education program (civilian PMEs, often State Department or Defense Department civil servants); officers currently active in the reserves or National Guard and taking correspondence or on-site courses at professional military education institutions but with a primary occupation outside the military (reserve and Guard elite); officers currently on active duty taking courses at professional military education institutions (elite military); civilians in a national telephone survey sample who have never served in the military (mass civilian nonveterans); and

[8] But Powell himself emphasizes that the doctrine was not intended to lead to a "no-casualties" approach. See Powell (2000).

[9] Feaver (2003). See also Kretchik (1997); Burns (2000); Record (2000); Ricks (2000); R. J. Smith (2000); Clark (2001); M. Smith (2001). The literature on the evolution of military efforts at force protection is vast. For a good bibliography, consult: *www.jfsc.ndu.edu/library/bibliography/fprotect.htm.*

civilians in a national telephone survey sample who report prior service in the military (mass civilian veterans). We use various statistical tools to analyze whether this military status correlates with casualty sensitivity.

On the other hand, the data require that we estimate casualty sensitivity with reference to a battery of hypothetical questions: "When American troops are sent overseas, there are almost always casualties. For instance, 43 Americans were killed in Somalia, 383 in the Gulf War, roughly 54,000 in Korea, roughly 58,000 in Vietnam and roughly 400,000 in World War II. Imagine for a moment that a president decided to send military troops on one of the following missions. In your opinion, what would be the highest number of American military deaths that would be acceptable to achieve this goal: (A) To stabilize a democratic government in Congo. (B) To prevent widespread 'ethnic cleansing' in Kosovo. (C) To prevent Iraq from obtaining weapons of mass destruction. (D) To combat the terrorist organization responsible for bombings at U.S. embassies. (E) To defend South Korea against an invasion by North Korea. (F) To defend Taiwan against invasion by China."

As many reviewers have noted, a hypothetical question may only uncertainly reflect attitudes toward actual casualties. One could argue, for example, that respondents might say that they were willing to tolerate casualties in the abstract, but when faced with the reality of body bags returning home, their tolerance would evaporate. If so, our analyses understate the true casualty sensitivity of the public. We believe the exact opposite is true: the responses to these hypothetical questions are likely to underestimate respondents' willingness to tolerate casualties in practice. American military casualties do not occur in a vacuum; they occur in the midst of military operations. In general, the president and other administration officials spend a great deal of time and energy explaining and justifying the importance of these military operations. Thus citizens will usually respond to U.S. casualties while they are also receiving strong messages justifying the casualties and the importance of the mission that they serve. If the casualties occur early in the mission, they are further framed by the halo of the rally 'round the flag effect. In our survey, however, respondents are allowed to make their own judgment about the importance of each mission without any rhetorical persuasion from policymakers invested in the operation. Moreover, while the "casualties" that respondents must consider in our survey are hypothetical abstractions, even the actual casualties suffered in military operations are not a concrete reality to the vast majority of American citizens. Most Americans only experience casualties as a story that they hear on the news. Military deaths are almost never someone they know, even less a harbinger of direct risk to themselves.

We further hedge against the problem of hypotheticals (and the separate problem of reliance on a single survey) by comparing our findings with those of other surveys, both hypothetical and those conducted during actual combat missions. We find that our results, within the limits of the data, are fairly robust. Thus while we are cautious in drawing firm conclusions from our data, we remain confident that our questions do capture respondents' views about the acceptability of U.S. casualties in military operations.

Dependent Variable: Casualty Sensitivity

The central dependent variable in our analysis is the willingness of respondents to accept casualties in American military operations. Casualty sensitivity is a difficult concept to capture. In particular, tolerance for casualties is likely to be highly dependent both on the operational success of the mission and on the particular goals being sought in the engagement. Thus in asking respondents about their willingness to accept casualties, we asked them to assume that the mission would be a success. Then we gave the respondents examples of the number of casualties suffered in previous American military engagements to help them set a reasonable baseline for the number of casualties that one might expect in different future engagements. Finally, we asked the respondents what they felt would be the highest level of American military deaths that would be acceptable to achieve six specific foreign policy goals.

Our hypothetical scenarios cluster into two groups. The first four scenarios we categorize as interventionist military missions, because they are what are known as, in military jargon, Operations Other Than War: operations short of high-intensity combat.[10] Moreover, each of them involves direct intervention inside another sovereign state. Although we categorize all four of these scenarios as interventionist, we also note a clear distinction between the Congo and Kosovo scenarios, on the one hand, and the Iraq and terrorism scenarios, on the other. Congo and Kosovo reflect humanitarian intervention scenarios consistent with our measurement of interventionism in chapter 2. Preventing Iraqi weapons of mass destruction (WMD) and combating terrorism do not fit precisely in this mold,

---

[10] Preventing Iraq from obtaining weapons of mass destruction may appear to come close to a realpolitik mission. However, the fact that we specified the goal as eliminating weapons of mass destruction means that the mission involves operations inside Iraq—much like the ill-fated United Nations UNSCOM mission in the wake of the Gulf War. This is distinct from the realpolitik goal of defending Iraq's neighbors from the threat of invasion—as was the U.S. goal prior to and during the 1991 Gulf War. The goal of regime change in Iraq, at stake in the most recent confrontation, is harder to classify, and a good case could be made to include it in either category.

since both of those operations concern potential military threats to the United States. We categorize the scenarios as interventionist because the military operations would involve internal intervention in other states, but we recognize that the scenarios represent something of a middle ground between interventionist and realpolitik operations. Thus these scenarios might be thought of as "intervention against terrorism" as opposed to "humanitarian intervention." It is also worth noting here that the responses to these questions were given prior to the attacks of September 11, 2001, on the World Trade Center and the Pentagon. It is possible that these terrorist issues would be viewed as realpolitik scenarios in a post-September 11th environment. It seems likely that tolerance for casualties to combat terrorism has increased in the wake of those attacks. Whatever the impact of September 11th on these views, it is interesting to note that the American public exhibited a reasonable willingness to suffer casualties in the war against terrorism even prior to those devastating attacks on the United States. We label the final two scenarios, Korea and Taiwan, realpolitik military missions, because they involve precisely the kind of high-intensity combat across international boundaries that constitutes the core mission of the U.S. armed forces. [11] Note that for reasons of space and cost, the survey of the general public only included three scenarios: Congo, Iraq, and Taiwan.

Responses to our question concerning acceptable casualties did not conform to anything like the normal distribution assumed by the ordinary regression model. Instead, responses conformed more closely to the assumptions of an event-count model in which the events (military casualties) are correlated with one another. That is, people tended to give answers regarding acceptable casualties in blocks of 100 or 1,000. Choosing an estimator to analyze data with such a skewed distribution is made more difficult because simple summary statistics like the mean, meidan, and mode may give misleading representations of the overall distribution

---

[11] We recognize that the terms "interventionist" and "realpolitik" may be problematic, but other terms that resonate with the general public, such as "traditional" and "nontraditional," are equally problematic. As we described in chapter 2, military missions can be arrayed on a scale with "realpolitik" missions at one end that involve the defense of territory (either U.S. territory or that of a friendly state) at one end and, at the other end, interventionist missions that require a deep involvement in reconstructing the domestic politics of another state. According to this scale, Korea represents the most realpolitik mission on our survey. Taiwan would be next because of its quasi-sovereign status. As we note above, terrorism and weapons of mass destruction would rank somewhere in the middle of the scale, because terrorism stands somewhere on the cusp between domestic and international politics. Finally, Kosovo and Congo would be the most interventionist missions because they explicitly involve the domestic restructuring of sovereign states. In any case, these terms were not used in the survey instrument itself and therefore simply reflect a distinction that emerged from the data when comparing responses across the range of different missions.

of responses. We believe the most comprehensive and reasonable representation of these responses is to group them into categories that are substantively meaningful and analyze the differences across these categories.[12] This approach seems warranted because the responses did fall into clusters. Moreover, the analysis of these broad categories of responses allows us to present the data in simple cross-tabulations for the reader to examine and allows us to use statistical estimators—such as ordinal logit—that analyze variations across all categories of responses rather than focusing simply on the mean, median, or mode of the distribution.[13]

We place the willingness to tolerate casualties into six categories: (1) zero casualties; (2) 1 to 50 casualties; (3) 51 to 500 casualties; (4) 501 to 5,000 casualties; (5) 5,000 to 50,000 casualties; and (6) more than 50,000 casualties. We chose these categories because they generally reflect the casualty numbers given to the respondents in the prompts for the questions, and so they also represent recent American experiences in terms of suffering military casualties. The first category obviously captures casualty-phobic respondents who are not willing to tolerate any U.S. deaths for that particular mission. The second category indicates that the respondent would tolerate casualties up to the levels encountered in operations like Somalia and Panama. The third category indicates that the respondent would tolerate casualties roughly comparable to those encountered in the Gulf War. The fourth category indicates that the respondent would be willing to tolerate more casualties than the United States suffered in the Gulf War, but not as many as were suffered in Korea or Vietnam. The fifth category indicates a tolerance for casualties up to the levels suffered in Korea and Vietnam, while the sixth category indicates tolerance for more casualties than the United States encountered in those conflicts and heading in the direction of what might be thought of as a "World War II–sized" price.

Responses tend to be clustered at the upper ends of these categories. That is, respondents tend to give answers like 50, 500, or 5,000. Thus our scale is a relatively conservative measure of casualty tolerance and

[12] In preliminary analyses, we reported means (Feaver and Gelpi 1999c) and also used a negative binomial estimator (Feaver and Gelpi 1999b), which is based on the mean. Although we were careful to emphasize that the precise numbers generated by these methods should only be interpreted loosely, nevertheless we now think those numbers were overly susceptible to misinterpretation, especially misinterpretations that exaggerate the willingness of the public to accept casualties. We are grateful to Eric Larson for alerting us to this problem.

[13] The responses fit a negative binomial distribution quite nicely. However, the negative binomial estimator models the mean of this overdispersed distribution. As we noted above, modeling the mean value may not be most appropriate or meaningful when the distribution of responses is badly skewed. At the end of this chapter we discuss a variety of robustness tests to demonstrate that our results are not affected by our choice of statistical procedures.

may tend to overemphasize casualty sensitivity by pooling numerous responses of 500 casualties with a few responses of "60" or "75" casualties. At the end of this chapter we examine a variety of different recodings of the casualty sensitivity variables as well as differing statistical estimators that are appropriate for analyzing these recoded variables. In that section, we demonstrate that our results are quite robust, are not due to the skewed distributions in the data, and are not dependent on our choice of coding procedures or statistical estimators.

Two difficult issues surrounding our casualty sensitivity data are the treatment of refusal and "zero" responses. The refusal rates for our six casualty scenarios were substantially higher than the refusal rates for most other questions on our survey. Specifically, refusal rates for these questions consistently ranged at approximately 30 percent, compared with a 5 percent to 10 percent refusal rate for most other questions on the survey. To a certain extent high refusal rates for this type of question are to be expected. The casualty scenario questions are complicated and require a good deal of thought from the respondents. R. Michael Alvarez and John Brehm (2002) analyzed our casualty sensitivity data and concluded that the general public showed great "equivocation," meaning that respondents likely held several possibly contradictory expectations and did not see a contradiction between them, but might if they had more information or were better educated; the elite responses showed "ambivalence," meaning the respondents views tapped into truly irreconcilable values. Either way, we would expect large numbers of refusals and this would not necessarily bias the analyses. Moreover, many of the respondents may not actually have formulated any specific attitudes regarding casualty sensitivity. Refusals by these kinds of individuals do not create a problem for our analysis because there *is* no attitude for us to measure. Indeed, if such individuals were to respond to those questions it would create greater problems for us by creating random noise in our data.

However, another possibility is that some of the respondents who refused to answer actually did have attitudes about casualty sensitivity, but chose not to reveal them. If there is no pattern underlying respondents' decisions to refuse, then our inferences from these data are not biased (although we obviously lose efficiency). But if the respondents who chose to refuse can be systematically predicted, then we risk biasing our inferences as well (Brehm 1993; King et. al. 2001). Of course we cannot provide a definitive solution to this problem, but at the end of this chapter we discuss a number of analyses that suggest that refusal rates do not significantly influence our results.

A related issue concerns the treatment of responses that zero casualties were acceptable to achieve a particular mission. On the one hand, this response may be a straightforward indication that the respondent is not willing to suffer any American casualties in order to achieve the given goal. On the other hand, anecdotal evidence suggests that some respondents may been objecting to the phrase "acceptable" casualties. While we were aware of and concerned about this difficulty prior to the implementation of the survey, other terms such as "tolerable" also exhibited some of the same problems. This issue may be endemic when measuring something as sensitive as casualty sensitivity. Notable minorities of each group of respondents reported that zero casualties was acceptable for each of the scenarios.[14] The size of these minorities were roughly comparable across all seven categories of respondents. The proportion was slightly higher among the active duty military than among the civilian elite, but none of these differences were statistically significant. The zero responses often came from the same set of respondents. In fact, 8.5 percent of our respondents answered zero to all of the scenarios. This blanket response of zero casualties—even for missions such as the defense of Korea and Taiwan—raises the concern that such respondents are quibbling with our phrasing casualties as "acceptable," rather than making an accurate statement of the costs they would be willing to suffer.

A careful look at our data indicates that responses that zero casualties were acceptable across all scenarios generally represent "spoiled ballots." Respondents who answered "zero casualties" for all six scenarios did not differ from other respondents in terms of other attitudes that are strongly tied to casualty sensitivity. For example, 66 percent of all-zero respondents agreed with the statement that the United States should use force to prevent aggression. This hardly differs from the 70 percent of other respondents who agreed with this statement. Moreover, all-zero responses were not related to respondents' attitudes toward the importance of the issue at stake in each of the scenarios, nor their views on the effectiveness of military force. As we shall see in chapter 5, these factors are strongly related to the willingness of other respondents to tolerate casualties. The all-zero respondents exhibit nearly identical variation in these other attitudes, yet they exhibited no variation in their response to the casualty questions. This rather odd pattern of response led us to the conclusion that these respondents were objecting to our phrasing of the questions regarding casualty aversion rather than expressing their attitude toward the human costs of war.

One final issue we faced were "spoiled ballots" that exaggerated respondents' willingness to tolerate casualties. For example, a few respondents indicated that they would tolerate more than a million casualties

---

[14] Specifically, 40 percent of the respondents stated that zero casualties were acceptable for the Congo scenario, 22 percent for Kosovo, 15 percent for Iraq, 10 percent for terrorism, 14 percent for Korea, and a surprisingly high 30 percent for Taiwan.

for all six scenarios. Although we cannot rule out the possibility that they would tolerate millions of casualties for any U.S. military operation, it seems likely that these respondents were also objecting to our phrasing of the question. There were only seven such cases, but their responses are so skewed from the rest of the distribution that they substantially alter the mean. For example, the inclusion of those seven responses alter the mean level of tolerance for casualties in Congo from approximately 1,900 to more than 2,400. This is an undue amount of influence for a few rather suspect responses.

Our solution to the problem of spoiled ballots is to exclude respondents who stated that they would tolerate zero casualties for all six scenarios and to exclude respondents who stated that they would tolerate more than a million casualties for all six scenarios. Of course no coding choice is going to be entirely satisfactory in this situation; we believe, however, that the exclusion of what appear to be spoiled ballots represents the fairest representation of attitudes that we are trying to measure. At the end of this chapter we explore a variety of treatments of the question refusals, zero responses, and the potentially exaggerated responses. Our results remain largely unchanged regardless of how these cases are treated. In particular, since the frequency of question refusals and all-zero responses is not significantly related to military status, these responses do not bias our estimates of the relative ranking of civilian elites, military elites, and the general public in terms of casualty tolerance.

Key Explanatory Variable: Military Status of Respondent

Consistent with our discussion in chapter 2, we divided the elite civilian and military samples into five principal categories of respondents. In addition, where possible, we also include attitudes of a sample drawn from the American public. These categories range across a continuum of exposure to and participation in the military. Thus we will refer to a respondent's position among these categories as his or her military status. The five categories of military status within the civilian and military elite are as follows.

Civilian Elite, Nonveterans.   These respondents were drawn from our sample of the civilian elite and stated on their survey that they had never served on active duty in the military or in the military reserves. This group represents the elite respondents with the lowest level of direct exposure to and experience in the military.

Civilian Elite, Veterans.   These respondents were drawn from our sample of the civilian elite and stated on their survey that they had at one time served in the active duty military or reserves. We distinguish them from the nonveteran civilian elite in order to determine whether previous military experience moderates the distance between civilian and military preferences on the use of force.

Civilian Elite, Professional Military Education.   These respondents were drawn from our military sample, but stated that they had never served in the active duty military or in the reserves. These respondents came into our sample because they were civilian elites (often civil service employees from the State Department or the Pentagon) who had been selected to attend one of the professional military institutes, such as the National Defense University or the Naval War College. Once again, we distinguish these respondents from the nonveteran civilian elite in order to determine whether exposure to military values and instruction serves to bridge the civil-military divide.

Elite Reserve and Guard.   These respondents were drawn from our military sample and indicated that they were currently serving in the military reserves. We distinguish reserves from active duty military in order to determine whether the higher level of exposure to civilian society and institutions that reservists experience shapes their attitudes to be more like those of civilian elites.

Elite Active Duty Military.   These respondents were drawn from our military sample and indicated that they are currently serving as active duty military personnel.

As noted above, where possible, we also include the responses of a sample drawn from the American public. Within the mass public we distinguish between two categories of military status:

Mass Nonveterans.   These are respondents from the national sample who stated that they had never served in the U.S. military.

Mass Veterans.   These are respondents from the national sample who stated that they had previously served in the U.S. military.
We begin our discussion with simple cross-tabulations of the responses of four major groups: civilian elites, military reservists, military officers, and the mass public. In our subsequent multivariate analyses, however, we also investigate possible opinion gaps between veterans and nonveterans within the civilian elite and the mass public. In addition, we will consider whether any gaps we observe may be a result of demographic differences across our samples.

Findings from the TISS Data on Casualty Attitudes

The TISS data allow us to answer two basic questions. First, what are elite opinions about casualty sensitivity in the general public? And second, who really expresses the most sensitivity to taking casualties? The data confirm the conventional wisdom's expectation on the first question but challenge it on the second.

What are elite opinions about casualty sensitivity in the general public?

Civilian and military elites were asked to gauge the willingness of the American public to tolerate casualties. Specifically, they were asked to indicate their level of agreement with the following statement, "The American public will rarely tolerate large numbers of U.S. casualties in military operations." As table 4.1 reports, there was a strong consensus across all categories that the American public was highly casualty sensitive. Strong majorities of our respondents agree with this statement regardless of their level of affiliation with the military. For example, 78 percent of the active duty military elite either somewhat agreed or strongly agreed with this statement. Similarly, 75 percent of elite civilian veterans and 80 percent of civilian elite nonveterans agreed with this judgment.[15] These results confirm the conventional wisdom: both civilian and military elites *believe* that the American public will not tolerate casualties.

Who really does express sensitivity to taking casualties?

Because casualty sensitivity is so difficult to measure, simple summary descriptive statistics are potentially misleading. The distribution of responses to our various military scenarios was highly skewed, so the mean values differ greatly from the median. Relying on the median as a measure of casualty sensitivity has some intuitive appeal in the context of democratic decision making, because it might be thought of as relating to the opinion of the "median voter." According to this view, the median might represent the point beyond which additional casualties would tip public support beneath the 50 percent threshold. The 50 percent threshold certainly has high salience in public punditry on public support for military operations, but in fact it has never proved decisive for the government's ability to intervene or to continue the use of force. After all, Presidents Harry S Truman and Lyndon Baines Johnson did not face substantial pres-

---

[15] A chi-squared test revealed that the differences across these categories were statistically significant. However, they are not substantively large.

TABLE 4.1
Elite Expectations about Casualty Sensitivity in the American Public

	Elite Military	Military Reserves	Civilian PME	Civilian Veteran	Civilian Nonveteran	Total
Agree Strongly	44.8%	45.6%	38.9%	33.2%	41.1%	41.8%
	276	176	42	99	275	868
Agree Somewhat	33.1%	31.6%	35.2%	41.6%	38.6%	35.9%
	204	122	38	124	258	746
Disagree Somewhat	15.6%	17.6%	19.4%	19.5%	13.6%	16.1%
	96	68	21	58	91	334
Disagree Strongly	6.2%	5.2%	6.5%	5.0%	5.4%	5.6%
	38	20	7	15	36	116
No Opinion	0.3%	0.0%	0.0%	0.7%	1.3%	0.6%
	2	0	0	2	9	13
Total	616	386	108	298	669	2,077

Note: Percentages calculated within each column.

sure to end the conflicts in Korea and Vietnam until popular support for the wars had fallen well below 40 percent. Thus it makes a difference how respondents are distributed around that median. Nonetheless, as a first cut of the data, we report the mean and median responses of three broad categories of respondents—active duty military, civilian elites (veterans and nonveterans), and the general public (veterans and nonveterans)—for our six scenarios in table 4.2. Because the question was open-ended, the modal answer is even more misleading; respondents were suggesting absolute numbers (and some suggested truly idiosyncratic numbers) against the backdrop of prompts indicating specific casualties in previous wars and natural focal points of round numbers (50, 100, 1,000 and so on). Given those conditions, it is not surprising that the modal answer in most cases was the most natural focal point of all, zero.

Table 4.2 suggests some broad observations that are borne out by the more sophisticated analysis presented below. First, there appears to be a rough consensus across the civilian and military subsamples in support of accepting some casualties in the high-intensity missions, Korea and Taiwan. Second, consistent with our results in chapter 2, military officers appear to be somewhat more tolerant of casualties in the realpolitik missions than are the civilian elite or mass respondents. The median response of military officers for the Korea scenario was ten times higher than the median among the civilian elite. And while the median military response for the Taiwan scenario was slightly lower than for the civilian elite sample, subsequent analyses of the full distribution of responses indicated that military officers overall were willing to tolerate slightly more casualties for this mission. Third, also consistent with chapter 2, this pattern

TABLE 4.2
Summary Statistics for Acceptable Casualties for Realpolitik and Interventionist Missions

	Active Duty Military		Civilian Elite		Mass Public	
	Mean	Median	Mean	Median	Mean	Median
Realpolitik Missions						
Defend South Korea	21,144	10,000	19,057	1,000		
Defend Taiwan	17,425	500	16,519	1,000	20,226	100
Interventionist Missions						
Democracy in Congo	283	5	357	10	6,890	100
Human Rights in Kosovo	1,061	50	4,237	100		
Iraqi WMD	6,017	500	17,008	1,000	29,964	500
Terrorism	6,580	100	9,142	150		

Note: WMD = weapons of mass destruction.

reverses when we turn to the interventionist scenarios. That is, civilian elite and mass respondents appear to be more willing to tolerate casualties than are military officers. The Iraqi WMD scenario presents one exception to this pattern, where we see the views of the public are generally quite similar to those of military officers—except for a relatively few very high responses that raise the mean for the mass sample.

Table 4.2 has contrary indications about whether the American public is reflexively casualty phobic. On the one hand, the modal response regarding Congo and Taiwan is zero. A sizable portion of the public does, in fact, conform to the conventional wisdom. With regard to Iraqi weapons of mass destruction, on the other hand, the modal response is 100 casualties, suggesting that there are some issues over which the public will tolerate casualties. Moreover, the mean and median responses provide further evidence that the public—as a whole—has nuanced attitudes toward casualties. The median response ranges from 100 to 500 casualties, suggesting that half of the public is willing to tolerate casualties that are in the ballpark of (or greatly exceed) the levels experienced in the 1991 Gulf War. The means are even more dramatic, although they are greatly influenced by a few very high responses that raise the mean. Nevertheless, our subsequent analyses suggest the presence of fairly reasoned and temperate responses by the mass sample.

Casualty Sensitivity for Realpolitik Missions

Since the summary statistics are misleading, we disaggregate the responses using the six categories of casualty tolerance that we discussed earlier. Table 4.3 compares civilian and military responses for the realpolitik mission of Korea. Table 4.4 accomplishes the same goal for the Taiwan mis-

TABLE 4.3
Casualty Tolerance for Defending South Korea by Military Status

Number of Casualties	Military Officers	Reservist Officers	Civilian Elites
Zero	4.6%	2.9%	18.8%
	18	8	115
1–50	3.3%	1.8%	5.6%
	13	5	34
51–500	9.0%	13.4%	15.2%
	35	37	93
501–5,000	29.5%	36.5%	25.4%
	115	101	156
5,001–50,000	43.1%	39.0%	29.9%
	168	108	183
50,001+	10.5%	6.5%	5.2%
	41	18	32
Total	390	277	613

Pearson chi-squared (20) = 145.29; $p < 0.00$.

sion. Table 4.3 demonstrates the high level of military support for casualties in the defense of Korea. Less than 5 percent of military officers state that no casualties would be acceptable, while nearly 55 percent stated that more than 5,000 casualties would be acceptable. This contrasts sharply with the nearly 19 percent of civilian elite respondents who stated that zero casualties would be acceptable in the defense of Korea and the limited 35 percent who would accept more than 5,000 casualties. Military reservists are generally similar to active duty officers on this issue.

Turning to the Taiwan scenario in table 4.4, we see a greater civil-military consensus, but despite the lower median score military officers tend to remain slightly more willing to tolerate casualties for this mission. About 25 percent of military officers stated that they would tolerate zero casualties for this mission as compared with 31 percent of civilian elites. Conversely, about 31 percent of military officers stated that they would tolerate more than 5,000 U.S. casualties to defend Taiwan, while only about 25 percent of civilian elite respondents expressed this view. The public expressed somewhat greater casualty sensitivity than either of the elite samples in this case. In particular, mass respondents tended to be willing to tolerate between 1 and 500 casualties and were less likely to tolerate casualties in the 501 to 50,000 range than were many elite respondents. Nearly 30 percent of the public rejected any U.S. casualties on this mission, indicating a certain degree of casualty phobia. At the same time, 30 percent of the public was willing to tolerate up to 1,000 casualties to defend Taiwan, indicating that a reservoir of support could also be rallied for such a mission.

TABLE 4.4
Casualty Tolerance for Defending Taiwan by Military Status ·

Number of Casualties	Military Officers	Reservist Officers	Civilian Elites	U.S. Public
Zero	25.8%	26.0%	31.3%	29.7%
	100	70	188	135
1–50	9.3%	4.5%	5.3%	15.9%
	36	12	32	72
51–500	12.4%	15.2%	14.6%	21.8%
	48	41	88	99
501–5,000	21.4%	25.7%	23.0%	15.0%
	83	69	138	68
5,001–50,000	23.8%	21.9%	20.8%	9.7%
	92	59	125	44
50,001+	7.2%	6.7%	5.0%	7.9%
	28	18	30	36
Total	387	269	601	454

Pearson chi-squared (20) = 145.29; $p < 0.00$.

Casualty Sensitivity for Interventionist Missions

As was the case in chapter 2, this pattern reverses when we turn our attention to interventionist missions. Table 4.5 displays the willingness of our civilian and military samples to tolerate casualties in defense of a democratic government in Congo. Not surprisingly, the overall level of tolerance for casualties is substantially lower for this mission than for Korea or Taiwan. More than 40 percent of the military officers, reservists, and civilian elites stated that no casualties would be acceptable in undertaking this mission. Nonetheless, civilian elites did express a greater willingness than military elites to suffer costs for this mission. Nearly one-third of the civilian elites stated that more than 50 casualties would be acceptable for an intervention in Congo whereas fewer than half as many military officers expressed this view. Interestingly, the American public appears the most willing to tolerate casualties for this mission. More than a quarter of the mass respondents stated that they would accept more than 500 casualties to accomplish this mission—intuitively, this is saying that Congo is worth a higher "price" than the 1991 Gulf War. By comparison, only 7 percent of civilian elites and 3 percent of military officers expressed this view.

The pattern of civilian tolerance for interventionist missions continues when we turn our attention to a hypothetical intervention in Kosovo in table 4.6. Nearly 60 percent of the civilian elite sample expressed a willingness to tolerate more than 50 casualties in accomplishing the Kosovo mission, whereas only about 40 percent of military officers shared this

TABLE 4.5

Casualty Tolerance for Defending Democracy in Congo by Military Status

Number of Casualties	Military Officers	Reservist Officers	Civilian Elites	U.S. Public
Zero	46.9%	42.1%	45.6%	26.5%
	187	120	285	114
1–50	36.6%	29.5%	22.9%	19.0%
	146	84	143	82
51–500	13.0%	23.2%	24.2%	27.8%
	52	66	151	120
501–5,000	2.8%	4.9%	6.1%	13.7%
	11	14	38	59
5,001–50,000	.5%	0%	1.3%	9.0%
	2	0	8	39
50,001+	.3%	.4%	0%	3.9%
	1	1	0	17
Total	399	285	625	431

Pearson chi-squared (20) = 145.29; $p < 0.00$.

TABLE 4.6

Casualty Tolerance for Defending Human Rights in Kosovo by Military Status

Number of Casualties	Military Officers	Reservist Officers	Civilian Elites
Zero	22.8%	21.0%	23.4%
	90	60	147
1–50	32.0%	24.1%	17.8%
	126	69	112
51–500	31.0%	35.0%	36.9%
	122	100	232
501–5,000	11.9%	17.1%	17.8%
	47	49	112
5,001–50,000	1.3%	2.4%	3.2%
	5	7	20
50,001+	1.0%	.3%	.8%
	4	1	5
Total	394	286	628

Pearson chi-squared (20) = 145.29; $p < 0.00$.

view. Interestingly, in both the Congo and the Kosovo scenarios, military reservists seem to hold opinions that stand somewhere between those of military officers and civilian elites.

Finally, in tables 4.7 and 4.8, we turn to the other interventionist missions regarding preventing Iraq from acquiring weapons of mass destruction and combating global terrorist organizations. Although these missions are "interventionist" because they involve U.S. military intervention

TABLE 4.7
Casualty Tolerance for Preventing Iraqi WMD by Military Status

Number of Casualties	Military Officers	Reservist Officers	Civilian Elites	U.S. Public
Zero	4.8%	4.3%	6.0%	4.8%
	19	12	37	22
1–50	12.5%	7.8%	8.7%	18.4%
	49	22	54	85
51–500	34.2%	30.2%	31.5%	31.1%
	134	85	195	144
501–5,000	32.9%	34.9%	35.2%	21.2%
	129	98	218	98
5,001–50,000	12.8%	19.6%	14.0%	16.2%
	50	55	87	75
50,001+	2.8%	3.2%	4.7%	8.4%
	11	9	29	39
Total	392	281	620	463

Pearson chi-squared (20) = 145.29; $p < 0.00$.
Note: WMD = weapons of mass destruction.

TABLE 4.8
Casualty Tolerance for Combating Global Terrorism by Military Status

Number of Casualties	Military Officers	Reservist Officers	Civilian Elites
Zero	6.2%	5.3%	5.4%
	24	15	33
1–50	32.0%	26.2%	25.9%
	124	74	159
51–500	40.3%	41.5%	42.3%
	156	117	260
501–5,000	14.7%	20.2%	20.2%
	57	57	124
5,001–50,000	4.4%	5.7%	4.6%
	17	16	28
50,001+	2.3%	1.1%	1.6%
	9	3	10
Total	387	282	614

Pearson chi-squared (20) = 145.29; $p < 0$.

inside other states, they stand somewhere in between the humanitarian interventions of Congo and Kosovo and the realpolitik scenarios of Korea and Taiwan. And just as one would expect, the pattern of casualty tolerance for these scenarios was somewhere between the realpolitik and humanitarian cases.

Overall, the results in tables 4.7 and 4.8 reveal a broad consensus across all three samples regarding Iraqi WMD and the war on terrorism. Substantial majorities of all three samples said they would be willing to suffer at least as many casualties as the United States encountered in the Gulf War in order to prevent Iraq from obtaining nuclear weapons. Similarly, substantial majorities of all the elite samples expressed a willingness to tolerate 50–501 casualties or more in combating global terrorism. It is important to note that these responses were given well before the attacks of September 11th. As we discuss in chapter 6, polling since September 11th confirms that casualty tolerance for the counterterrorism mission has increased substantially. Our results indicate, however, that civilian elites, military officers, and the mass public were already willing to pay a price to prevail in the war on terror even before those devastating attacks.

Although the responses in tables 4.7 and 4.8 reveal a broad consensus regarding the war on terror, our subsequent analyses indicate that this consensus is actually created by the strong demographic differences across our samples. Once we account for these demographic patterns, we find that the civil-military gap regarding casualties in a war on Iraq or global terrorism looks very much like the patterns we observe for humanitarian intervention in Kosovo or Congo.

Multivariate Analyses

The cross-tabulations in tables 4.2 to 4.8 give us a good substantive sense of the overall distribution of responses, but they are not well suited for judging which of the "gaps" that we observe are purely due to chance and which are likely to reflect general patterns of opinions. Thus we analyze each of the casualty sensitivity scenarios with an ordinal logit estimator. This estimator will allow us to determine which opinion gaps are statistically significant, and it will allow us to determine the extent to which gaps may be accounted for or hidden by demographic differences across our samples.

We represent the seven categories of military status respondents in our logit analyses in the following manner. First, we created three dummy variables denoting whether the respondent was a member of the civilian elite, the mass public, or the military reserves. Active duty military remained as the excluded category with which the other major groups of respondents were compared. Within the civilian elite sample, we created additional dummy variables denoting whether the respondent was a veteran or attended a professional military educational institution; this allowed us to see whether these peculiar ties to the military altered the attitudes of civilian respondents. Thus the coefficients for civilian elite veterans and civilian PMEs compared the attitudes of those groups with the responses of civilian nonveterans. Similarly, within the mass public sample, we created a second dummy variable denoting whether the respondent was a veteran. Once again, the coefficient for this variable indicated whether veterans in the mass public differ from nonveterans in terms of their sensitivity to casualties.

Interactive dummy variables are necessary, but they complicate the interpretation of the coefficients generated by the logit analyses. The coefficient for the civilian elite captures the difference in attitudes between civilian elite nonveteran respondents and our sample of military officers. The civilian elite veteran coefficient captures the difference in attitudes between civilian veterans and civilian nonveterans. Thus if one wants to compare elite civilian veterans with military officers, one must add the two coefficients for the civilian elite and civilian veterans. This combined effect represents the gap between elite civilian veterans and the military. The coefficient for civilian PMEs should be interpreted in precisely the same manner—with the obvious exception that it refers to the views of civilian PMEs rather than civilian veterans. The mechanics of this interpretation may be clarified through an example. Imagine that the coefficient for the civilian elite was 0.5 and the coefficient for the civilian PMEs was −0.4. This set of coefficients would indicate that the average response of civilian elite nonveterans was 0.5 units *higher* than that of the active duty military elite. In addition, the average response for the civilian PMEs was 0.4 units *lower* than that for the civilian elite nonveterans, which would make it 0.1 (0.5 − 0.4) units higher than the average for the active duty military. The coefficients for the mass public and mass veterans should be interpreted in an analogous manner. Thus the coefficient for the mass public captures the difference in attitudes between military officers and members of the mass public who are not veterans. The coefficient for mass veterans measures the gap between members of the mass public who served in the military and those who did not. Thus to compare the views of military officers and mass veterans, we must add the coefficients for the mass public and mass veterans. Finally, the coefficient for the military reservists simply captures the difference between those respondents and active duty military officers.

Demographic Control Variables

The elite civilian, military, and mass public samples within the TISS survey differ substantially in their demographic profiles. It is not surprising, for example, to find that our sample of military officers has a higher proportion of male respondents than either the civilian elite or mass samples. Moreover, military officers tend to be younger and are more likely to be from ethnic or racial minority groups than either of the other two samples. Thus in addition to evaluating the raw differences in opinion between civilian and military respondents, we also make some assessment regarding whether these gaps are a result of serving in the military or are a result of the demographic differences across the samples. Note that in the next chapter, we explore the influence of other controls, both demographic (such as the extent of contact with the military) and attitudinal (such as views on foreign policy), to probe the determinants of casualty sensitivity more deeply.

Accounting for the gap in this statistical manner does not in any way make the civil-military gap "disappear." Instead, these analyses shed light on possible causes of the civil-military gap and suggest the potential causal impact of military experience on respondents' attitudes. We remain cautious, however, in attributing a causal relationship between military experience and respondents' attitudes, even if the civil-military gap remains significant after accounting for control variables. These multivariate analyses indicate that civilian and military respondents differ in their attitudes, even after accounting for the impact of other factors. Our data do not allow us to determine whether these attitudes were caused by military experience or whether individuals who hold those attitudes are more likely to choose military service. Strong inferences about the causal impact of military experience on foreign policy attitudes will have to await tailored studies that can assess attitude changes over time.

We include four demographic control variables in our analyses:

Gender. The respondent's gender is recorded as follows: male = 0, female = 1.

Age. The respondent's age in years based on his or her reported year of birth.

Minority. Respondents were coded as being part of a minority group if they identified themselves as African American, Hispanic, or Native American (value of 1). A value of 0 was coded otherwise.

Level of Education. Respondents were asked the highest level of education that they completed. Responses were coded as follows: less than high school = 1, high school = 2, some college = 3, college graduate = 4, graduate work = 5.

Analyses of Realpolitik Scenarios

To a large extent, the multivariate analyses confirm the results from the cross-tabulations. For our analysis of realpolitik missions, table 4.9 indicates that civilian elite nonveterans are significantly less willing to support casualties in the defense of Korea than are military officers ($b = -1.22$, $p < .01$). Notice, however, that both civilian veterans and civilian PMEs are significantly closer to military officers in their views. Military reservists are also slightly less willing to tolerate casualties than are military officers ($b = -.24$, $p < .10$). These results demonstrate a fairly clear linear trend between exposure to the military and tolerance for casualties in Korea. Military officers express the greatest support, followed by military reservists, civilian PMEs, elite civilian veterans, and finally elite civilian nonveterans. This same relative ranking of respondents persists even when we account for demographic differences across samples, although not all the gaps remain statistically significant. The distinction between civilian non-veterans and military officers, however, remains significant, as does the gap between civilian nonveterans and civilian PMEs. The inclusion of demographic controls also reveals two results that are remarkably consistent across all our analyses of casualty sensitivity. The coefficients for gender and age are negative and statistically significant. Thus female respondents and older respondents are less willing to tolerate casualties across all types of missions.[16] These results mean that when civilians show a greater willingness to tolerate casualties, they do so *despite* the fact that military officers tend to be younger and are more likely to be male than either of our civilian samples—two demographic features that are strongly associated with casualty tolerance.

The results for the Taiwan scenario follow generally the same pattern, though not all the gaps are statistically significant. As the third column of table 4.9 indicates, the civilian elite nonveterans are less supportive of casualties in defense of Taiwan than are military officers ($b = -.30$, $p < .05$). The mass public is also significantly less supportive of casualties for this realpolitik mission than are military officers ($b = -.47$, $p < .01$). Importantly, however, the gap between the mass public and civilian elites is not statistically significant. Thus the greater gap in casualty tolerance is civilian vs. military rather than mass vs. elite. Civilian veterans and PMEs are more willing to tolerate casualties than civilian nonveterans, but this gap is not statistically significant, while military reservists were virtually indistinguishable from active duty officers. All of these gaps become statistically insignificant and substantively small once we account for the impact of demographic differences. That is, the civil-military gap over casualty sensitivity in Taiwan appears to be a result of the fact that there are more female respondents and older respondents in the civilian sample. This difference does not erase the civil-military gap, of course, but it suggests that these differences may be a result of patterns of military recruitment and retention.

Analyses of Interventionist Scenarios

Also consistent with our previous cross-tabulations, the civil-military gap reverses direction when we turn our attention to interventionist scenarios. We begin by examining the two humanitarian intervention scenarios: Congo and Kosovo. As the first column of table 4.10 indicates, elite civilian nonveterans are significantly more willing to tolerate casualties in defense of democracy in Congo than are military officers ($b = .29$, $p < .05$).

---

[16] Eichenberg (2002) finds a similar gender effect on casualty tolerance in his analysis of support for using force.

TABLE 4.9
Exploring Casualty Sensitivity on the Korean and Taiwan Missions

	Korea		Taiwan	
Respondent's Military Status				
Civilian Elite Nonveteran	−1.22***	−0.67***	−0.30**	0.13
	(0.14)	(0.17)	(0.13)	(0.15)
Civilian Elite Veteran	0.45***	0.22	0.19	0.16
	(0.17)	(0.18)	(0.16)	(0.17)
Civilian Elite Military Education	0.82***	0.56**	0.25	0.03
	(0.23)	(0.24)	(0.23)	(0.24)
Military Reserve	−0.24*	−0.15	0.02	0.14
	(0.14)	(0.15)	(0.14)	(0.15)
Mass Public			−0.47***	−0.17
			(0.13)	(0.19)
Mass Veterans			−0.27	−0.36
			(0.22)	(0.23)
Demographic Variables				
Gender		−1.31***		−0.61***
		(0.17)		(0.12)
Age		−0.02***		−0.02***
		(0.01)		(0.004)
Minority		−0.36		−0.13
		(0.25)		(0.16)
Education		0.31**		0.01
		(0.14)		(0.09)
Number of Observations	1,280	1,250	1,710	1,680
Chi-squared	90.29***	166.42	27.57	75.46

Note: Standard errors for coefficients in parentheses. All tests for statistical significance are two-tailed.
* = $p < .10$.   ** = $p < .05$.   *** = $p < .01$.

In this case, neither civilian veterans nor civilian PMEs differ significantly from civilian nonveterans. Military reservists also are more willing to tolerate casualties than military officers ($b = .30$, $p < .05$). This combination of coefficients indicates a consensus among all elite respondents except for military officers—who are significantly more casualty phobic than other elites.[17] Consistent with the results in table 4.4, members of the mass public tend to be more willing to tolerate casualties than any of the elite

---

[17] This finding cannot be an artifact of confusion over what is meant by "casualties." The popular usage of casualties is as a synonym for fatalities; the only subgroup likely to use the Department of Defense official terminology in which casualties refers to fatalities plus wounded gives *lower* figures of "acceptable casualties." If the elite military are thinking fatalities plus wounded while the mass and elite civilians are thinking fatalities, and if the former are still giving lower numbers than the latter, the true fatality phobia gap is even larger than we estimate.

TABLE 4.10
Exploring Casualty Sensitivity on the Congo and Kosovo Missions

	Congo		Kosovo	
Respondent's Military Status				
Civilian Elite Nonveteran	0.29**	0.55***	0.48***	0.86***
	(0.13)	(0.15)	(.13)	(0.17)
Civilian Elite Veteran	−0.002	0.005	−0.21	−0.13
	(0.17)	(0.18)	(0.16)	(0.18)
Civilian Elite Military Education	0.01	−0.16	−0.33	−0.56**
	(0.24)	(.24)	(0.24)	(0.25)
Military Reserve	0.30**	0.38***	0.30**	0.44***
	(0.14)	(0.15)	(0.14)	(0.15)
Mass Public	1.45***	1.68***		
	(−0.15)	(0.21)		
Mass Veterans	−0.15	−0.19		
	(.22)	(0.24)		
Demographic Variables				
Gender		−0.39***		−0.32*
		(.13)		(0.16)
Age		−0.01***		−0.02***
		(0.005)		(0.01)
Minority		0.29*		0.46*
		(0.17)		(0.24)
Education		0.06		0.25*
		(0.09)		(0.14)
Number of Observations	1,738	1,704	1,308	1,276
Chi-squared	140.00	157.17	14.04	32.37

Note: Standard errors for coefficients in parentheses. All tests for statistical significance are two-tailed.
* = $p < .10$.   ** = $p < .05$.   *** = $p < .01$.

groups. As was the case with elite respondents, mass veterans and nonveterans do not differ significantly in their tolerance for casualties in Congo.

The inclusion of demographic controls substantially increases the appearance of the civil-military gap. As we noted previously, older respondents and female respondents express a lower tolerance for casualties. Accounting for these influences nearly doubles the size of the opinion gap between the civilian elite and military officers ($b = .55$, $p < .01$). That is, when we compare military officers with younger males in the civilian elite sample, we find the officers are much less tolerant of casualties than similar respondents in the civilian sample. The gap between military officers and the mass public becomes slightly larger once we account for these demographic differences ($b = 1.68$, $p < .01$), but this gap does not appear to be as substantially affected as the civil-military gap among elites.

The multivariate results regarding humanitarian intervention in Kosovo are quite similar to those for Congo. If we keep in mind that the overall tolerance for casualties in Kosovo was significantly higher than for the Congo scenario, we find that the relative ranking of the different civilian and military groups remains identical. That is, civilian elites (b = .48, $p < .01$) and military reservists (b = .30, $p < .05$) are significantly more tolerant of casualties resulting from intervention in Kosovo than are military officers, and civilian veterans and PMEs do not differ significantly from other civilian elites. Moreover, the apparent size of the civil-military gap nearly doubles once we account for demographic differences (b = .86, $p < .01$). One slight difference between the two scenarios is that civilian PMEs are significantly closer to military officers than are civilian nonveterans once we account for demographic influences.

Finally, we turn our attention to the "intervention against terror" scenarios of Iraqi WMD and global terrorism. As we discussed previously, the results for these scenarios stand somewhere in between the humanitarian intervention scenarios and the realpolitik scenarios. As was the case in table 4.7, table 4.11 indicates a broad consensus across both mass and elite respondents concerning the tolerance of casualties in Iraq. Only military reservists differ from this consensus, expressing greater tolerance for casualties than the other groups (b = .36, $p < .01$). Once we include demographic control variables, however, we can see that this consensus is created by the demographic differences among these groups. That is, military officers remain less tolerant of casualties than are young male civilian elites. This gap is reflected in the positive and statistically significant coefficient for the civilian elite in the second column of table 4.11 (b = .39, $p < .01$). Similarly, the positive coefficient for the mass public (b = .35, $p < .10$) indicates that the military officers express less tolerance for casualties in Iraq than do younger male members of the public.

The analyses for the global terrorism scenario are virtually identical to those regarding Iraqi weapons of mass destruction. That is, we observe a broad consensus, with only military reservists expressing a greater tolerance for casualties than other groups (b = .27, $p < .10$). But we also find that this consensus is created by demographic differences between military officers and civilian elites. After accounting for these differences, we can see that military officers were less supportive of casualties in the war on terrorism than were demographically similar respondents among the civilian elite.

Overall, these multivariate analyses tend to confirm the results we obtained in chapter 2 regarding broader foreign policy attitudes, and they tend to confirm the cross-tabulations of casualty sensitivity responses in tables 4.2 to 4.8. That is, military officers tend to place greater importance on realpolitik missions and express a greater willingness to tolerate casualties in support of those missions. Civilian elites tend to place greater importance on missions of humanitarian intervention and express greater tolerance for casualties in support of those missions. Interventionist mis-

TABLE 4.11
Exploring Casualty Sensitivity on the Iraq and Terrorism Missions

	Iraqi WMD		Terrorism	
Respondent's Military Status				
Civilian Elite Nonveteran	0.14	0.39***	0.17	0.47***
	(0.13)	(0.15)	(0.13)	(0.17)
Civilian Elite Veteran	0.20	0.09	0.24	0.24
	(0.16)	(0.17)	(0.16)	(0.18)
Civilian Elite Military Education	−0.05	−0.15	0.15	0.03
	(0.23)	(0.24)	(0.23)	(0.24)
Military Reserve	0.36***	0.43***	0.27*	0.38**
	(0.14)	(0.14)	(0.14)	(0.15)
Mass Public	−0.03	0.35*		
	(0.13)	(0.20)		
Mass Veterans	0.27	0.12		
	(0.22)	(0.24)		
Demographic Variables				
Gender		−0.49***		−0.41**
		(0.12)		(0.17)
Age		−0.01*		−0.01*
		(0.004)		(0.01)
Minority		−0.18		0.13
		(0.17)		(0.24)
Education		0.10		0.21
		(0.09)		(0.14)
Number of Observations	1,719		1,283	1,251
Chi-squared	35.13		7.97	19.31

Note: Standard errors for coefficients in parentheses. All tests for statistical significance are two-tailed. WMD = weapons of mass destruction.
* = $p < .10$.   ** = $p < .05$.   *** = $p < .01$.

sions in the war on terrorism stand in between these extremes, and so civilian and military respondents find common ground in their support for casualties in these cases. However, civil-military differences continue beneath the surface, since this consensus is produced by demographic differences between the military and civilian society. Once we account for these differences, the relative levels of support for these missions looks much like the pattern for humanitarian intervention. This civil-military gap was more salient than the differences between the mass and elite samples. Contrary to the conventional wisdom, the public only expressed greater casualty sensitivity than military officers with regard to intervention in Taiwan, and the public did not express greater casualty sensitivity than civilian elites for any of the scenarios.

Testing the Robustness of the Civil-Military Gap

Given the sensitivity of the subject and the difficulty in measuring this concept, we must be very careful before concluding that any segment of American society is or is not highly sensitive to suffering casualties. The fact that we are coping with first-of-a-kind data on casualty sensitivity only adds to our caution in drawing conclusions. In order to increase our confidence that our results are not an artifact of idiosyncrasies in the data or our statistical method, we replicated these analyses with several different methods of recoding the data and several different statistical estimators. Specifically, we examined a second categorization of the casualty responses, we analyzed the logged values of the casualty responses, and we examined the untransformed responses themselves.

Our alternative ordinal scale also coded responses into six categories. The responses were assigned to categories in the following manner: (1) zero casualties; (2) 1 to 99 casualties; (3) 100 to 999 casualties; (4) 1,000 to 4,999 casualties; (5) 5,000 to 9,999 casualties; and (6) 10,000 casualties or more. Analyses of this alternative scale were virtually identical to those described above.

Much of the literature on casualty sensitivity has focused on the log of the number of casualties suffered as the critical variable in altering support for a military operation (J. Mueller 1973, 1994). Mueller hypothesized a logarithmic relationship between casualties and support because the first few casualties in any operation would be more salient and shocking to the public. As casualties continue to mount, however, Mueller expected that citizens would become desensitized and would only respond to larger numbers of casualties. Thus we analyzed the logged values of the casualty responses using regression analysis. These results followed a very similar pattern to those described above, but they tended to indicate a larger civil-military gap—especially with regard to the Taiwan scenario. Despite the prevalence of the logged value of casualties as a measure of casualty sensitivity in the existing literature, we present our logit analyses because we believe they are a more conservative depiction of the civil-military gap.

Finally, we analyzed the untransformed casualty responses through the use of a statistical procedure known as the negative binomial estimator. The negative binomial estimator is one of the family of "event-count" estimators. That is, this estimator assumes that respondents are giving a count of the number of casualties that they would accept. The negative binomial distribution also assumes that these "events" occur in clusters that are correlated with one another. That is, if one "event" is observed, the probability that a second event will also be observed increases. This matches the clustered nature of our casualty responses, and statistical analyses revealed that the negative binomial distribution provided a good fit for our data.[18] The results of the negative binomial analyses were also quite similar to the logit analyses described above. Like the analyses of logged casualty values, however, the negative binomial analyses tended to show a larger and more statistically significant civil-military gap. They also tended to indicate a greater level of casualty tolerance among the mass public. Again we report the logit analyses which represent more conservative estimates of the opinion gaps.

Next we addressed the issue of refusal rates for the casualty questions on the TISS survey. In order to examine whether these refusals represented a problem for our analyses, we created a dummy variable that was coded 1 if a respondent refused any of the casualty questions. A value of 0 was coded for respondents who answered all six scenarios.[19]

None of our categories of military status were significantly related to refusing to answer the casualty questions except for the military reserves, who were less likely to refuse than any other subgroup. For that matter, very few of the control variables analyzed in this or the next chapter were significantly related to refusal either. Some prominent exceptions are worth noting, however. First, women were more likely to refuse to answer at least one of the casualty questions. What implications do these refusals have for our results concerning the impact of gender? That depends upon what attitudes (if any) are being withheld. If women who have a high tolerance for casualties feel that it is socially unacceptable to reveal this attitude on an anonymous survey, then we may be exaggerating the gender effect. This scenario strikes us as unlikely, however. It seems to us more plausible either that women are less likely to have well-formed attitudes on casualty tolerance, because they spend less time thinking about military affairs, or that women are more casualty averse but do not wish to share this fact on a survey. In this case, our estimates are either unbiased or actually understate the gender gap.

Republicans, in contrast, are somewhat less likely to refuse the casualty questions, and those who hold realpolitik military values are likewise less likely to refuse. Both of these effects are statistically quite tenuous, however, and should be viewed with care. The results on this point are not strong enough to suggest a substantial selection bias problem.

A more encouraging result from this analysis is that by far the best single predictor of refusing a casualty question is the respondent's level

[18] We relied primarily on the negative binomial estimator for our preliminary analyses of the data (Feaver and Gelpi 1999b). Alvarez and Brehm (2002) also use this estimator for their analyses of our casualty data.

[19] A separate equation was estimated to include the mass data because they were only asked three of the scenarios. The results were nearly identical.

of education. In general, less well educated respondents were substantially more likely to refuse to respond to these questions. This result is encouraging, because we would expect that those with lower levels of education would be less likely to have a well-formed attitude to a highly complex question like how many casualties are acceptable in a given foreign military conflict. Thus if the respondents are reporting their attitudes honestly, then we would expect to see a significant relationship between education and refusal rates. Overall, these analyses leave us encouraged that our findings do not appear substantially biased by the refusal rates for the casualty question.

Finally, we reexamined our treatment of the responses that zero casualties were acceptable to achieve all of the missions we addressed. As we discussed above, we believe that the pattern of these all-zero responses suggests that the respondents are objecting to our phrasing of American deaths as "acceptable" rather than offering a judgment of their actual willingness to suffer the human costs of war. Much like the instances of question refusal, we find that the variables that generally predict casualty tolerance do not seem to predict the all-zero responses. In fact, the determinants of the all-zero responses showed greater similarity to the analyses of question refusal than they did to the analyses of the other casualty responses. Like the analyses of the question refusals, both gender and level of education appear to be related to the all-zero responses. With regard to gender, our decision to remove the all-zero cases has the effect of dampening the gender gap in the analyses in tables 4.9 to 4.11. Nonetheless, the gender gap remains significant. Once again, the fact that education is the powerful predictor of an all-zero response—even though education did not have a consistent impact on the overall level of casualty tolerance—suggests that these respondents are rejecting our phrasing of the question or have not formed attitudes about this complex issue. For this reason we believe that excluding these respondents gives us the most valid overall measurement of respondents' attitudes.

Nonetheless, it is important to determine the extent to which the inclusion of these all-zero respondents could influence our results. Thus we performed all of the analyses we have described—including the logit analyses, the regression analyses, and the negative binomial analyses—on all of the casualty responses—including the "all zeros." The basic pattern of results remains remarkably stable with the inclusion of these cases across all of the estimation techniques. Civilian elites still tend to exhibit higher tolerance for casualties in support of humanitarian intervention; military officers tend to be more willing to tolerate casualties in support of realpolitik missions. We also continue to find that the American public is not reflexively averse to casualties—even in these hypothetical scenarios. Of course, including these all-zero responses does lower our overall estimate of the willingness of our respondents to tolerate casualties. For example, the inclusion of the cases shifts the median response for the Congo scenario to zero for all groups. Nonetheless, even in this case, 45 percent of the public expressed a willingness to tolerate casualties in Congo and more than a third expressed a willingness to tolerate more than 50 casualties without any prompting as to why the United States would have any interest in performing such a mission. Moreover, this willingness to suffer casualties for intervention in Congo continues to exceed the support expressed by either of the elite samples.[20]

Finally, we sought to investigate the combined impact that question refusals and all-zero responses might have on our results by estimating a series of Heckman selection models. This procedure begins with all possible respondents—including those who refused to answer and the all-zero respondents—and estimates a selection equation that describes the selection into the sample of cases that appear in our cross-tabulations. The Heckman model then controls for this selection process while estimating the equation for the remaining casualty responses. This statistical procedure is the appropriate method for correcting for the selection bias that may be induced by the question refusals and spoiled ballots (Achen 1986). The Heckman models provide further support for the models presented in tables 4.9 to 4.11. Specifically, the selection models indicate that the civil-military gaps described in our analyses are not induced by the pattern of question refusals or spoiled ballots. In fact, accounting for this selection process increases the size and significance of the civil-military gap in some instances. Moreover, the results of the Heckman model suggest that the question refusals and spoiled ballots may cause us to underestimate the public's willingness to tolerate casualties. Specifically, the Heckman models indicate that after this selection process is accounted for, the public is significantly more willing to tolerate casualties in Iraq than are elite respondents. The Heckman model also indicates no significant difference between mass and elite respondents with regard to Taiwan.

Why Does the Conventional Wisdom Differ?
Another Look at Other Data

The conventional wisdom says the American public is overwhelmingly casualty phobic, essentially exhibiting a zero tolerance for combat fatalities. Our data show that while there is indeed a nontrivial portion of the public that might fit that description, the majority of the public is some-

---

[20] Inclusion of the all-zero responses also made the bivariate gap between the mass public and military officers significant for the Iraqi WMD scenario. Nonetheless, a majority of mass respondents remained willing to tolerate a substantial number of casualties in order to prevent Iraq from gaining weapons of mass destruction.

thing else entirely. On a range of missions, sizable majorities of the public are willing to tolerate substantial casualties. In the next chapter, we explore some of the determinants of these attitudes more deeply. In the remaining part of this chapter, we explore the apparent inconsistency between our conclusion and the conventional wisdom.

To be sure, we are not the first to observe that the conventional wisdom grossly overstates the public's casualty phobia. Bruce Jentleson (1992, 1998) has argued that the public is "pretty prudent." Some forms of military operations will receive more support—such as those designed to restrain rogue states—while others that are only dealing with humanitarian concerns or intervening in messy civil wars will receive less support. Our findings suggest that there may be more support even for these lower-priority missions, yet overall Jentleson's assessment of a prudent public that weighs costs and benefits, rather than a mercurial public with a zero-tolerance for casualties, is consistent with our own.

Benjamin Schwarz (1994) has argued that the public prefers victory rather than defeat, and so casualties do not cause support for an operation to evaporate. On the contrary, Schwarz argues that casualties can actually lead the public to support an escalation of the conflict in order to overcome the enemy. Likewise, James Burk (1999, 55) claims that "public support for military deployments [in Lebanon and Somalia] was neither as unsteady nor as uncritically contingent on the absence of casualties as many have claimed"; indeed, Burk (77) notes that after the bombing of the Marine barracks in Beirut, public opinion "moved in a direction opposite to what the casualties hypothesis predicts." Eric Larson (1996) challenges this escalation claim, but nevertheless concludes that casualties do not lead inexorably to a collapse of public support for an operation; on the contrary, Larson writes, "When we take into account the perceived benefits of the operation, broadly conceived as the importance of the interests at stake and the principles being promoted, the evidence of a recent decline in the willingness of the public to tolerate casualties appears rather thin. The historical record in fact suggests a rather high degree of differentiation in the public's willingness to tolerate casualties, based upon the merits of each case" (99–100). Larson views his own study as a middle ground between those who argue with Schwarz that casualties generate a rally 'round the flag escalatory pressure and those who argue that casualties generate a "crescendo in demands for immediate withdrawal" (xv).[21]

Steven Kull and I. M. Destler (1999:106) go even further and argue that "polls show little evidence that the majority of Americans will respond to fatalities by wanting to withdraw U.S. troops immediately and, if any-

---

[21] Larson rejects the escalation hypothesis, even though he acknowledges that some cases, like Lebanon, actually reflect the escalation dynamic described by Schwarz. Compare Larson (1996, 49) with Burk (1999, 64–67).

thing, are more likely to want to respond assertively." Kull and Destler
track this dynamic through a mix of survey data, including polls during
actual military operations and hypothetical questions about possible casualties. They even found strong support for the Bosnian mission in a February–March 1998 poll that otherwise indicated a majority of Americans
mistakenly believed U.S. soldiers were being killed in the operation; and
there was no significant correlation between respondents who wrongly
thought the United States was suffering casualties and respondents who
opposed the Bosnian mission (Kull and Destler 1999, 109).[22] Larson
(2000) however, claims Kull and Destler have exaggerated public tolerance for casualties.

Despite these iconoclastic reviews of public opinion data, the conventional wisdom clings tenaciously to the idea of a reflexively casualty-phobic public, and we would argue that this is largely due to two factors:
first, a stubborn misreading of the Somalia case, exhibit A for the casualty-phobia thesis; and second, a misreading of John Mueller's findings
about public support during World War II, Korea, and Vietnam.

Somalia looms very large in the conventional wisdom. In their inter-
views with political and media elites, Kull and Destler (1999, 91) found
that all media respondents and nearly 75 percent of elites overall believed
unequivocally that the Somalia case illustrated the public's reflexive opposition to taking any casualties. When the U.S. soldiers died in October
1993, it is alleged, the public turned virulently against the Somalia mission
and demanded an immediate withdrawal. An analysis of polls on Somalia
by Louis Klarevas (2000, 528) offers a ringing endorsement of this conventional view, concluding that there is now a "Somalia syndrome," in which
"the American public will be supportive (or at least tolerant) of a post–
Cold War peace operation—even when the overall policy objective involves
more expansive peace-enforcement goals—so long as American soldiers are
not losing their lives in the pursuit of interests not considered vital."

But the Somalia case does not in fact conform to the casualty-phobia
hypothesis. Klarevas (2000) shows that public support for the presence
of U.S. troops in Somalia dropped from 74 percent in December 1992,
at the start of the humanitarian relief operation, to 43 percent in mid-
September 1993, *before* the 18 soldiers died in the October raid. Support
dropped to 36 percent *after* the October fatalities, but even Klarevas, who
otherwise accepts into the casualty-phobia conventional wisdom, is
obliged to recognize this as modest: "Because support had diminished by
September, support did not drastically drop following the October 3 battle in Mogadishu" (526). On the contrary, in the immediate aftermath of

---

[22] For a debate over the generalizability of these findings, see Clark and Dautrich (2000)
and Murray (2000); for the rejoinder, see Kull and Ramsay (2000).

the raid, majorities wanted to capture or punish the warloard Mohammed Farah Aideed—the very mission the public did not support prior to the raid (Burk 1999; Kull and Destler 1999, 106). Of course this escalation imperative was not overwhelming. Larson (1996, 67), for instance, claims that this support "evaporated" if the survey questions linked such a mission to a delay in the withdrawal from Somalia. But it is striking that the public held these views even though virtually no major opinion leaders were talking about capturing and punishing Aideed in the aftermath of the raid. Republicans in Congress called for abandonment of the Aideed hunt and immediate withdrawal. Democrats and the White House called for abandonment of the Aideed hunt and slow withdrawal. Both sets of political elites, in other words, were offering the cut-and-run strategy, whereas a sizable portion of the public was supporting the win-and-leave strategy. Since Larson elsewhere argues that a lack of consensus at the leadership level should erode support for military operations at the mass level, the potential public support of military escalation to punish Aideed in the absence of any political leadership in that direction is all the more striking. Had the White House sought to mobilize support for the punishment option, Larson's (1996, 67–71, 94–95) own data suggest that this effort would have likely succeeded. Contrary to Larson's interpretation of Somalia but consistent with his overall model, the data show that public support for the mission was available, despite casualties, but merely never mobilized by the Clinton administration.

If anything, the Somalia case supports not the conventional wisdom but rather two other views. First, Somalia confirms that if the president (and by extension the rest of the political elite) does not attempt to mobilize public support in the midst of a costly military operation, then the public support will not long be mobilized on its own. There was one important audience that was deeply casualty phobic, reacting immediately and reflexively to the sight of bodies being dragged through the streets of Mogadishu: the president, his closest advisors, and members of Congress. They all lost whatever political will they had remaining for the Somalia mission after the Ranger raid and made no attempt to frame the casualties as the necessary price for victory and thereby tap into the reservoir of public support that might otherwise have been available (Dauber 2001).

Second, the public supports missions that are successful, not necessarily those that are cost free. Klarevas (2000) claims that public support for Somalia eroded over the summer of 1993 "in large part" because of the gradual mounting fatalities: 24 Pakistani peacekeepers killed in June; 4 Italian soldiers and 4 journalists killed in July; 4 American soldiers killed in August, followed by 6 more wounded the same month; and 3 American soldiers killed in September. But it is more likely that these deaths eroded support indirectly, by signaling that the operation was a mess. As headlines from that period attest, the hunt for Aideed looked like a failure, not really because soldiers were dying, but because Aideed kept slipping away—because the missions kept failing to capture him. Throughout September 1993, the public was reading such stories as "Rangers Net 17 but Miss Aideed Again; Mogadishu Warlord Frustrates Elite GIs," and "Aideed Hunt's Still On, Peacekeepers Insist" (Richburg 1993; Watson 1993), and the obvious implication was that American forces were engaged in an exercise in futility. Somalia, in other words, provides more evidence of a defeat phobic public than a casualty phobic public.

Other public opinion data from recent U.S. military operations corroborate the view that the American public is more defeat phobic than casualty phobic. For example, public support for the U.S. intervention in Panama remained almost unwavering at 80 percent or higher despite the 23 casualties suffered (Larson 1996, 113). Of course 23 casualties is a small number, but it is nearly identical to the number of casualties that allegedly caused the public to call for a U.S. withdrawal from Somalia. The same pattern is evident in the 1983 intervention in Lebanon, despite the fact that many more American lives were lost. In that case Larson (1996, 112) notes that public support for the operation actually increased from 37 percent to 45 percent following the bombing that killed more than 200 Marines. Only after President Ronald Reagan abandoned the operation and announced the withdrawal of U.S. forces did public support for the mission decline. Similarly, one poll taken by the *Los Angeles Times* in November 1990 indicated that 56 percent of respondents would be willing to accept 1,000 casualties or more in order to defeat Iraq—a result remarkably similar to the TISS data on Iraq reported above. In the 1990 case, the hypothetical poll results were borne out by the war itself. Public support for the Gulf War remained high despite the 383 casualties.

The conventional wisdom may be misreading Somalia—and other recent military operations—because of an even more deeply entrenched misreading of the Vietnam and Korean cases. Table 4.12 describes the results of several polls asking the public about support for the Korean and Vietnam wars along with the cumulative number of American battle deaths suffered at the time of each poll. In the Korea case, it is striking that in August of 1950—about a month or two into the war effort—public support remained a remarkably high 66 percent despite the more than 4,600 battle deaths suffered by the United States. Moreover, by August 1950 U.S. forces had slowed the North Korean advance and had successfully set up a perimeter around Pusan, from which they planned to retake the peninsula. Thus while the initial phase had obviously taken the United States by surprise, the rally 'round the flag phenomenon and the ability of the U.S. military to stabilize the situation on the battlefield arguably stiffened the public's tolerance of casualties.

TABLE 4.12
Public Support for Military Operations and
Cumulative Casualties in Korea and Vietnam

	Korea			Vietnam	
Date of Poll	Cumulative Combat Deaths	Percentage Supporting	Date of Poll	Cumulative Combat Deaths	Percentage Supporting
Aug. 1950	4,631	66	Aug. 1965	166	61
Dec. 1950	13,991	39	Nov. 1965	924	64
Feb. 1951	16,716	41	Mar. 1966	2,415	59
Mar. 1951	17,602	43	May 1966	3,191	49
Apr. 1951	18,674	45	Sept. 1966	4,976	48
Jun. 1951	20,641	42	Nov. 1966	5,798	51
Aug. 1951	21,459	47	Feb. 1967	7,419	52
Mar. 1952	25,617	37	May 1967	10,341	50
Sept. 1952	28,185	39	Jul. 1967	11,939	48
Oct. 1952[1]	29,202	36	Oct. 1967	13,999	44
Oct. 1952[2]	29,874	37	Dec. 1967	15,695	46
			Feb. 1968	19,107	42
			Mar. 1968	20,658	41
			Apr. 1968	22,061	40
			Aug. 1968	27,280	35
			Oct. 1968	28,860	37
			Feb. 1969	32,234	39
			Sept. 1969	38,581	32
			Jan. 1970	40,112	33
			Mar. 1970	40,921	32
			Apr. 1970	41,479	34
			May 1970	42,213	36
			Jan. 1971	44,109	31
			May 1971	44,980	28

Note: Data are from J. Mueller (1973), reprinted in Larson (1996).

The most substantial drop in public support for the war in Korea occurred between August and December 1950. During this period the United States suffered nearly 10,000 battle deaths, and the conventional view attributes the collapse of public support to the infliction of these casualties. However, something even more consequential was going on at precisely this same time: Chinese forces unexpectedly intervened in the conflict in November 1950 and inflicted a series of devestating defeats on the badly overextended American forces from late November 1950 through mid-January 1951—including the loss of Seoul. The casualties were suffered in battlefield defeats, not in battlefield victories. The drop in public support for the war was an unwillingness to take casualties in a losing cause, not an unwillingness to take casualties, period. In fact, as the United States stabilized the front, stopped the Chinese advance, and recaptured Seoul, public support for the war increased somewhat—despite the fact that casualties continued to mount. Nonetheless, after the Chinese intervention it became clear that America's attempt to "roll back" communism would not succeed, and so public support for the war remained low.

A similar pattern holds for the public's response to the war in Vietnam. Once again, the data reported by Larson (1996) and Mueller (1973) in table 4.12 seem to indicate a general decline in support for the war as casualties mounted. But a reexamination of the data shows that the severity of this decline is not constant over time; on the contrary, the Tet offensive of 1968 marked a turning point in the relationship between public opinion and casualties. After Tet, casualties had a much more corrosive effect on presidential approval. While the U.S. military claimed that Tet was a tactical success for American armed forces, it was not perceived that way by the media or the mass public. Rather, Tet was framed as a massive (and surprise) setback, all the more shocking because the U.S. military had been claiming that the South was largely pacified. Consistent with the defeat-phobic hypothesis, the public was substantially more sensitive to suffering casualties after the war effort was deemed a failure. For example, nearly 46 percent of the public still supported the war in Vietnam in December of 1967, despite the fact that the United States had suffered more than 15,000 combat deaths. After Tet, however, as U.S. casualties mounted, public support declined until barely 30 percent of the public supported the war by September 1969.

The importance of framing the wars in Korea and Vietnam as winning or losing causes is confirmed by some basic statistical analyses of these data. Table 4.13 presents several regression analyses of the relationship between U.S. casualties and support for the wars in Korea and Vietnam. Consistent with Mueller (1973), we regressed the log of cumulative casualties on support for each war. As the conventional wisdom would expect, the coefficient for the relationship between casualties and public support for the war in Korea is statistically significant ($b = -33.11$, $p < .01$). But if we drop the first phase of the war and analyze the relationship between casualties and support for the war from December 1950 on, the relationship between casualties and support becomes insignificant ($b = -15.86$, n.s.). In other words, the famous finding that casualties eroded public support for the war in Korea is entirely a function of events during the first seven months of the conflict, precisely the period when the United States looked to be losing the Korean War.

TABLE 4.13
Public Support for War in Korean and Vietnam before and after Battlefield Setback

	Korea		Vietnam	
	All Observations	Post-PRC Attack	All Observations	Pre- and Post Tet
Log Cumulative Casualties	−33.11***	−15.86	−14.96***	−9.23***
	(5.38)	(9.91)	(1.44)	(1.55)
Log Casualties × Post-Tet				−18.71***
				(6.49)
Tet offensive				76.08**
				(29.01)
Constant	184.37***	109.33**	104.39***	85.44***
	(23.01)	(42.96)	(5.95)	(5.69)
Number of Observations	11	10	24	24
f-statistic/Chi-squared	37.91***	2.56	108.52***	82.89***

Note: Standard errors for coefficients in parentheses. All tests for statistical significance are two-tailed.
* = $p < .10$ ** = $p < .05$.   *** = $p < .01$.

With regard to Vietnam, table 4.13 confirms the traditional view that overall support for the Vietnam War declined as a function of the log of cumulative casualties ($b = −14.96$, $p < .01$). But when we distinguish between the period before and after the Tet offensive, the results change markedly. Table 4.13 reports a model including a control dummy variable for the Tet offensive interacting with the log of casualties. In this model, the coefficient for the log of casualties captures the impact of casualties on support for the war in Vietnam prior to the Tet offensive. The coefficient for the interaction term represents the additional impact of casualties on support after Tet. The total impact of casualties after the Tet offensive, therefore, is the sum of the two coefficients. It is evident that, viewed this way, the public's sensitivity to casualties depended significantly on the perceived success of the military operation. Prior to the Tet offensive, the log of cumulative casualties did have a significant impact on public support for the war ($b = −9.23$, $p < .01$). But after Tet, the impact of casualties on support tripled in size. The coefficient for the interaction term is $−18.71$ ($p < .01$), indicating that the overall coefficient after the Tet offensive was $−27.94$ ($p < .01$).

These data indicate that Korea, Vietnam, and Somalia do teach a consistent lesson about the public's tolerance for military operations. The lesson, however, is not that the American public is reflexively casualty phobic. The lesson of Korea, Vietnam, and Somalia is that the American public demands success.

Casualties and Presidential Approval

In short, while our analyses of the TISS questions on casualty tolerance run sharply contrary to the conventional wisdom regarding popular casualty phobia, our findings are in fact consistent with a careful analysis of the public's actual responses to American casualties in military operations over the past fifty years. It remains the case, however, that data on the public's tolerance for casualties are spotty and plagued by problems of comparability. As both Larson (1996) and Mueller (1973, 1994) note, the specific wording of questions changes significantly, and the questions are asked infrequently and at irregular intervals. Thus comparisons across multiple military operations in Korea, Vietnam, Panama, the Gulf War, and Somalia are necessarily rough and contingent, because the phrasing of the questions is so different. Moreover, the fact that the polls are taken at irregular intervals—often in response to international events—creates an incomplete and potentially biased image of the public's attitudes toward casualties.[23]

But while questions about specific military operations may be intermittent and inconsistent, survey questions about presidential approval are not. Presidential approval also represents an important dependent variable for judging the public's casualty sensitivity sensitivity. After all, presidents care about public attitudes toward specific military operations, because they believe that those attitudes are linked to their overall public support. If the public's attitudes toward casualties and support for U.S. military operations do not have an impact on presidential approval, then the electoral connection is considerably more tenuous. Put another way, popular presidents can pursue unpopular policies more easily than unpopular presidents can. Thus in order to gain a more systematic and consistent view of the impact of casualties on public opinion, we conducted a combined analysis of the impact of casualties on presidential approval from 1949 to 1994.

We measured both presidential approval and U.S. military casualties in quarterly aggregations. As with the data in table 4.12, U.S. casualties are measured as cumulative across each military intervention. After each intervention ends, however, the measure for U.S. casualties returns to zero and begins to aggregate again with the next operation. Next, we coded a dummy variable that identified when U.S. military operations were not successful. Consistent with our earlier analyses of Korea and Vietnam, Korea was coded as "not successful" beginning with the Chinese interven-

[23] The irregular spacing of polls also creates problems in correcting for temporal dependence—which almost undoubtedly plagues the analysis of attitudes that so obviously change over time.

tion in November 1950 and Vietnam was coded as "not successful" begin-ning with Tet. In terms of the subsequent U.S. military interventions be-tween 1975 and 1994, the *Mayaguez*, Grenada, Panama, the Gulf War, and Kosovo were coded as successful.[24] The failed Iranian hostage rescue and the 1983 mission to Beirut were coded as unsuccessful.

In addition to estimating the impact of casualties on approval, we also controlled for several well established temporal patterns in presidential approval. First, presidential approval patterns since World War II have tended to follow a curvilinear pattern over each presidential administra-tion (Stimson 1976). That is, approval begins at a relatively high point in the wake of a successful election and then tends to decline over time. As the next election approaches, however, presidents have generally been able to raise their approval ratings once again in an effort to retain office—either for themselves or for their party. We capture this effect by including a variable that counts the number of quarters since the previous presidential election. In order to capture the curvilinear effect, we also include the square of this variable. Moreover, because these data are quarterly aggrega-tions of both approval ratings and casualties, we are likely to encounter high levels of autocorrelation. We correct for this problem through the use of the Prais-Winsten generalized least-squares (GLS) estimator.

The results of our analyses of military casualties and presidential ap-proval are displayed in table 4.14. The negative coefficient for the quarter of the administration and the positive coefficient for its square indicate the cyclical nature of presidential approval (Stimson 1976). More im-portant for our purposes, the first column indicates that casualties do not have a consistently negative impact on presidential approval. In fact, the coefficient for casualties is slightly positive ($b = 1.02$, $p < .10$). This coeffi-cient indicates that on average a one-unit increase in the log of the cumula-tive casualties would actually increase presidential approval by about one percentage point. However, as the second column of table 4.14 indicates, this pattern changes when we distinguish between casualties that were suffered during operations that were perceived as successful and opera-tions that were perceived as unsuccessful. The positive and significant coefficient for the log of cumulative casualties ($b = 2.22$, $p < .01$) indicates that when military operations were perceived as successful, presidents ap-peared to receive an increase in support as casualties increased. In con-trast, the negative coefficient for the interaction between casualties and

[24] President Gerald Ford's response to the attack on the *Mayaguez* could arguably be coded as a failure, since more U.S. military personnel were killed in the operation than U.S. citizens were rescued. However, the *Mayaguez* incident was not generally viewed as a failure at the time—perhaps because the president was viewed as taking decisive action in the wake of the recent fall of Saigon.

TABLE 4.14
Presidential Approval and Cumulative Casualties: Success and Failures

	1949–1994	1949–1994	1949–1974	1975–1994
Independent Variables				
Log Cumulative Casualties	1.02*	2.22***	1.12	2.84**
	(0.59)	(0.70)	(0.98)	(1.16)
Casualties × No Success		–2.40***	–2.40***	–5.87*
		(0.77)	(0.83)	(3.25)
Qtr. of Administration	–3.32***	–3.41***	–3.86***	–2.30*
	(0.70)	(0.69)	(0.23)	(1.19)
Qtr. of Admi. Squared	0.16***	0.16***	0.19***	0.10
	(0.04)	(0.04)	(0.05)	(0.07)
Constant	65.89***	67.1***	71.78***	60.74
	(4.82)	(4.49)	(6.78)	(4.86)
Number of Observations	184	184	104	80
F-statistic/Chi-squared	23.08***	20.68***	16.38***	5.82***
Estimated Rho	0.90	0.90	0.92	0.78
Initial Durbin-Watson Statistic	0.27	0.25	0.25	0.45
Transformed Durbin-Watson Statistic	1.75	1.73	1.64	1.65

Note: Standard errors for coefficients in parentheses. All tests for statistical significance are two-tailed.
* = $p < .10$.   ** = $p < .05$.   *** = $p < .01$.

an unsuccessful operation ($b = -2.40$, $p < .01$) indicates that presidents did not receive this boost if the operation was considered unsuccessful. By summing these two coefficients, we can see that casualties had virtually no impact at all on approval if the operation was unsuccessful.

The mildly positive impact of casualties for successful operations may be somewhat surprising, given the fact that the conventional wisdom has focused on the public's alleged casualty phobia. But this positive impact is easily explained by the extensive literature on the rally 'round the flag effect (Ostrom and Job 1986; James and Oneal 1991; Russett 1990). That is, our measure of the impact of casualties on presidential approval also captures the boost that a president may receive from engaging in international conflict. As the rally literature expects, this boost evaporates if the use of force is unsuccessful.

Table 4.14 can also shed light on other observable implications of our basic hypothesis that success trumps casualties. If the positive coefficient for casualties is due to a rally around the flag, then we would expect this coefficient to be larger for the post-Vietnam era. After all, American military operations since Vietnam have been relatively brief operations in which the number of U.S. casualties suffered has been relatively low. These are the cases in which a positive relationship between casualties and approval is well explained by the rally 'round the flag phenomenon. However, we would still expect casualties to reduce presidential approval if the mission is viewed as unsuccessful, because this failure would undermine the rally effect. Between 1949 and 1975, in contrast, U.S. military casualties were almost exclusively suffered in two long wars with fairly high numbers of casualties. Since the consensus in this literature is that the rally 'round the flag effect lasts only a few months, these observers would not expect a positive relationship between casualties and presidential approval in Korea and Vietnam even while these operations were successful (Russett 1990; Lian and Oneal 1993). Moreover, this literature also suggests that rally effects are most likely when the costs of the military operation are low. Clearly the costs in Korea and Vietnam were not low.

Thus combining the rally 'round the flag literature with our previous expectations regarding the differing impact of casualties in successful and unsuccessful operations leads us to several expectations. First, we expect a postive relationship between casualties and presidential approval for successful military operations between 1975 and 1994. Second, we would expect either a slightly negative relationship or no relationship between casualties and approval for the 1949–1974 period while those operations were successful. Third, we would expect a strongly negative relationship between casualties and presidential approval whenever the military operation is viewed as unsuccessful.

The analyses in columns 3 and 4 of table 4.14 support all three of these expectations. For the era of Korea and Vietnam (1949–1974), casualties did not have a significant impact on presidential approval when those military operations were successful ($b = 1.12$, n.s.). After the Chinese intervention and the Tet offensive changed the public perceptions of Korea and Vietnam, however, casualties began to reduce presidential approval ratings. The coefficient for the interaction term is negative and statistically significant ($b = -2.40, p < .01$). Adding the two coefficients together reveals that each increase of one unit in the log of casualties reduced presidential approval by about 1.3 percent after Tet and the Chinese intervention. In the post-Vietnam era, however, the pattern is slightly different. Here we see that casualties actually increase presidential approval if the operation is viewed as successful ($b = 2.84, p > .05$). This is consistent with the rally effect we expected. When the operation is not successful, however, the relationship flips and becomes negative. The coefficient for the interaction term is strongly negative ($b = -5.87, p < .10$). The statistical significance of this coefficient is somewhat eroded by the small number of unsuccessful operations, but adding the two coefficients indicates that each one-unit increase in the log of casualties decreased presidential approval by an average of about 3 percent. Thus moving from a situation of no conflict to an unsuccessful military operation of 100 casualties would reduce the president's approval rating by an average of 6 percent.

We hesitate to push these analyses too far. Much depends on our coding of successful and unsuccessful military operations, and of course the view that an operation is a failure is partly reflected in the very same public opinion polls that evaluate presidential popularity. A tactical success like Tet can function as a failure because the public viewed it that way. To avoid a tautology, we must be certain to measure success and failure independent of public attitudes toward the president in the wake of the operation—something that we can only do imperfectly. Nevertheless, within the limits of the method, these results are important and consistent with the overall conclusion that the American public does not demand that its leaders use force without suffering any casualties. Instead, the public—as a whole—appears able to draw reasonable distinctions between successful and unsuccessful military operations. A substantial proportion of the public is willing to support a military operation despite U.S. casualties if the operation appears to be succeeding. If the operation is not successful, however, the American public is—understandably—much less tolerant of casualties. The key challenge for political leaders, then, is not simply to minimize casualties but to frame casualties as the necessary price for success (Dauber 2001). If casualties are seen in this light, the public is willing to pay the human costs of victory.

Summary, Caveats, and Speculations

A clear and statistically significant pattern has emerged concerning civilian and military willingness to accept casualties. Active duty military elite respondents appear to have a rather realpolitik view of American security requirements. They are willing to expend American lives in defense of foreign policy priorities that have long been established as central to American national security. The civilian elite and members of the mass public also support the defense of these realpolitik national security interests, although they appear to be less willing than are military officers to suffer casualties in defense of long-established American allies such as Korea and Taiwan. At the same time, civilian elites and the mass public appear to have broadened their sense of America's national security requirements beyond the realpolitik geopolitical goals of the cold war. These respondents appear significantly more willing to risk American lives in defense of new national priorities such as the spread of democracy, the defense of human rights, stopping the spread of nuclear weapons, and combating terrorism. Active duty, elite military officers show much greater reluctance to accept casualties on missions of humanitarian intervention, although they are more willing to tolerate casualties for interventionist missions in the war on terrorism.

These findings run counter to the conventional wisdom, but they are not in fact inconsistent with the bulk of the polling data, properly understood. On the contrary, we detect in the polls overall a four-part division of public opinion. At one end of the spectrum is a group that supports almost every use of force. It is striking that in virtually every cold war and post–cold war military operation, support for the use of force almost never dropped below 30–35 percent. These respondents might be considered the "solid hawks," for they appear to be remarkably indifferent to stakes, costs, or prospects for victory. At the other end of the spectrum are the "solid doves," a group of maybe 10–30 percent that opposes virtually every use of force. As discussed in chapter 6, even the post-September 11th Afghanistan mission, which arguably tapped into the strongest public support possible, was opposed by a consistent 10–15 percent of the American public, depending on the poll. Neither of these groups can be considered casualty sensitive in the purest sense; they either support or oppose U.S. military operations, period.

In between are two other groups, the casualty phobics and the defeat phobics. Roughly 20 percent of the public *is* casualty phobic in the sense of the conventional wisdom. They support a military mission until the question mentions hypothetical casualties. They respond "zero" to hypothetical questions about acceptable casualties, and they do mean "no casualties are acceptable." They withdraw support when the costs mount in an actual mission. They have been the central preoccupation of the conventional wisdom and of policymakers for the past decade.

Lost in the mix is another, slightly larger group of defeat phobics, people who support military missions provided that they are successful. These people supply the short-term "escalation dynamic" seen in many polls and identified by Schwarz (1994), where support can be found for reversing a temporary setback with an escalation that will seek victory. This segment of the American public will not panic at the sight of body bags, but will turn on a mission that appears to have no prospect of meaningful victory.

Of course, as Larson (1996, 2000) argues persuasively (and as we analyze directly in chapter 5), another dynamic is also present in the data—case-specific ends-means calculations of whether this specific military mission is "worth it." The ends-means dynamic probably interacts with the quadripartite pattern we see in the data. The more tangential the operation is to perceived national interests, the smaller will be the pool of solid hawks and the larger the pool of solid doves. It may also be the case that individuals find themselves moving from one camp to the other depending on the mission—there is no reason why someone cannot be a solid hawk on Afghanistan, defeat phobic on Iraq, casualty phobic on Haiti, and a solid dove on Rwanda, But these individual ends-means calculations appear to aggregate into something like a rough pattern that shapes public attitudes on any use of force. Given the prominence of the casualty debate in recent uses of force, our findings on casualty sensitivity are noteworthy and run contrary to the prevailing perspective in the policy community. There is a widespread consensus that the American public will no longer accept casualties. The elites think that the American public will not accept casualties in the Iraqs and Congos of the world. Our data suggest otherwise and instead support the iconoclastic studies that have also found the public more casualty acceptant even in so-called interventionist missions (Jentleson 1992, 1998; Burk 1999; Kull and Destler 1999). Of course some support will erode as casualties mount, but our data suggest the baseline of support is higher than elites believe—even civilian elites who themselves express a high support for casualties.[25]

Our study suggests that decision makers are forming policy on the basis of questionable presuppositions. In this sense, casualty aversion is real, regardless of poll results, in one important way: recent administrations have conducted policy so as to minimize casualties. Regardless of whether the public is sensitive to casualties, it is true that President Clinton was sensitive and thus policy was skewed accordingly. But the data suggest that the attitudes of the civilian public, mass and elite, are more nuanced than policymakers (or the elite) appear to understand. Estimates of acceptable casualties vary in logical ways, and most important, as we shall demonstrate in chapter 5, these estimates vary with attitudes toward the stakes involved in the conflict. Thus if policymakers can make the case that the operation is important, then we would expect the public to show a willingness to shoulder greater costs.

Moreover, the effort by policymakers to deliver a cost-free military operation, in order to keep the casualty-phobic segment of public support, may actually work against the mission. If the resulting constraints and half measures undermine the prospects for victory or result in mixed results on the battlefield, then policymakers may unintentionally lose the defeat-phobic segment of the American public. Properly mobilized, the public will pay the price of victory, and policymakers need not fear otherwise.

Some significant caveats are in order. We recognize that analysis of first-of-a-kind hypothetical questions faces numerous limitations. Our results, though robust to extensive sensitivity analysis, must at some level remain tentative until they are replicated by other secondary analysis of our data and, more important, by additional surveys using our instrument. Since our findings run against the conventional wisdom, we have highlighted where the results must be held tentatively and where future research

---

[25] Although we did not ask about Kosovo in the mass survey, some other surveys of the general public during the actual conflict found higher than expected support for casualties (Cox 1999).

should focus to resolve remaining ambiguities. Casualty sensitivity is itself a sensitive issue, reflected in the high refusal rates to our casualty questions and the fair number of sabotaged ballots, that is, responses that are clearly absurd, such as casualty estimates larger than the population of the United States. During pretesting we encountered some resistance to the wording of the question—are casualties ever "acceptable"—and found similar problems with other wordings such as "tolerable" or "reasonable." In our discussion we treat "acceptance" and "tolerance" as synonyms but recognize that some respondents may draw subtle distinctions. We are confident, however, that our measure is generally valid and that our findings about the underlying determinants of casualty sensitivity are robust, because the results persist even after extensive sensitivity analyses that treat nonresponses and zeros in different ways. Our findings are robust, but are best thought of as a point of departure for follow-on studies, which we discuss in chapter 6.

At some fundamental level, of course, casualty sensitivity may be unobservable or unverifiable. The possibility of contradictory effects renders the arguments inherently difficult to test even if data on all component parts—civilian attitudes, military attitudes, policymaking deliberations over trade-offs, implementation, and actual casualties—are available (which they are not). Moreover, what is hypothesized is intentions regarding casualties but what is observed is actual casualties. Actual casualties in an operation are a function of what policymakers direct, of course, but they are also a function of the fog of war. Perhaps this is the best way to summarize the striking changes since World War II: civilian casualties were the intended effects of the fire bombing of Tokyo, but for at least the first two months of NATO's war against Serbia, to pick just one example, civilian casualties were principally due to the fog of war.

In sum, American policymakers find themselves trapped in a paradox, but one largely of their own making. On the one hand, as the only superpower, the United States is freer to use its military to intervene in conflicts around the world—more free, in fact, than at any time in its history. On the other hand, policymakers in Washington fear that the American public will not support such interventions without the backdrop of the urgent global threat posed by a countervailing superpower, such as the one that preoccupied American strategy during the cold war. The result is a curious mix of ever more frequent foreign interventions conducted under ever more constrained circumstances. The Clinton administration embarked on the quest for the most elusive holy grail of foreign policy, cost-free influence.

NATO's intervention in Kosovo provided only the most striking example of this dilemma. The American-led alliance drove Serbian troops out of Kosovo without suffering any U.S. combat fatalities, a testament to

American military professionalism and prowess. U.S. costs were low, and that is to be applauded. But at the same time, the foreign policy community, both inside and outside the U.S. government, generally believed that Americans *demanded* such a casualty-free victory as the price of supporting any military intervention abroad. This belief is not to be applauded. If true, it would pose a grave challenge to America's position in the world and could paralyze American foreign policy.

Fortunately, these influential elites are wrong. They have bought into a powerful myth, born during the Vietnam War and cemented during the ill-fated Somalia action of October 1993, that Americans are casualty-phobic. Although the myth has become conventional wisdom, it remains generally unsupported by public opinion polls. A careful analysis of surveys shows that the general public appears to be more willing to tolerate combat losses than civilian policymakers or senior military officers would expect.

CHAPTER FIVE

EXPLORING THE DETERMINANTS

OF CASUALTY SENSITIVITY

T HE PREVIOUS CHAPTER established that civilian and military elites have accepted the conventional wisdom that the general public is highly casualty phobic. The conventional wisdom is, we argue, a myth. Although a portion of the public is casualty phobic, overall the general public expresses a remarkable willingness to accept casualties (that is, combat fatalities) when necessary for victory. The public appears to be defeat phobic, not casualty phobic.

Moreover, our analyses in chapter 4 revealed that, on the whole, civilian elites, military officers, and the mass public all generally appeared willing to tolerate casualties on the order of another Desert Storm in support of realpolitik missions such as the defense of Korea. Nonetheless, consistent with our analyses in chapter 2 regarding foreign policy preferences, we found that military officers tended to be more willing than civilian elites to tolerate casualties in achieving realpolitik missions. And consistent with the analyses in chapter 3, we found that the civil-military gap flips directions when we switch to asking about interventionist missions such as the defense of human rights, missions in which military officers, become the least willing to tolerate casualties. We found a greater consensus across civilians, military officers, and the mass public with regard to security-related interventions against Iraqi weapons of mass destruction and global terrorism. To some extent these scenarios stood in between the realpolitik and humanitarian intervention scenarios. However, we found that this overall consensus was actually a function of demographic differences across the samples. When we compared military officers with younger males in the civilian elite sample, we found that these responses followed a pattern that was similar to the humanitarian intervention responses—the military was more casualty sensitive.

In this chapter we take a look at why civilian and military elites differ in their tolerance for casualties. First, as we noted in chapters 2 and 4, there are substantial demographic differences between our civilian and military samples. As a group, military officers are younger, more predominantly male, and more likely to be African American or Hispanic than our sample of civilian elites. We continue to account for these differences in the analyses in this chapter. Second, our analyses in chapter 2 identified a civil-military opinion gap regarding when and how military force ought to be used. Civilian and the military elites did not always agree on the importance of realpolitik and interventionist foreign policy goals, the effectiveness of military force, and the Powell Doctrine. Perhaps the civil-military gap over casualty sensitivity is a result of these differing attitudes toward the use of force. Third, perhaps other attitudes held by civilian and military respondents can account for the civil-military gap. For example, we know that elite military officers are substantially more likely to identify themselves as Republican than are civilian elites (Holsti 2001). Perhaps these or other political or social attitudes can explain the difference in casualty sensitivity. Finally, we also address the extent to which respondents are socially connected to those individuals who are most likely to be at risk in U.S. military operations. Perhaps the military is more sensitive to casualties in interventionist missions because these casualties are a more concrete reality to them than they would be to someone with little connection to the military.

Briefly, our findings indicate that casualty attitudes appear to be a function of what might be called rational calculations. Those who place greater importance on interventionist missions and those who express greater faith in military force as a foreign policy tool also express a greater tolerance for casualties on interventionist missions. This pattern leaves the impression that elite attitudes toward casualties are fairly sophisticated and well considered. Although these differing views of when and how to use military force do explain part of the civil-military gap, they cannot account for all of it. Second, several other attitudes, such as party identification and trust of political leaders, correlate with casualty sensitivity as well, but these attitudes also cannot account for the entirety of the civil-military gap. Instead, the best explanation of the gap is the extent to which respondents are socially connected to those who would be at risk in a military operation. People, whether civilians or military, who are socially connected to other military personnel tend to be more casualty sensitive than people who are not.

Finally, we turn to a series of in-depth analyses of the attitudes of the military respondents. These analyses indicate that casualty sensitivity does not appear to be the result of "self-preservation" fears of military respondents. For example, we find that respondents from the Marines—and sometimes the Air Force—tend to be the most willing to tolerate casualties on interventionist missions. Yet the Marines and arguably the Air Force officers are relatively likely to be placed at risk in such operations. Moreover, we find no consistent difference in casualty sensitivity between the combat arms and other branches of the services (such as combat support and combat service support). Younger officers—who are more likely to see combat—are also more willing to tolerate casualties. Moreover, those who state that they joined the military to "serve their country" express no greater willingness to tolerate casualties than those who say that they joined because they were drafted or joined in order to avoid the draft. If the elite military showed casualty sensitivity out of a desire for self-preservation, we would expect casualty sensitivity to be higher among younger officers from the combat arms, especially in the Marines and Air Force, and among those who did not volunteer to serve. We find no support for any of these claims.

In fact, our analyses of casualty tolerance within the military reveals relatively few robust patterns. Nonetheless, we continue to find that tolerance for casualties is a result of respondents' views about the importance of the potential benefits from an interventionist mission. We also find that casualty tolerance is associated with political attitudes, such as the confidence military officers express in civilian policymakers and the officers' beliefs about the casualty tolerance of the American public. We close by evaluating whether career incentives resulting from a "zero defects" mentality within the military may be shaping military officers' attitudes on casualties and conclude that the evidence is ambiguous on this point.

The chapter proceeds as follows. We begin with a brief review of expectations derived from the conventional wisdom and existing literature. We next turn to an analysis of the TISS data, opening that section with a brief discussion of the way we operationalize the key variables introduced as possible correlates of attitudes on casualties. In this chapter, however, we omit any explanation of how we arrived at our basic measure of casualty sensitivity itself, covered extensively in the previous chapter. Our statistical analysis of the TISS data has two parts. First, we compare the civilian and military elites to determine whether the civil-military gap is a result of differing estimates of the benefits of interventionist operations; other, more general political and social attitudes; or a respondent's personal connection to the military.[1] Second, we look more closely at military attitudes, exploring differences across various services and branches within the services and examining whether military perspectives on other military policies are correlated with casualty sensitivity. We conclude with a brief summary of the results.

General Expectations about the Determinants of Casualty Attitudes

The conventional wisdom may expect the public to be casualty phobic, but it is somewhat less certain *why* the public is this way. The most common explanation is the influence of media, especially television's ability

---

[1] Unfortunately, the TISS survey of the mass public was not extensive enough to provide data to measure these other attitudes. Consequently, in this chapter, we focus our analyses on a comparison of the elite samples.

to dramatize the costs of war; this is the meaning of General Shelton's "Dover test," referring to televized images of flag-draped coffins arriving at Dover Air Force Base (Cuningham 2000; Shelton 2000). When the media brought the Vietnam War into America's living room, the terrible human costs of war became real and the American public confronted this reality for the first time. This has given rise to an alleged "CNN effect," apparently demonstrated in the Somalia disaster, in which media images of human suffering supposedly lead the American public to demand entry into conflicts they might otherwise ignore as inconsequential to the national interest, and then media images of U.S. casualties lead the American public to demand retreat from those commitments without a victory (Kennan 1993; Neuman 1996).

Analysts have found very little support for the crude version of the CNN effect—that the public responds viscerally to gruesome images on television and whipsaws policymakers with wild swings in mood (Larson 1996; Strobel 1997; Burk 1999; Kull and Destler 1999; Kull and Ramsay 2000). Indeed, the supposedly paradigmatic case, Somalia, is not in fact consistent with the CNN hypothesis and does not demonstrate that casualty phobia on the part of the general public is driven by images of the human costs of war (Dauber 2001). Kull and Destler (1999) argue that the public reduced support for the Somalia operation not because of the 18 Ranger deaths in October 1993 but rather because they were told by the political elite that the mission could not succeed, regardless of the price. The Clinton administration made no effort to frame the casualties in any way other than as a disaster that proved the Somalia mission had drifted dreadfully off course. If the administration had rather chosen to galvanize public opposition to Aideed—highlighting the soldiers' deaths in a "dastardly" ambush and the way Aideed's forces desecrated the bodies of the American dead—one can imagine that public opinion might have tolerated (even demanded) a greatly expanded effort to catch and punish Aideed, even one that involved greater casualties.

Although there is little evidence of a CNN effect that is driving casualty attitudes among the general public, there is evidence to suggest that the CNN effect may operate directly on the policymakers themselves. It is noteworthy that President George H. W. Bush reported that he was stimulated to intervene in Somalia by watching the news accounts of the starving children. He phoned Secretary of Defense Cheney and General Powell and said, "Please come over to the White House. . . . I—we—can't watch this anymore. You've got to do something" (Hines 1999). Bush was not alone. When asked by an interviewer what effect the gruesome TV footage had on his decision to withdraw troops, President Clinton took pains to draw a parallel with Bush's reasoning. "We live in a time when electronic images have great power. I mean, CNN went to

Somalia and dramatized the problems of the people and that's one reason the world community got interested in helping them. Next door in the Sudan there are also a lot of people starving, and people don't know about it. I just think, it's irresistible . . . to show vivid images but I just think it is important that we be reminded that the same television power is what got the country and the world community in [*sic*] the first place" (unattributed 1993, A12).

Another plausible source of casualty sensitivity might be technological determinism: perhaps Americans have become averse to taking casualties because they *can* avoid them, because America's overwhelming technological advantage allows it to dominate the enemy and fight on its terms (Toffler and Toffler 1993; Hyde 2000; K. Mueller 2000). By this account, the dramatic post–cold war intensification of a long-standing sensitivity to casualties coincides with the equally dramatic unipolar moment: no peer competitor can challenge the United States and compel it to take casualties. A related explanation is what might be called the creeping curse of success. Since Vietnam, fatality rates have been several orders of magnitude off historical levels for combat operations (see table 5.1),[2] precisely because they have not involved the United States in a prolonged conflict against a peer competitor. Beginning with the 1989 invasion of Panama (or arguably earlier, with the 1983 invasion of Grenada), the United States has taken steadily fewer casualties in each of its uses of force. The spike of deaths during Desert Storm actually reinforces the point, since the level was low compared with any reasonable measure of effort (sorties flown, soldiers deployed, and so on), certainly lower than historical rates and well below even the most optimistic estimates prior to the conflict (Biddle 1996). Perhaps the low casualty rate came to be linked with the success of the military operation; perhaps the conflict was a victory not just because the United States prevailed but also because the

[2] Figures are total battle deaths and other deaths, as reported by the Directorate for Information Operations and Reports (Statistical Information Analysis Division), U.S. DoD (*www.web1.osd.mil/mmid/casualty*). The website did not include Bosnia data; the number reported here was given to us in a telephone conversation with OSD-Public Affairs, October 6, 1999. Note that the number of deaths reported for Korea here is different from the figure used in the TISS survey instrument. The stem to the question on casualties in the TISS survey reminded respondents about how many Americans died in previous wars, giving rough estimates that allowed for broad comparisons. The number used for Korea on the TISS survey was "roughly 54,000," somewhat higher than the number reported here. The reason for the discrepancy is that, due to an error by an anonymous government clerk, for years the official accounts of Korean War casualties used the 54,000 figure, which included roughly 18,000 deaths that occurred during the Korean War period but outside the theater and for reasons having nothing to do with the Korean War. The Department of Defense officially revised the Korean War estimates in June 2000, long after our survey instrument was used. For more on the Korean War casualty controversy, see Vogel (2000).

TABLE 5.1
U.S. Fatalities in Prominent Armed Conflicts

World War II (1941–1946)	405,399
Korea (1950–1953)	36,913
Vietnam (1964–1973)	58,177
Lebanon (1983)	265
Grenada (1983)	19
Panama (1989)	23
Persian Gulf War (1990–1991)	383
Somalia (1992–1994)	43
Bosnia (1992–1995)	3
Haiti (1994–1996)	4
Kosovo (1999)	2

Source: See note 2.

United States prevailed with very low casualties. Each successive military operation set a benchmark for the next, leading to a lower and lower tolerance of casualties.

Casualty sensitivity has also been linked to the decline in the birth rate in Western countries. Edward Luttwak makes the provocative argument that Western postindustrial societies are casualty phobic because infant mortality is down, leading to less experience with the death of children and, because of smaller families, fewer children to sacrifice in war. He calls this effect "motherism": "When it was normal to lose one or more children to disease, the loss of one more youngster in war had a different meaning than it has for today's families, which have two or three children, all of whom are expected to survive, and each of whom represents a larger share of the family's emotional economy" (Luttwak 1994, 25). Death is no longer a familiar part of the family experience, and thus dying in combat is viewed as an "outrageous scandal" rather than an "occupational hazard." Luttwak offers caveats for his argument by saying that this constraint can be overcome if political leaders make the case that the particular use of force involves a vital national interest, but he argues that this represents a dramatic change from periods when great powers were relatively unconstrained in the use of force in pursuit of important but not vital interests. Although Luttwak does not do so, one could draw a further inference from his argument: perhaps women are more casualty sensitive than men.

Charles Moskos (1998) puts forward yet another plausible explanation of casualty phobia in the mass public. He accepts the argument that the public willingness to take casualties is based on whether or not the mission is perceived to be in the national interest. The greater the national interest at stake, the greater the willingness of the public to take casualties.

Moskos goes on to assert, however, that the general public's perception of the national interest is not intrinsic to the issue at stake, but is rather a function of whether the elite is willing to die for the cause: "The answer to the question of what are national interests is not found in the cause itself, but in who is willing to die for that cause. Only when the privileged classes perform military service does the country define the cause as worth young people's blood. Only when elite youth are on the firing line do war losses become more acceptable. This explains the seeming paradox of why we have a lower acceptance of combat casualties with a volunteer military than we had with a draft Army" (1998, 25). Moskos argues that public support for the large wars of the twentieth century correlated with the exposure of elites to combat. Support for Vietnam, in his view, dropped once elite youth starting evading the draft in large numbers. With the all-volunteer force, children of the elite have essentially avoided service in the military altogether. "Citizens accept hardships," Moskos says, "only when their leadership is viewed as self-sacrificing."

Moskos thus traces a fairly straight line from the growing "experience" gap between civilian elite and the military to a supposed growing unwillingness among the public to take casualties. In effect he claims that the civil-military experience gap directly affects estimations of the benefits that accrue from military operations and the costs associated with those operations. The general public lowers its estimation of the benefits and raises its estimation of the costs if it sees that elite children are not willing to risk their lives to advance U.S. policy.

Two implications of this view deserve special emphasis. First, the argument implies a fairly monotonic trend in casualty sensitivity over time. If elite patterns of national service change, of course, casualty sensitivity should change as well. But given a fairly fixed pattern of elites' increased avoidance of national service from the mid-1960s until today, we should see a similar pattern of ever-increasing casualty sensitivity. Significantly, if this argument is correct, casualty sensitivity should not vary with other measures of the stakes involved. The public should be as casualty phobic in securing access to Persian Gulf oil as they are in protecting Tutsis from ethnic cleansing. Since the same low number of elites are at risk in either operation, according to Moskos, the public should view the operations as equally unworthy of American lives. Second, this argument holds that casualty sensitivity should be greater in the mass public than in the elite. The root of casualty phobia is the awareness in the general public that the elites are free riding on the system. By implication, elites will be willing to accept the casualties because it is not really "their" citizens but other American citizens who are paying the costs.

Neither of these implications of Moskos's argument is supported by our analyses in chapter 4. In fact, both mass and elite respondents appeared to draw sharp distinctions between realpolitik and interventionist scenarios. Moreover, elites were generally more casualty sensitive than the masses. In this chapter, we assess a further implication of Moskos's conjecture. Moskos is positing a variant of a general rational calculation on the part of the public—the public supports casualties when it is perceived to be in the national interest. The key variant is that—according to Moskos—the public does not make distinctions among missions according to the specific merits of each case, but instead uses the overall willingess of elites to place themselves and their children at risk as a simpler proxy measure for the importance of the interests at stake. If this is so, then respondents' own estimates of the importance of interventionist and realpolitik goals should not be associated with their willingness to tolerate casualties.

Moskos's conjecture is a special case of yet another, broader, hypothesis about the determinants of casualty sensitivity: that tolerance for casualties is a direct function of the respondent's perception of the national interest at stake in the mission (Larson 1996, 2000; Strobel 1997; Burk 1999; Kull and Destler 1999). The public is willing to take casualties if the national security interest at stake is high, but as the security interest declines so too does the willingness to pay a human cost in defense of it. The TISS data are uniquely suited for testing this hypothesis, since we can measure each respondent's perceived importance and expressed casualty tolerance for various missions. We are unable, however, to test a corollary offered by Larson (1996, 2000): that the public is willing to take casualties if the mission is supported by a consensus among the political elite. Larson's argument is sensible, but very difficult to test. Every U.S. use of force since World War II has been hotly contested within the political elite. It is endemic in democratic politics, especially within the United States, that important foreign policies will be vigorously debated with loud voices on every side of an issue. Even when a consensus arguably was present—for instance, in the immediate aftermath of North Korea's invasion of South Korea or in the 1964 Gulf of Tonkin resolution—it was quickly replaced with prominent voices expressing doubt about the operation. Without a valid and independent measure of consensus, the theory is virtually impossible to test systematically. Moreover, as Larson (1996, 91–92) himself concedes, the lead-up to the 1991 Gulf War demonstrates that an adroit president can mobilize public support even in the midst of what can only be described as vigorous political dissensus. Nevertheless, we believe that consensus is probably an important ingredient in stiffening public resolve. The more prominent, credible, and powerful the critics of a particular military operation, the more doubt this is likely to sow in the public's mind and hence the greater reluctance to pay a huge price for that mission.

Chapter 4 introduced yet another determinant of casualty acceptance, perceived success: if the mission is successful, or there is a reasonable expectation of success, or at least the political elite make a plausible case to the public that success is within reach, then the public will accept casualties. This kind of casualty acceptance is likewise difficult to isolate, since a low casualty count may itself be a measure of success. In effect, this view also argues for an eminently rational public, unwilling to pay much when the operation is not worth it or is likely to fail. To the extent possible, we test this hypothesis in chapter 4.

Finally, because of the paucity of empirical studies on the subject, there is little in the literature to guide us on the determinants of military attitudes. Nevertheless, we can tease out some conjectures from other arguments in the literature. For instance, one possible cause of military casualty sensitivity is the transition in military mindset from what has been called an "institutional" approach to military service—one emphasizing the heroic goals of defending the nation—to an "occupational" approach that emphasizes the career-enhancing benefits of service in the military (Moskos 1977; Segal 1986; Moskos and Wood 1988). An implication of this thesis might be that the American military is taking on a mercenary cast and is less prepared to take casualties than it once was. This expectation is reinforced in the literature bemoaning the loss of the "warrior" culture in the U.S. military, which implies, perhaps unintentionally, that casualty phobia may be as least as great in the military as among the civilians (Collins 1998; Lanman 1998; Webb 1998; Hillen 1999).

The TISS Data on the Determinants of Casualty Attitudes: Explaining Our Method

Of course, the core claim of many of these arguments—that the American public is absolutely casualty phobic—was already rebutted by the analyses of the TISS data presented in the previous chapter. If the phenomenon an analyst posits is nonexistent, our confidence in the explanation for the phenomenon posited by the analyst naturally diminishes. Nevertheless, it is possible that, for example, Luttwak is wrong that the public is casualty phobic, but might still be right that public support for casualties is higher among those who are childless and therefore less likely to have a direct personal stake in any casualties that might result.

Because of limitations on the number of questions that could be asked, the data cannot assess all of these expectations. Nevertheless, the data are a rich resource for evaluating more generally the determinants of attitudes on casualties. As explained in the previous chapter, our measure of casualty sensitivity is an ordinal logit estimator of clusters of responses to a series of hypothetical questions on the highest number of casualties the respondent would consider acceptable to accomplish a given mission. The missions range in intensity but fall into two broad categories: the high-intensity missions of defending South Korea and Taiwan, on the one hand,

and, on the other, a range of lower-intensity missions running from preventing Iraq from obtaining weapons of mass destruction to stabilizing a democratic government in Congo. The multivariate analysis reported in this chapter assesses whether military status (operationalized as discussed in the previous chapter) correlates with casualty sensitivity, even after controlling for other plausible factors that might account for the civil-military gap such as demographic variables, estimates of the benefits of a military operation, and other political and social variables.

Once again, we should note that introducing these control variables is not a method of assessing whether the civil-military gap is "real." For example, a statistical analysis revealing that civilian and military respondents have similar attitudes once we account for the impact of gender would not constitute evidence that the civil-military gap is unreal or ephemeral. After all, the military elite is more than 90 percent male, and hypothetical statistical comparisons about what military opinions would be like if there were a more even gender balance cannot change that fact. The hypothetical equalization of the civilian and military samples through the introduction of control variables does not alter the size or nature of the civil-military gaps that we discussed in chapter 4. Instead, these analyses may help us to understand why such a gap exists.

The coefficients reported in the logit analyses represent the "direct effects" of the independent variables on respondents' sensitivity to casualties. That is, they capture the effects of each independent variable while holding the other variables constant. Thus if the introduction of control variables causes the coefficients for military status to become substantively small and statistically insignificant, then these control variables represent an explanation for *why* civilian and military opinions differ. These statistical explanations for the gap can come in essentially two logical forms. First, it is possible that the control variables represent independent causal effects that happen to be correlated with military status. In this case, the civil-military gap is spurious in the sense that it is caused by other variables that simply happen to be correlated with military status. Second, it is possible that these control variables might represent intervening links between military status and attitudes toward casualties. In this case, military experience causes a change in respondents' attitudes, and these attitudes, in turn, cause a change in attitudes toward casualties. The distinction between these "spurious" and "intervening" explanations is theoretical rather than statistical. That is, the distinction rests on a claim about whether military status could be a cause of the control variable in question. We begin to examine this distinction below, but more definitive conclusions will have to await future research.

Explanatory Control Variables

The measurement of the demographic control variables is specified in chapter 4. We divide the other control variables into three categories: (1) attitudes toward the use of force; (2) political and social attitudes; and (3) connection to persons at risk in military operations. We discuss our results in the next section.

Attitude toward the Use of Force (1): Importance of the Issue at Stake

One would expect that respondents' willingness to suffer costs in the use of force would be dependent at least in part on their view of the importance of the potential benefits. Because there is substantial variation in the six casualty scenarios we presented to the respondents, we use three different variables to capture the importance that respondents place on the issues at stake in each scenario. For the Congo and Kosovo scenarios, we rely on the scale we constructed in chapter 2 regarding the importance that respondents place on human rights as a foreign policy goal. For the Iraqi weapons of mass destruction and terrorism scenarios, we constructed a scale measuring the importance that respondents placed on fighting terrorism and the spread of weapons of mass destruction.

As we discussed in chapter 2, our human rights scale captures the extent to which the respondent believes that the defense of human rights around the globe is an important foreign policy priority for the United States. Our measure is constructed as the mean of the respondents' support for the following goals for American foreign policy: (1) helping to improve the standard of living in developing countries; (2) combating world hunger; (3) fostering cooperation to solve common problems such as food, inflation, and energy; (4) promoting and defending human rights in other countries; and (5) addressing humanitarian needs abroad.[3] For each of these questions the respondents' answers were coded as follows: very important = 4, somewhat important = 3, no opinion = 2, not important = 1. We identify the respondents' mean response as their level of support for international human rights.

For the Iraq and terrorism scenarios, we measured the extent to which respondents feel that defending against international terrorism the spread of nuclear weapons is an important foreign policy goal for the United States. This measure is constructed as the respondents' judgment of the severity of the following potential threats to American national

---

[3] The exact question wording is reproduced in chapter 2.

security: (1) the spread of nuclear weapons; (2) the proliferation of weapons of mass destruction to less-developed countries; (3) international terrorism; (4) the expansion of Islamic fundamentalism; and (5) terrorist attacks on the United States.[4] For each question responses were coded as follows: very serious = 5, moderately serious = 4, somewhat serious = 3, no opinion = 2, not at all serious = 1. We identify respondents' mean answer to these five items as their level of concern for nuclear proliferation and terrorism.

For the Korea and Taiwan scenarios, we use the same scale we used in chapter 2 to measure the extent to which respondents support what might be considered realpolitik geopolitical goals for American foreign policy. The scale is created from respondents' level of agreement with the following statements: (1) the United States should contain communism; (2) the United States should maintain superior military power worldwide; (3) there is considerable validity in the "domino theory"; (4) Russia is generally expansionist; (5) there is nothing wrong with using the CIA to undermine hostile governments; (6) the United States should take all steps to prevent aggression by any expansionist power; (7) any Chinese victory is a defeat for America's national interest; and (8) the emergence of China as a military power is a threat to the United States.[5] We identify respondents' mean answer to these eight items as their level of concern for realpolitik goals.

Attitude toward the Use of Force (2): Effectiveness of Military Force

As we noted in chapter 4, substantial evidence suggests that the willingness to tolerate casualties depends significantly on the prospects for success in the military operation. Thus we would expect that respondents' beliefs about the effectiveness of force should influence their responses to the various casualty scenarios. Unfortunately, the TISS survey did not ask respondents to give their views of the effectiveness of military force for missions of humanitarian intervention. Thus we rely on slightly different

---

[4] Exact question wording from the TISS survey questionnaire: Question 1: "Here is a list of possible foreign policy goals that the United States might have. Please indicate how much importance you think should be attached to each goal." q01g: "Preventing the spread of nuclear weapons." Question 3: "This question asks you to evaluate the seriousness of the following as threats to American national security." q03b: "The proliferation of weapons of mass destruction to less-developed countries." q03e: "International terrorism." q03j: "Expansion of Islamic fundamentalism." q03k: "Terrorist attacks on the United States." Although these items address two somewhat distinct concepts, respondents seem to link terrorism and the spread of nuclear weapons quite closely. Interitem correlations are quite high, and the overall alpha for the scale is 0.73.

[5] For specific question wording, see the note 7 in Chapter 2.

measures to capture respondents' views of the effectiveness of military force in addressing each scenario. For the Congo and Kosovo scenarios we measure the perceived effectiveness of force through responses to a question regarding the appropriateness of using the military for humanitarian intervention.[6] Fortunately, the TISS survey did ask respondents about their views regarding the effectiveness of military tools relative to other nonmilitary tools in combating weapons of mass destruction, for coping with terrorism, and for containing China. Thus we relied on these responses to measure the perceived effectiveness of force for the Iraq, terrorism, Korea, and Taiwan scenarios.[7] Responses could be "much more," "somewhat more," "equally," "somewhat less," "much less," and "no opinion." No opinion responses were recoded as "equally effective."

Attitude toward the Use of Force (3): The Powell Doctrine

Although support for the Powell Doctrine does not directly address attitudes toward casualties, it may have an indirect impact on willingness to support certain scenarios. For example, if one is a strong supporter of the Powell Doctrine and one also believes that a "quick and massive" use of force in Congo is unlikely, one might become less willing to tolerate casualties for that mission. Moreover, as we discussed above, critics of the Powell Doctrine have suggested that Powell's ideas were driven by an excessive focus on avoiding American military casualties—regardless of the implication for enemy casualties. This criticism became pointed enough that Powell felt compelled to respond to this charge. Thus we examine whether support for the Powell Doctrine may be a cause of casualty sensitivity—especially in interventionist scenarios.

We rely on the same scale of support for the Powell Doctrine used in chapter 2. Recall that the TISS survey included questions concerning two key assertions of the doctrine: (1) military force should be used in pursuit of total victory; and (2) military force should be used quickly and massively rather than gradually. We code respondents' level of support for the Powell Doctrine as their mean level of support for these two statements.[8]

---

[6] The specific question on the TISS survey was question q07e, "The following are some possible uses of the military. Please indicate how important you consider each potential role for the military. To address humanitarian needs abroad."

[7] The specific questions on the TISS survey were questions q04a, q04b, and q04d: "Reviewing some of the earlier list of possible threats to national security, how effective is the use of military tools compared to non-military tools for coping with them? A. The emergence of China as a great military power. B. The proliferation of weapons of mass destruction to less-developed countries. D. International terrorism."

[8] For specific items and question wording, see chapter 2. The correlation between these two responses is 0.43.

As was the case with the realpolitik variable, responses were coded as: agree strongly = 5, agree somewhat = 4, no opinion = 3, disagree somewhat = 2, disagree strongly = 1.

Political and Social Attitude (1): Party Identification

Perhaps the most basic political attitude is party identification, and as we have noted, existing research indicates that the military is substantially more Republican than civilian society (Holsti 2001). Thus controlling for party self-identification can help to ensure that the civil-military gaps we observe are not simply a function of underlying partisan gaps. We capture party identification with two dummy variables. Respondents who identified as "Independent" or who failed to list a party identification were left as the comparison group. The "Democrat" dummy variable takes on a value of 1 if the respondents recorded their party identification as "Democrat." A value of 0 was coded otherwise. Likewise the "Republican" dummy variable takes on a value of 1 if the respondents recorded their party identification as "Republican." A value of 0 was coded otherwise.

Political and Social Attitude (2): Confidence in Political Leaders

One of the received lessons of Vietnam was that the United States should not use force unless its leaders have the commitment to support the war to its conclusion. Tolerating casualties thus requires some level of trust and confidence in political leaders to see the mission through to a successful outcome. The TISS survey asked respondents to rate their confidence in the following institutions: (1) the Presidency; (2) Congress; (3) the executive branch of the federal government; and (4) the U.S. Supreme Court. For each institution, respondents could offer a great deal of confidence (3), only some confidence (2), or hardly any confidence (1). We identify the mean of these responses as the respondent's level of confidence in political leaders.[9]

Political and Social Attitude (3): Perception of Mass Public's Casualty Sensitivity

America's experience in Vietnam would seem to demonstrate that the United States has difficulty prosecuting a war if the overwhelming majority of the public opposes its policy. As we discussed in the previous chap-

[9] "No opinion" responses were coded as missing. The exact question wording for the stem: "The following is a list of some institutions in this country. As far as these institutions are concerned, would you say you have a great deal of confidence, only some confidence, or hardly any confidence in them?" In the TISS survey questionnaire these are questions q32b, q32d, q32e, and q32h (alpha = 0.72).

ter, both civilian and military leaders are deeply concerned about the public's tolerance for casualties. Thus we would expect that elite tolerance for casualties will depend in part on their beliefs about public tolerance for casualties. As chapter 4 indicates, elite respondents were asked whether they agreed with the statement: "The American public will rarely tolerate large numbers of US casualties in military operations." Responses were coded as: agree strongly = 5, agree somewhat = 4, no opinion = 3, disagree somewhat = 2, disagree strongly = 1.

Connection to Those at Risk in U.S. Military Operations (1): Extent of Military Contact

Despite the availability of media images and information about casualties, the fact remains that for most civilian Americans the casualties of war will remain relatively abstract costs. However, these costs become more concrete to the extent that respondents actually know individuals who serve in the military and might be at risk in a military operation. We would expect that these kinds of personal links to the military may reduce respondents' tolerance for casualties as their calculations about costs move from the abstract to the more concrete. For instance, Scott Gartner, Gary Segura, and Michael Wilkening (1997) found that geographic proximity to the costs of war seemed to matter in the early stages of the Vietnam War; respondents from counties with higher casualty rates were less likely to approve of the conflict.

Respondents were asked to describe the people they came into contact with in social or community groups and at work in terms of whether these people were generally from the military or from civilian society. Responses in both categories were coded as: all military = 5, mostly military = 4, about equal = 3, mostly civilian = 2, all civilian = 1.[10] In addition, respondents were asked to think of their three closest adult friends and to report on how many of them were members of the military.[11] We identify the mean response to these three questions as the respondent's level of military contact.

---

[10] "No opinion" responses were recoded as "about equal." The specific wording for questions q28 and q29 was: "Now consider the people you come in contact with in the *social or community* groups to which you belong. Are they all civilians, mostly civilians with some military, about equal civilians and military, mostly military with some civilians, or all military? For the purposes of this question, 'civilian' here refers to civilians other than civil servants or contractors working for the military." And "Now consider the people you come in contact with at work. Are they all civilians, mostly civilians with some military, about equal civilians and military, mostly military with some civilians, or all military? For the purposes of this question, 'civilian' here refers to civilians other than civil servants or contractors working for the military."

[11] The specific wording for q30 was: "Think of three adult friends you most enjoy spending time with. How many of these friends currently serve or have served previously in the

Connection to Those at Risk in U.S. Military
Operations (2): Parenthood

We tested Luttwak's (1994) expectation that the fear of losing children
will undermine tolerance for casualties. In fact, respondents with children
may feel more of a connection to those at risk for two differing reasons.
First, parents of small children may identify with military parents who
are going off to war and who represent potential combat fatalities. Second, parents of older children may not want to place their offspring at
risk, or they may identify with those parents who are sending their children to war. In either case, the experience of parenthood may make the
thought of casualties in war more concrete and more disconcerting. Respondents were asked whether or not they had any children. Those who
stated they did were assigned a value of 1. A value of 0 was assigned
otherwise.

The TISS Data on the Determinants of Casualty Attitudes: Results

Table 5.2 presents our analyses of casualty sensitivity for the Korea and
the Taiwan scenarios. The first and third columns present analyses that
include our controls for attitudes toward the use of force and other political and social attitudes. The results in the second and fourth columns of
results present analyses that also include respondents' connection to those
at risk.

Across both the Korea and the Taiwan scenarios, the importance that
respondents place on realpolitik foreign policy issues has a positive and
statistically significant impact on tolerance for casualties. Similarly, respondent's views of the effectiveness of military force in coping with
China also had a positive impact on tolerance for casualties. Support for
the Powell Doctrine does not have a significant impact on tolerance for
casualties for either the Korea or the Taiwan scenario, but as we discussed
above, we expected the Powell Doctrine to depress casualty tolerance for
scenarios in which the quick and massive use of force is unlikely. That is
clearly not the case with Korea and Taiwan, so the insignificant coefficients are not surprising. In fact, this combination of results represents
strong support for the argument that civilian and military elites gave careful and thoughtful responses to the TISS casualty questions. Tolerance
for casualties appears to be a well-considered balancing of the costs and
benefits of military operations.

---

military? Zero, one, two, three, uncertain." This variable was recoded on a five-point scale
before taking the mean of the three items.

TABLE 5.2

Determinants of Casualty Sensitivity in the Korean and Taiwan Scenarios

	Korea		Taiwan	
Respondent's Military Status				
Civilian Elite Nonveteran	−0.68***	−1.00***	0.56***	0.18
	(0.18)	(0.24)	(0.18)	(0.24)
Civilian Elite Military Education	0.49**	0.64**	−0.18	−0.04
	(0.24)	(0.26)	(0.25)	(0.26)
Civilian Elite Veteran	0.16	0.18	0.04	0.08
	(0.19)	(0.20)	(0.19)	(0.19)
Military Reserve	−0.12	−0.32*	0.22	−0.0004
	(0.15)	(0.18)	(0.15)	(0.18)
Demographic Variables				
Gender	−1.45***	−1.48***	−1.09***	−1.12***
	(0.17)	(0.18)	(0.17)	(0.18)
Age	−0.02***	−.02**	−0.04***	−0.03***
	(0.01)	(0.01)	(0.01)	(0.01)
Minority	−0.40	−0.46*	−0.21	−0.25
	(0.25)	(0.25)	(0.25)	(0.25)
Education	0.30**	0.26*	0.28*	−0.27*
	(0.15)	(0.15)	(0.15)	(0.15)
Attitudes toward the Use of Force				
Importance of Realpolitik	0.28***	0.30***	0.53***	0.55***
	(0.10)	(0.10)	(0.10)	(0.10)
Effectiveness of Force	0.10**	0.09*	0.11**	0.10**
	(0.05)	(0.05)	(0.05)	(0.05)
Powell Doctrine	−0.08	−0.07	−0.02	−0.02
	(0.05)	(0.05)	(0.05)	(0.05)
Political and Social Attitudes				
Democrat	−0.04	−0.04	0.09	0.06
	(0.17)	(0.17)	(0.17)	(0.17)
Republican	−0.39***	0.35***	−0.17	−0.18
	(0.13)	(0.13)	(0.13)	(0.13)
Confidence in Leaders	0.09	0.10	0.17	0.19
	(0.13)***	(0.13)	(0.13)	(0.13)
Mass Sensitivity	−0.20	−0.20***	−0.19***	−0.18***
	(0.04)	(0.05)	(0.04)	(0.04)
Connection to Those at Risk				
Contact with Military		−0.15**		−0.18**
		(0.08)		(0.08)
Parent		−0.02		−0.08
		(0.15)		(0.15)
Number of Observations	1,213	1,181	1,191	1,159
Chi-squared	201.86	200.84	127.09	127.97

Note: Standard errors for coefficients in parentheses. All tests for statistical significance are two-tailed.
* = *p* < .10.   ** = *p* < .05.   *** = *p* < .01.

The results in table 5.2 do not indicate consistent partisan differences over tolerance for casualties. With regard to Korea, Republicans are less supportive of casualties than are Independents or Democrats, but this gap is not significant with regard to Taiwan. Moreover, confidence in political leaders does not have a significant impact on casualty tolerance in either realpolitik scenario. These results could indicate that elite respondents are generally confident that the United States will uphold its security commitments to these friendly states. The elite view of the public's willingness to tolerate casualties has a strong and consistent impact on the elite's tolerance for casualties in Korea and Taiwan. The negative coefficients for perceptions of mass sensitivity indicate that the respondents who agreed with the statement "the American public is rarely willing to tolerate casualties in military operations" were themselves also less willing to tolerate casualties. One interpretation of this relationship is that the myth of popular casualty phobia is causing political and military elites to be more sensitive to casualties as well. Anecdotal evidence from the policymaking debates would tend to support this view. However, we should also acknowledge that the causal influence could flow in the opposite direction. That is, elites may perceive the public as casualty phobic because they project their own views onto the public.

Contact with those at risk in military operations also seems to have a significant impact on elite tolerance for casualties. Specifically, the coefficients for social contact with the military are negative and statistically significant for both the Korea and the Taiwan scenarios. Respondents who indicated that they have greater social contact with the military tended to be less willing to tolerate casualties on these missions. Interestingly, this result holds despite the fact that members of the military themselves are generally more tolerant of casualties in these scenarios. This pattern is consistent with the notion that contact with the military makes the abstract notion of casualties more concrete and therefore more costly. Parenthood in contrast, does not appear to have any impact on casualty tolerance for the realpolitik cases.

Finally, it is important to note the impact that these control variables have on the estimated size of the civil-military gap. With regard to Korea, the effects are fairly straightforward. Controlling for attitudes toward the use of force and other political and social attitudes had virtually no impact on the size of the civil-military gap. The coefficient for the civilian elite was −.67 after accounting for demographic controls in chapter 4, and the coefficient is −.68 in the first column of table 5.2. Introducing the extent to which respondents are connected to those at risk, however, increased the estimated size of the gap. With regard to Taiwan, the bivariate gap between civilian elites and the military was negative and significant. In chapter 4 we showed that this gap was largely a function of demographic differences across the samples, but now table 5.2 indicates that civilian elites are actually more willing to tolerate casualties in Taiwan once we account for their attitudes toward the use of force and other political and social attitudes. Accounting for the connection to those at risk, however, eliminates the gap.

Next we turn our attention to the impact of these control variables on attitudes toward casualties in support of humanitarian interventions in the Congo and Kosovo. The results of these analyses are displayed in table 5.3. Once again, these analyses strongly support the claim that respondents base their attitudes toward casualties on a careful balancing of the costs and benefits of intervention. Specifically, the coefficients for the importance of human rights issues are positive and statistically significant for both the Congo and the Kosovo scenarios. That is, respondents who view human rights as an important goal for U.S. foreign policy tend to be more willing to tolerate casualties in these scenarios. Similarly, those expressing the opinion that humanitarian intervention is an important mission for the U.S. military were also willing to tolerate casualties in both these scenarios. Finally, the coefficient for support of the Powell Doctrine is negative and statistically significant for both the Congo and the Kosovo scenarios. That is, respondents who are supportive of the Powell Doctrine tend to be less willing to accept casualties in Congo and Kosovo. This negative effect would seem to be a result of the fact that supporters of the Powell Doctrine find the massive and overwhelming use of force unlikely in these cases.

The evidence on partisan gaps remains inconsistent. We find no significant partisan differences with regard to Congo. In the case of Kosovo we find that Democrats are significantly more supportive of casualties than are Republicans or Independents. It is important to note, however, that the TISS survey was implemented in the months leading up to U.S. intervention in Kosovo. Thus it seems likely that Democratic support for casualties in this case represents a show of support for President Clinton as he prepared for war. Unlike the realpolitik scenarios of Korea and Taiwan, confidence in political leadership has a significant impact on support for casualties in humanitarian interventions. The coefficients for political confidence are positive and significant in all of the analyses in table 5.3, indicating that those who express greater confidence in the institutions of political leadership also express a greater tolerance for casualties in Congo and Kosovo. This result seems to indicate that policymakers should pay careful attention to shoring up confidence in their commitment to humanitarian missions before they attempt such operations. Consistent with the analyses of the Korea and Taiwan scenarios, we continue to find that perceptions of public casualty phobia is a powerful predictor of elite attitudes toward casualties.

We also continue to find that social contact with members of the military tends to reduce support for casualties in both Congo and Kosovo. In both

TABLE 5.3
Determinants of Casualty Sensitivity in the Congo and Kosovo Scenarios

	Congo		Kosovo	
Respondent's Military Status				
Civilian Elite Nonveteran	0.50***	0.23	0.71***	0.41*
	(0.19)	(0.25)	(0.18)	(0.24)
Civilian Elite Military Education	−0.13	−0.02	−0.49*	−0.36
	(0.26)	(0.27)	(0.25)	(0.26)
Civilian Elite Veteran	0.18	0.26	0.12	0.10
	(0.20)	(0.20)	(0.19)	(0.19)
Military Reserve	0.52***	0.35*	0.54***	0.32*
	(0.16)	(0.19)	(0.15)	(0.18)
Demographic Variables				
Gender	−0.64***	−0.60***	−0.55***	−0.59***
	(0.18)	(0.19)	(0.17)	(0.17)
Age	−0.01*	−0.02*	−0.02***	−0.02***
	(0.01)	(0.01)	(0.01)	(0.01)
Minority	0.30	0.23	0.31	0.22
	(0.25)	(0.26)	(0.25)	(0.26)
Education	0.27*	0.23*	0.09	0.04
	(0.16)	(0.16)	(0.15)	(0.15)
Attitudes toward the Use of Force				
Importance of Intervention	0.26**	0.28**	0.17*	0.17*
	(0.10)	(0.10)	(0.10)	(0.10)
Effectiveness of Force	0.22***	0.23***	0.25***	0.26***
	(0.06)	(0.06)	(0.05)	(0.06)
Powell Doctrine	−0.13***	−0.13***	−0.14***	−0.13***
	(0.05)	(0.05)	(0.05)	(0.05)
Political and Social Attitudes				
Democrat	0.21	0.20	0.40**	0.42**
	(0.17)	(0.17)	(0.16)	(0.17)
Republican	−0.09	−0.08	−0.13	−0.11
	(0.13)	(0.13)	(0.13)	(0.13)
Confidence in Leaders	0.42***	0.42***	0.46***	0.48***
	(0.13)	(0.13)	(0.13)	(0.13)
Mass Sensitivity	−0.15***	−0.14***	−0.14***	−0.15***
	(0.04)	(0.04)	(0.04)	(0.04)
Connection to Those at Risk				
Contact with Military		−0.15*		−0.14*
		(0.08)		(0.08)
Parent		0.23		0.05
		(0.16)		(0.15)
Number of Observations	1,238	1,204	1,237	1,202
Chi-squared	116.86	118.20	149.66	148.92

Note: Standard errors for coefficients in parentheses. All tests for statistical significance are two-tailed.
* = $p < .10$.   ** = $p < .05$.   *** = $p < .01$.

cases the coefficients are negative, although their statistical significance is somewhat attenuated in comparison with the realpolitik scenarios. Once again, parenthood has no impact on casualty tolerance.

The impact of these control variables on the size and direction of the civil-military gap is quite interesting. Controlling for attitudes toward the use of force and other political and social attitudes has virtually no impact on the civil-military gap. Civilian elites remain significantly more willing than military officers to tolerate casualties for interventions in Congo and Kosovo *even* after we control for attitudes toward the use of force, confidence in political leadership and perceptions of mass sensitivity. Controlling for social contact with the military, however, has the effect of substantially reducing our estimate of the civil-military gap for these cases. With regard to the Congo, the coefficient for the gap between the civilian elite and military officers drops to less than half its previous size—from .50 to .23—and it becomes statistically insignificant. Similarly, with regard to Kosovo the coefficient for the civilian elite drops from .71 to .41 and its statistical significance is substantially eroded. These results strongly suggest that one important cause of the civil-military gap regarding casualty sensitivity may be a lack of personal contact between the military and civilian society. Put another way, these results suggest that increasing personal interactions between the military and civilian society may have the effect of reducing the civil-military opinion gap. We should be careful to note, however, that we cannot make strong claims of causal direction here. It is possible, for example, that contact with members of the military has no impact on civilian attitudes and that our observed relationship is due to the fact that civilians who socialize with members of the military do so because they already share attitudes and opinions with those in uniform.

We next turn our attention to an analysis of tolerance for casualties in intervening against potential terrorist threats and against Iraqi weapons of mass destruction. Consistent with our previous results, we continue to find that respondents' views of the importance of the issues at stake have a significant impact on tolerance for casualties. Specifically, the coefficients for the importance of the terrorist threat and Iraqi weapons of mass destruction are consistently positive and statistically significant, indicating that those who view these issues as important aspects of U.S. foreign policy also tend to be more willing to tolerate casualties. Respondents' views on the effectiveness of military force show a similar, though slightly less robust, pattern. With regard to the Iraq scenario, the coefficient for the effectiveness of force in combating weapons of mass destruction is positive, though it does not achieve statistical significance. In the global terrorism scenario, however, the coefficient for the perceived effectiveness of force in addressing terrorism is strongly positive and statistically significant. As was the case with realpolitik scenarios, support for the Powell Doctrine did not have an impact on support for casualties in Iraq or

TABLE 5.4
Determinants of Casualty Sensitivity in the Terrorism and Iraq Scenarios

	Iraqi WMD		Terrorism	
Respondent's Military Status				
Civilian Elite Nonmilitary	0.55***	0.32	0.63***	0.40
	(0.18)	(0.24)	(0.18)	(0.24)
Civilian Elite PME	−0.26	−0.08	−0.16	−0.06
	(0.25)	(0.26)	(0.25)	(0.26)
Civilian Elite Veteran	0.10	0.18	0.10	0.14
	(0.18)	(0.19)	(0.19)	(0.20)
Military Reserve	0.49***	0.35*	0.39**	0.26
	(0.16)	(0.18)	(0.16)	(0.19)
Demographic Variables				
Gender	−0.59***	−0.57***	−0.51***	−0.48***
	(0.17)	(0.18)	(0.18)	(0.18)
Age	−0.02**	−0.02***	−0.01**	−0.02**
	(0.01)	(0.01)	(0.01)	(0.01)
Minority	0.08	0.03	0.16	0.13
	(0.25)	(0.26)	(0.25)	(0.25)
Education	0.29	0.29*	0.22	0.19
	(0.15)	(0.15)	(0.15)	(0.15)
Attitudes toward the Use of Force				
Importance of Intervention	0.70***	0.69***	0.48***	0.49***
	(0.12)	(0.12)	(0.12)	(0.13)
Effectiveness of Force	0.07	0.06	0.18***	0.18***
	(0.05)	(0.05)	(0.05)	(0.05)
Powell Doctrine	−0.02	−0.01	−0.04	−0.03
	(0.05)	(0.05)	(0.05)	(0.05)
Political and Social Attitudes				
Democrat	0.08	0.07	−0.28*	−0.29*
	(0.16)	(0.17)	(0.17)	(0.17)
Republican	−0.13	−0.15	−0.24*	−0.28**
	(0.13)	(0.13)	(0.13)	(0.13)
Confidence in Leaders	0.04	0.03	0.18	0.14
	(0.13)	(0.13)	(0.13)	(0.13)
Mass Sensitivity	−0.27***	−0.27***	−0.23***	−0.23***
	(0.04)	(0.04)	(0.04)	(0.04)
Connection to Those at Risk				
Contact with Military		−0.13*		−0.11
		(0.08)		(0.08)
Parent		0.32		0.23
		(0.16)		(0.16)
Number of Observations	1,220	1,186	1,214	1,181
Chi-squared	105.15	110.49	88.41	89.75

Note: Standard errors for coefficients in parentheses. All tests for statistical significance are two-tailed.
* = $p < .10$. ** = $p < .05$. *** = $p < .01$.

against terrorism. Once again, these results could indicate a greater confidence among elite respondents that the United States may be willing to use force on a large scale in these scenarios.

The evidence concerning a partisan gap over casualty tolerance continues to be inconsistent. With regard to Iraq we find a partisan consensus. Neither Democrats, Republicans, nor Independents express a greater or lesser willingness to tolerate casualties. But our analysis also indicates that Independent respondents tend to be more tolerant of casualties for the global terrorism scenario. Confidence in political leadership did not have a significant impact on tolerance for casualties with regard to either Iraq or terrorism. However, elites' perception of public casualty phobia continues to be a powerful and robust predictor of elite attitudes on these issues.

Finally, respondents' connections to those at risk continue to have an impact on casualty tolerance. As was the case in all four previous scenarios, the coefficients for social contact with the military are negative for both the Iraq and the terrorism scenarios. The statistical significance of these effects is somewhat attenuated in these instances. The coefficient is significant at the .10 level in the Iraq scenario and does not quite achieve that level for the terrorism scenario. Still, the pattern is quite consistent with earlier results regarding both realpolitik and humanitarian interventionist missions. As was the case with humanitarian intervention in Congo and Kosovo, controlling for social contact with the military appears to account for the civil-military gap over casualty tolerance. For example, the coefficient for the gap between military officers and civilian elites drops by more than half, from .55 to .32, in the Iraq scenario, and this gap becomes statistically insignificant. With regard to global terrorism, the coefficient for the civilian elite drops by one-third, from .63 to .40, and also becomes statistically insignificant. Once again, this pattern of results suggests that increasing contact between the military and civilian society may lessen the opinion gap with regard to the use of force. Of course this inference remains vulnerable to the fact our results may be due to self-selection rather than any causal impact of contact with the military.

Patterns of Tolerance for Casualties

What inferences can be drawn from these analyses about the determinants of casualty tolerance among civilian elites and military officers? We emphasize five consistent patterns.

First, tolerance for casualties among civilian and military elites appears to be a careful and well-considered balancing of the merits of each military operation, its role in defending American national interests, and the costs of undertaking such an action. In particular, respondents draw a strong connection between their views on whether a particular military operation addresses important American interests and whether they would tolerate casualties in that operation.[12]

Second, elite attitudes toward casualties are powerfully tied to their views about the public's willingness to tolerate casualties. We cannot be certain about the direction of causal influence, but the strong correlation between elite casualty tolerance and elite perception of mass casualty tolerance indicates that the myth of popular casualty phobia is strongly related to the elite debate over casualties and military intervention. The strong tie between these attitudes demonstrates the importance of informing elites about the true structure of public attitudes so that policy debates do not founder on misperceptions and oversimplifications of public attitudes.

Third, we find little consistent evidence for partisan differences over casualties. This result is especially interesting when compared with the consistent support we find for a civil-military gap. Consistent with our analysis in chapter 3 regarding American militarized disputes, we find that the civil-military divide may be more important in understanding American debates over the use of force than is the partisan divide.

Fourth, we find little support for Luttwak's (1994) claim that our unwillingness to place our children at risk is an important cause of casualty phobia. Parenthood did not have a significant impact on any of our casualty analyses. However, since we did not have a direct measure for whether the respondent personally had children at risk, we can not dismiss the possibility that the Luttwak effect operates in that subset of the population who are parents of servicemen and -women.

Finally, consistent with Gartner, Segura, and Wilkening (1997), we find at least some tentative evidence that the civil-military gap regarding tolerance for casualties may be due, in part, to a lack of contact between the military and civilian society. That is, we find evidence to suggest that increasing civil-military contact at an informal and social level may serve to ameliorate civil-military divisions over the use of force—at least with regard to interventionist issues. In the conclusion, we discuss how these findings relate to the renewed debate over whether to revive the draft as a way of reining in a political leadership allegedly cavalier about casualties because it lacks a personal connection to people in uniform (Fears 2003; Glastris 2003; Rangel 2003). Given the severe difficulties in drawing causal inferences from these data, however, we can only flag this relationship as one that merits further study and debate.

---

[12] Michael Alvarez and John Brehm (2002, 208–9) analyzed these same data and concluded that the military elite respondents were "ambivalent" about casualties, meaning that as they gained more information, the variance of the respondents would increase. This is not necessarily inconsistent with our finding that the views fit an overall rational cost-benefit calculation.

How Big Is the Civil-Military Divide?

The analyses in tables 5.2 to 5.4 can tell us about the direction of the relationships between variables and also about the statistical significance of those relationships. But it is difficult to infer the substantive size of these effects from the logit coefficients. In order to evaluate the substantive significance, table 5.5 presents the marginal effects that emerge from the statistical models in this chapter. Since our analyses revealed that social contact with members of the military may be part of the causal chain that produces the civil-military gap, we generate our predicted effects from the equations in tables 5.2 to 5.4 that do not include military social contact. Moreover, since the results were generally quite similar for the two realpolitik scenarios, the two humanitarian intervention scenarios, and the two interventions against terrorism, we present the marginal effects for one of each of these pairs of scenarios. Thus we consider the marginal impacts of military status, gender, age, the importance of the issue at stake, and the perception of the public's tolerance for casualties for the Korea, Kosovo, and Iraq cases (see table 5.5). Predicted effects were generated by varying certain variables in the model while holding others constant and then creating predicted values. We varied the importance of the issue at stake from approximately 2 standard deviations below the mean to 2 standard deviations above, and we varied perception of mass support for casualties from strongly agree to strongly disagree.

These results indicate that the civil-military gap over casualty sensitivity remains substantial even after we account for the influence of many demographic and attitudinal controls. Moreover, the results indicate that the impact of military status is substantial relative to the impact of other statistically significant coefficients such as age or the importance of the issue at stake. For example, with regard to the Korea scenario, our model predicts that a military officer will be about 17 percent more likely (that is, summing 11.3 and 5.6 from the last two columns) than a civilian nonveteran to tolerate 5,000 casualties. Only the gender gap is substantially larger than this effect. Specifically, the model predicts that a female respondent would be about 33 percent less likely to tolerate 500 or more casualties than would a male respondent. The size of the civil-military gap is quite similar to the impact of age on attitudes: a sixty-five-year-old respondent is about 14 percent less likely to tolerate 5,000 or more.

This same pattern of results also holds when we turn to more interventionist missions. With regard to Kosovo, military officers were a little more than 17 percent more likely than civilian nonveterans to demand that military operations be conducted with fewer than 50 casualties. This gap is slightly larger than the impact of gender and age on the Kosovo

TABLE 5.5
Effects of Statistically Significant Determinants of Casualty Sensitivity

Change in Independent Variable	Change in Probability of Casualty Tolerance Response					
	None	1–50	51–500	501–5,000	5,001–50,000	50,000+
Korea						
Civil-Military Gap	−3.8	−1.5	−5.0	−6.7	11.3	5.6
Male to Female	18.0	5.1	9.3	−4.9	−23.4	−4.9
Age 35 toAge 65	4.0	1.6	4.6	4.2	−10.5	−3.9
Importance of Issue	−5.9	−2.3	−6.6	−6.0	15.1	5.7
Mass Sensitivity	3.9	1.5	4.6	4.3	−10.4	−3.9
Kosovo						
Civil-Military Gap	11.1	6.2	−6.3	−9.0	−1.5	−0.5
Male to Female	8.2	5.1	−4.4	−7.2	−1.3	−0.4
Age 35 to Age 65	8.2	7.3	−1.7	−10.8	−2.3	−0.8
Importance of Issue	−4.3	−3.6	1.4	5.2	1.0	−0.3
Mass Sensitivity	4.9	4.4	−1.1	6.4	−1.3	−0.4
Iraqi WMD						
Civil-Military Gap	1.9	3.5	7.7	−4.0	−7.0	−2.1
Male to Female	2.1	3.8	8.1	−4.4	−7.3	−2.1
Age 35 to Age 65	1.2	2.3	6.8	−0.1	−6.9	−2.5
Importance of Issue	−5.0	−9.0	−18.2	9.3	17.4	5.6
Mass Sensitivity	1.9	3.8	11.4	−0.7	−11.9	−4.5

Note: WMD = weapons of mass destruction.

scenario. Each of these variables increased the probability that respondents would demand less than 50 casualties by about 15 percent. Finally, the pattern continues to hold as we examine the effects of the civil-military gap on the scenario of preventing Iraq from obtaining weapons of mass destruction. In this case, the substantive impact of the civil-military gap is somewhat lower, but it remains true to the previous pattern. Specifically, military officers were about 13 percent more likely than civilian nonveterans to indicate that this mission should be accomplished with less than 500 casualties. This is almost identical to the impact of gender. Female respondents were about 14 percent more likely to demand that the United States suffer less than 500 casualties in the Iraq scenario.

But Why Is the American Military Elite So Casualty Sensitive?

As one final cut at our data, we separated out the responses of military officers from the rest of our data and examined the responses of military officers for possible explanations of casualty sensitivity within the military. Due to space constraints, we do not report all the analyses of the military sample. Instead, we summarize our results regarding four potential sources of military casualty snsitivity. The first set of explanations focuses on the respondent's structural position within the military. In particular, we hope to determine whether casualty sensitivity within the elite military depends upon the particular service of the respondent (that is, Army, Navy, and so on), the arm of service (combat arms versus support), and the officer's rank. Underlying these variables is the possibility that casualty sensitivity within the U.S. military is a result of a "zero defect" mentality imposed on junior officers seeking careers in the military, or the result of a personal desire to avoid risk of injury or death.

A second set of explanations are demographic differences. In addition to looking at the impact of age, gender, and race within the military, we also take another look at the issue of parenthood. Perhaps the effects of family ties that Luttwak (1994) proposed are felt only within the military, by those who would suffer the risks of combat.

Third, we continue to look at foreign policy priorities and the "rational" calculations about the acceptable costs of casualties. It is important to reexamine even those demographic and attitudinal factors that showed up as significant in the full sample; it is possible, for instance, that these factors showed up as significant in the full sample because they are strongly operative with civilians and only weakly or perhaps not at all operative with the military.

Fourth, we look at the impact of several attitudes that soldiers may have toward the military as an institution and toward their civilian leaders. Perhaps feelings of alienation from military leadership and civilian government may account for the unwillingness of military officers to tolerate casualties.

A number of the control variables used in this analysis are the same ones we relied on in tables 5.2 to 5.4. However, we do introduce a number of new variables that are only relevant to military respondents.

Military Rank.   This is the highest rank that the respondent stated he or she had attained in the U.S. military. This variable is coded across the entire TISS dataset, and so it varies from 1 to 25 across both officers and enlisted personnel. The military elite, however, comprises only the officers or so-called O-level ranks. Thus in this analysis military rank varies from "O–3" level (value of 18) to "O–10" level (value of 25).

Branch of Service.   Respondents were asked "what is or was your primary service?" We created dummy variables identifying those who stated that the Navy, the Air Force, or the Marines was their primary branch of the service. Respondents from the Army were left as the comparison category.

Combat Arms.   We created a dummy variable which identifies respondents who stated that their primary arm or specialty within the service was "combat arms or platform."

Military Alienation.   This variable captures the extent to which members of the military feel separated from and abandoned by civilian society. Respondents were asked whether they felt that most members of civilian society have a great deal of respect for the military, and whether most members of the military have a great deal of respect for civilians. In addition they were asked whether civilians appreciate the military values of commitment and unselfishness and whether the American people understand the sacrifices made by members of the U.S. military.[13] Responses were coded as: agree strongly = 1, agree somewhat = 2, no opinion = 3, disagree somewhat = 4, disagree strongly = 5. We identify the mean of these responses as the respondent's level of military alienation.

Joined Military to Serve Their Country.   We created a dummy variable identifying all respondents who stated that their primary motivation for joining the military was "to serve my country."

Joined Military to Avoid Draft/Drafted.   We created a dummy variable identifying all respondents who stated that their primary motivation for joining the service was either: "to avoid being drafted into another service" or "I was drafted."

Because of space constraints, we do not present tables for these statistical analyses. Instead we briefly summarize the results below.

Respondent's Position in the Military Structure

Perhaps the most important result to emerge from these analyses is that tolerance for casualties does not appear to be a function of respondents' desires for self-preservation or a desire to avoid the risks of combat. The coefficient for service in the combat arms, for example, is not statistically significant for the Congo, Iraq, terrorism, or Korea scenarios. In the Kosovo the coefficient is negative and does just barely achieve significance

---

[13] Specific question wording from the TISS survey questionnaire: Question 33: "Here are some statements people have made about the U.S. military. For each, please indicate whether you strongly agree, somewhat agree, somewhat disagree or strongly disagree." q33a: "Most members of the military have a great deal of respect for civilian society." q33b: "Most members of civilian society have a great deal of respect for the military." q33h: " Even if civilian society did not always appreciate the essential military values of commitment and unselfishness, our armed forces could still maintain required traditional standards. " q33i: "The American people understand the sacrifices made by the people who serve in the U.S. military." Alpha = 0.66.

at the .10 level, but only with regard to the Taiwan scenario do military respondents who served in the combat arms appear to be substantially more averse to casualties than other members of the military. Thus we can observe no general pattern whereby those who serve in the combat arms (and are therefore more likely to experience the risks of combat) are generally less willing to tolerate casualties.

Further evidence against the self-preservation hypothesis can be found in an examination of the differing tolerance for casualties across the services. Marines were significantly more tolerant of casualties in the Iraq and Taiwan scenarios and slightly more tolerant of casualties in the Congo and terrorism scenarios. It is the Marines, however, who are arguably most likely to be sent on these missions.[14] Respondents from the Air Force were also more willing to tolerate casualties in the Iraq and Kosovo scenarios, and once again these missions would be likely to rely heavily on air strikes made by Air Force pilots. It is worth noting that for the Taiwan scenario respondents from the Navy were significantly more willing to tolerate casualties than any other branch of the service. Once again, this scenario would probably be the most likely to draw the Navy into heavy combat.

It seems plain, then, that casualty sensitivity within the military is not a result of a simple desire to avoid the risks of combat. Our results are less clear, however, about whether the desire to avoid casualties is a result of career incentives and a developing "zero defects" mentality within the officer corps (that is, an unrealistic attitude that no problem of any kind is tolerable under any circumstances). On the one hand, if incentives for promotion were structured so as to reduce tolerance for casualties, we might expect to see higher-ranking officers express less willingness to tolerate casualties. The promotion process might actually change officers' preferences and cause them to internalize the "zero defects" mentality, or it might select those officers who exhibited the "zero defects" approach. However, the coefficient for the respondent's rank is only statistically significant in the Taiwan scenario. This might have led us to dismiss the "careerism" explanation, except that the statistical insignificance of rank is caused by the inclusion of a single crucial control variable: age. If we drop age from the analysis, then the coefficient for rank becomes negative and statistically significant in all six scenarios.

The coefficient for age remains negative and statistically significant in three of the six scenarios even when both variables are in the analysis.

---

[14] We hesitate to push this interpretation too hard, however. Some might be prepared to dismiss the Marines as a natural outlier on any scenario, and we cannot speculate with any reliability about what casualties the Air Force elite officers had in mind. To reach the kinds of high casualty numbers reflected in Air Force elite officer responses would probably in-

This result is consistent with the interpretation that casualty sensitivity in the military is associated with age, but not with rank per se. From this perspective, our results provide little evidence of creeping perfectionism among the elite officers we surveyed. However, the correlation between age and rank is very high. The R^2 from a simple bivariate regression of rank on age is more than 0.45. Given this strong association, the rather uneven distribution of the dependent variable, and the relatively small number of cases we have with our more limited focus on the military elite, we remain cautious about drawing strong conclusions about the impact of rank on tolerance for casualties. Moreover, there is an alternative interpretation one could offer for any rank effect: perhaps more senior officers will more acutely feel the weight of responsibility of ordering others (more junior officers) to risk their lives. Consequently, we prefer to withhold judgment about the possibility of a growing "zero defects" mentality as a source of military casualty aversion. Our data cannot support such a claim at this time, but future research should look more carefully at this issue in order to better understand the intricate relationship between age, rank, and military casualty aversion.

The Impact of Demographic Factors within the Military

One interesting comparison between the analyses of the military elite and the comparison of the civilian and military samples is the role of the gender gap. The coefficient for gender is only statistically significant in the terrorism, Korea, and Taiwan scenarios. The substantive size of this gap, however, only appears to narrow with regard to the Iraq scenario. The coefficients for the Congo and Kosovo scenarios are not statistically significant, but they remain substantively large. In light of the small number of women among elite military officers and the large number of variables in our analyses, these results would seem to provide a tentative indication that a gender gap persists even among military officers. We would expect that women in the military are not, on average, representative of typical women in civilian society. Nonetheless, some gender gap persists, at least with regard to the issue of casualty tolerance. Given that we have only 53 women in our sample of the military elite, however, our results should be viewed with caution.

It is worth noting here that the Military Culture and Climate Survey conducted by the Study on Military Culture in the 21st Century at the Center for Strategic and International Studies found a pronounced gender

---

volve a ground war in which the casualties would be largely Army and Marines, not Air Force personnel.

gap.[15] The survey asked several thousand Army personnel, running through all the enlisted ranks to the staff officer level, their level of agreement with the following statement: "If necessary to accomplish a combat/lifesaving mission, I am prepared to put my life on the line." On a scale of 1 = strongly disagree and 6 = strongly agree, the mean response of Army males was 4.9 (or "agree") and the mean response of Army females was 4.2 (or "slightly agree"). The effect is even more stark if one looks only at the enlisted ranks. Nearly 13 percent of Army enlisted women answered "disagree strongly" when asked if they were prepared to put their life on the line to accomplish a combat mission, compared with 7 percent of Army men, and roughly 28 percent of Army enlisted women answered in the negative (combined disagree strongly, disagree, or disagree somewhat) compared with only 13 percent of Army men. The gender gap on casualty sensitivity persists even among women who voluntarily serve in the military. Of course, since women are excluded from the positions most involved in combat and therefore most likely to have the highest casualty rates, it may be that Army women have internalized an expectation that they need not die to perform their mission, and the lower responses may reflect this internalization more than a fundamental casualty phobia.[16]

Another important result from the demographic variables is the impact of parenthood on casualty tolerance. We found little support for this argument in our comparison of the civilian and military samples. This same pattern continues within the military elite. In fact, military respondents with children were actually more willing to accept casualties in the Congo scenario. This pattern of responses undermines Luttwak's claims about the unwillingness of Americans to place their families at risk for their country.

The Impact of Attitudes toward the Use of Force

Although the impact of demographic factors such as race and gender were attenuated within the military sample, the impact of respondents' foreign policy priorities and their views about the effectiveness of military force remained consistent with the previous analyses. The coefficient for support for the issue at stake in the scenario was positive and statistically significant in all six of the scenarios. These results continue to underline our conclusion that the respondents were capable of making careful and sophisticatedly "rational" calculations about the merits of individual missions and their willingness to suffer costs in order to achieve foreign policy goals.

---

[15] Data proprietary to the Study on Military Culture in the 21st Century at the Center for Strategic and International Studies. Used by permission.

[16] We are grateful to Owen Jacobs for suggesting this alternative interpretation of the data.

The Impact of Social and Political Attitudes

The impact of party identification may be more substantial in our analysis of the military than the pattern we observed in the analysis of our full sample. We do not find strong support for partisan differences over casualty sensitivity within the military, but Republicans in the military sample do tend to be more sensitive to suffering casualties across all six scenarios. This partisan gap is statistically significant in the terrorism, Korea, and Taiwan scenarios, and it is nearly significant in the Iraq scenario. Given the disproportionate number of Republicans in the military sample, we are hesitant to press this finding very far, but the results suggest that partisan differences within the military merit further attention. Democrats did not differ significantly from Independents in the military across any of the six scenarios.

The impact of the military's confidence in political leaders precisely mirrors the impact of the confidence in political leaders variable in the broader analysis. That is, confidence in political leadership increases the willingness of military officers to tolerate casualties in the humanitarian intervention scenarios of Congo and Kosovo. It does not have a significant impact on the other four scenarios. Our analysis indicates that lack of confidence has a corrosive effect on the military's willingness to suffer casualties in interventionist military operations. Although the Clinton administration suffered perhaps unusually bad relations with the military, this lack of trust might be viewed—at least in part—as a continuing legacy of the Vietnam era. Military elites are understandably wary of being left without political support in the midst of military operations. Consequently military officers who lack confidence in their civilian leaders are reluctant to suffer casualties because of their fear of being abandoned under fire.

Finally, while military officers' attitudes toward civilian elites have a substantial effect on their willingness to risk casualties, the specific reasons that officers expressed for joining the military did not influence their sensitivity to casualties. Specifically, those who expressed the view that they had joined the military in order to "serve their country" were no more willing to tolerate casualties than were those who said that they were drafted or joined in order to avoid being drafted. This result could be construed as further evidence against the argument that careerist incentives are causing the military to be casualty shy. If that were so, then we would expect those who expressed a desire to "serve their country" would be more willing to tolerate casualties.[17]

---

[17] We also included a dummy variables identifying respondents who stated that they joined the military "to gain skills valued in the civilian job market," those who primarily

Summary and Conclusions

In this chapter we have sought to examine the reasons behind the civil-military gap in casualty sensitivity that we described in chapter 4. Although we do not claim to have a definitive answer to this question, our analysis of the impact of control variables on casualty tolerance as well as our examination of casualty sensitivity within the military have led us to four primary conclusions.

First, our results indicate that the civil-military gap regarding casualty sensitivity is not a simple spurious result of demographic or other factors. A substantial opinion gap exists even after we account for the impact of numerous demographic and attitudinal factors. In fact, the demographic differences across the civilian and military samples largely served to mitigate civil-military difference in casualty sensitivity. Thus there does appear to be something about the experience of being in the military that has an impact on respondents' willingness to tolerate casualties in interventionist military operations.

Second, our analyses consistently indicate that respondents are making careful, rational calculations about the merits of specific military operations when they make judgments about their tolerance for casualties. One of the strongest predictors of casualty sensitivity for the interventionist missions was the level of importance that respondents place on achieving interventionist foreign policy goals. This result may not seem terribly surprising since it is anticipated by several other studies (Larson 1996; Burk 1999; Kull and Destler 1999), but it is important for two reasons. On the one hand, it shores up our confidence in our basic measure of casualty tolerance, namely a hypothetical question in a survey; if we got incoherent results, we would be less sure that our hypothetical question was tapping into anything meaningful. On the other hand, it increases our conviction that the conventional wisdom about the American public's knee-jerk response to casualties is wrong. Tolerance for casualties is a rather complex attitude. Estimating one's tolerance for casualties involves placing oneself in an inevitably hypothetical scenario, making an estimate of the importance of the issues at stake, comparing this value to the cost of casualties lost, and producing some estimate of the net value of military missions. American policymakers—and some scholars as well—seem to suggest that the American public is incapable of making this kind of assessment. The (false) premise of the CNN effect is that Americans will see casualties on television and will become viscerally incapable of making any reason-

---

sought "to have a career in the military," and those who joined in order "to obtain an education." None of these reasons for joining had a consistent effect on casualty tolerance.

able calculations about whether to continue to support a military operation. Our analyses suggest that policymakers ought to give their constit-
uents more credit.

Third, other political and social attitudes are also associated with casualty sensitivity. Our evidence regarding partisan gaps is inconsistent, but
confidence in political leadership played an important role with regard
to support for casualties in humanitarian missions. One of the strongest
patterns we discovered is that elite respondents' beliefs about the willingness of the American public to tolerate casualties were powerfully associated with their own sensitivity to casualties. One explanation of this relationship is that elites continue to be trapped by the myth of popular
casualty phobia. Their continued faith in this myth may have led them
to curtail their own tolerance for casualties. Alternatively, the myth of
popular casualty phobia may be difficult to shatter precisely because
elites created this belief as a way of justifying their own unwillingness to
tolerate casualties.

Fourth, the extent of respondents' personal connection to those who
serve in uniform may provide an important mechanism for ameliorating
civil-military opinion gaps regarding casualty sensitivity. Respondents'
extent of social contact with the military appeared to account for much
of the civil-military gap across all six casualty scenarios. We contend that
contact with the military may have this effect because it makes the abstract notion of casualties into something much more concrete. Casualty
sensitivity is also powerfully driven by demographic factors such as age,
race, and gender. We found that respondents with children, however, were
no less willing to tolerate casualties. This result casts doubt on Luttwak's
(1994) hypothesis that "motherism" has caused a reduction in America's
tolerance for casualties.

Although these analyses shed a great deal of light on the sources of
attitudes toward casualties, they could not provide a complete explanation for the civil-military gap we observed in chapter 4. Consequently, we
turned our attention to an analysis of casualty sensitivity *within* our military sample. This secondary analysis produced three results. First and
foremost, casualty sensitivity within the military does not appear to be a
simple result of the desire to avoid the risks of combat. The primary evidence against this claim is that respondents who were most likely to be
exposed to combat consistently gave estimates of tolerable casualties that
were equal to or higher than those who would be less likely to fight. Those
serving in combat arms, for example, differed little in terms of their tolerance for casualties. The Marines, in contrast, were often among the most
willing to suffer casualties despite the fact that they are arguably more
likely to be the first troops placed at risk. Similarly, respondents from the
Air Force gave higher estimates of acceptable casualties for missions that

would rely heavily on placing pilots at risk, and those from the Navy expressed the greatest willingness to suffer costs in the defense of Taiwan—primarily a naval mission. Thus while the military may be accused of being reluctant warriors, they cannot be accused of cowardice, since the first lives they are willing to lay on the line are their own.

Second, casualty sensitivity within the military is substantially shaped by military attitudes toward political leaders. Military officers who lack confidence in the institutions of political leadership are substantially less willing to tolerate casualties on interventionist military missions. This result provides yet another reason to try to mend the cultural fences between the military and civilian society. The failure to address broader issues of respect, trust, and confidence across the civil-military divide may eventually have a substantial and detrimental impact on American foreign policy by rendering the military unwilling to suffer casualties.

Third, our results find relatively little support regarding the impact of career incentives on military casualty sensitivity. Scholars have worried that the competitive desire for career advancement within the military has led to the construction of a "zero defects" mindset in which any casualties in military operations are viewed as unacceptable signals of failure (Record 2000). We ourselves raised this possibility in an earlier discussion of the TISS data (Feaver and Gelpi 1999b). It is still possible that the military holds a pernicious "zero defects" mindset in which casualties have become synonymous with mission failure. If so, however, that attitude is not a principal driver of military attitudes on casualties more generally. And we found only weak or no linkages between casualty sensitivity and any career mentality among officers. Our results suggest that respondents who say they joined the military "to serve their country" are no more willing to accept casualties than are respondents who say they joined for more instrumental reasons. Moreover, we find that higher-ranking officers are no less tolerant of casualties than are junior officers. Rank does become strongly significant when we remove age from the analysis, however, and so because of the close association between age and rank we hesitate to draw firm conclusions on this point.

CHAPTER SIX

CONCLUSION

WE HAVE ARGUED that civilians and the military in the United States have systematically different opinions on whether and how to use force and on their professed willingness to bear the human costs of war. These different opinions seem to have profoundly shaped the way the United States has used military force for most of its history, from 1816 to 1992.

According to our data, the differences between civilian elites and elite active duty officers on when to use force are neither dramatically large nor terribly surprising. Yet a discernible pattern emerges in the survey data, and this pattern is consistent with the general thrust of the case study literature. Elite military officers are more inclined toward a realpolitik view of the use of force—willing to use force for traditional national security threats like defense of allies and of geostrategic access to vital markets but more hesitant about using force for humanitarian missions and the "less-than-vital-interest" scenarios of intervening in foreign civil wars that have dominated the global agenda in the past decade. Civilian elites who have never served in the military are somewhat more interventionist, embracing a wider range of missions for the military, but veterans seem to resemble more closely the active duty military officers. At the same time, officers serving in the military reserves give essentially the same answers as those serving on active duty.

A related pattern emerges in attitudes about how to use force. Civilian elites who are nonveterans are more willing to use force gradually or incrementally, while elite military officers show greater support for the "decisive force" option made famous by the so-called Powell Doctrine. Again veterans in the civilian elite give responses that more closely parallel those of elite active duty military officers than those of nonveterans in the civilian elite. Thus far, our findings are more or less what one would expect, given the general theoretical literature on civil-military relations and the numerous case studies of civil-military decision making on the use of force since 1945.

We also found that the veteran's effect seemed to reverse in the mass public. Veterans in the elite more closely matched the military viewpoint—relatively dovish on interventionist missions, relatively hawkish on realpolitik missions, opposed to constraints on the use of force in any mission. Veterans in the mass, however, had a different profile—relatively hawkish on all missions but continued opposition to constraints on the use of force. These findings are somewhat tentative because they come from pooling a variety of different surveys, none of which was designed like the TISS study to explore civil-military differences. Nevertheless, they are suggestive of a possible mass-elite dynamic that interacts with the civil-military dynamic in interesting ways.

More dramatically, we have shown that this civil-military opinion gap seems to matter in decisive ways when it comes to determining how the United States has actually used military force for most of its history. Using the presence of veterans in the political elite as a proxy for the civil-military gap, we demonstrated that there is a strong correlation between the opinion gap and the empirical record of the initiation of the use of force by the United States from 1816 to 1992: as the percentage of veterans serving in the executive branch and the legislature increases and other things being equal, the probability that the United States will initiate militarized disputes declines substantially.[1] At the same time, however, as the percentage of veterans increases, so too does the likelihood that any use of force will be at a higher level of escalation, other things being equal; conversely, the lower the proportion of veterans, the lower the level of force the United States will use in the dispute.

Our findings on casualty sensitivity are equally interesting: the belief that the U.S. public is especially casualty phobic is widely accepted by policymakers, civilian elites, and military officers (both active duty and reservists), but it is not supported by our public opinion data. To be sure, a portion of the public does appear to be casualty phobic, but the data indicate that the public as a whole will accept casualties that are necessary to accomplish a variety of missions. On realpolitik missions such as the defense of South Korea and Taiwan, there is something resembling a broad consensus across civilian and military groups that these goals are worth the loss of substantial numbers of American lives, at least as many as were suffered in Desert Storm. No such civil-military consensus exists, however, with regard to interventionist missions such as nation building in Congo or protection against genocide in Kosovo, precisely the missions that have dominated American foreign policymaking in the decade between the end of the cold war and the terrorist attacks of September 11th. Contrary to the conventional wisdom, on these types of missions, the public is more casualty acceptant than are military officers, both active duty and reservists. There is not much evidence that the hands of political leaders or the military are tied by a public afflicted with a body-bag syndrome. On the contrary, casualty aversion—which is evident both in the

---

[1] As explained in chapter 3, a "militarized dispute" is defined by the presence of a threat to use military force, a threatening mobilization or movement of forces, or an actual use of force. See Bennett and Stam (2000).

behavior of decision makers and in the attitudes of military officers—appears to be a self-imposed restriction.

The public's attitudes on casualties is probably a function of simple rational calculations. Elites who think the national interest is not engaged by certain missions do not support casualties in those missions. Elites who think that force is not very effective have a lower acceptance for casualties. Moreover, elite attitudes toward casualties are strongly related to their overall views about public casualty phobia. The causal arrow may run in either direction, but there is a strong correlation between elite casualty tolerance and elite perception of mass casualty tolerance. At the same time, casualty sensitivity appears to be strongly related to a personal connection to the military. People who report high levels of social contact with the military are also likely to be the most casualty averse. A civil-military contact gap may be shaping a civil-military casualty tolerance gap.

When it comes to opinion on the use of force, the public appears to break down into four distinct groups. On any given use of force, the president can probably count on roughly 30–35 percent of the public that are solid hawks, relatively indifferent to stakes, costs, or prospects of victory. The president can also expect a group of solid doves, ranging from 10 to maybe 30 percent of the public, who oppose the use of force regardless. The president must mobilize two other groups. One group is indeed casualty phobic, and its proportion may be as high as 20 percent, depending on the mission; its members support a hypothetical military mission until the question mentions hypothetical casualties or give zeros when asked how many casualties are acceptable. Hypothetical questions probably exaggerate the degree of public casualty phobia since they are imposed on the respondent without either the rally 'round the flag effect or the frame of "these casualties are necessary for victory" that an effective president would set in the context of an actual mission; but this group is nonetheless a concern for political leaders. The remaining 15–40 percent of the public is best thought of as defeat phobic, people who support military missions provided that they are successful. These people supply the short-term "escalation dynamic" seen in many polls, where support can be found for reversing a temporary setback with an escalation that will seek victory. This segment of the American public will not panic at the sight of body bags, but will turn on a mission that appears to have no prospect of meaningful victory. Of course, the relative size of the groups varies with the case; for missions of obvious import (defeating Al Qaeda) the solid hawks and defeat phobics are doubtless larger, whereas the ranks of the solid doves and casualty phobics will swell on missions of dubious import (restoring President Aristide to Haiti).

An Artifact of the Pre-September 11th World?

Our argument leans heavily upon the TISS survey data, which were collected in 1998–99. Much has happened since then, and on September 11, 2001, by some accounts, the world changed. Is our argument still relevant to American civil-military relations now that the country has embarked on a global war against terrorists and a renewed conflict with Iraq? Of course, a definitive answer would require additional TISS-like surveys of civilian and military opinion, which to date have not been conducted. Nevertheless, the available evidence suggests that our basic findings are robust and can even help make sense of the post-September 11th developments.

Certainly the finding that active duty military and veterans may approach the use of force differently from nonveterans finds ample support in the reporting on debates over the war on terrorism and especially the debate on Iraq. Indeed, the internal and public debate over Iraq that dominated headlines in 2002 had a pronounced civil-military subtext. Inside the administration, the doves were championed by Secretary of State Powell, the most senior and most prominent veteran on the Bush team, who was then obviously reluctant to press a preemptive war against Iraq. According to numerous reports, Powell was allied with the senior military leadership, who shared his skepticism about launching such a war (Kessler 2002a,b,c; Milbank 2002b; Ricks 2002a, b). At the same time, the most prominent hawks inside the administration included the senior nonveterans. The line-up was not perfect—veteran Secretary Rumsfeld was widely considered to be a hawk and nonveteran National Security Advisor Condoleezza Rice came down somewhere in between the two camps—but the pattern was so obvious that it became a staple of commentary on the debate (Bamford 2002; Dewar 2002; Kessler 2002a,b,c; Kiely 2002, McGregor 2002; Van Deerlin 2002). Outside the administration, some of the loudest dove voices were prominent veterans—General Zinni, General Clark, Senator Chuck Hagel—and several of them commented on the apparent correlation between veteran status and opposition to expanding the war on terrorism to include Iraq (MSNBC 2002; Salinero 2002).

At the same time, civilians and the military have clashed over how to use force, especially over plans on Iraq. According to the leaks about the internal debate, the senior military proposed plans that followed the Powell Doctrine script: a large military buildup prior to a massive invasion—decisive force. Civilian hawks, however, pressed the military to innovate with plans that would involve substantially smaller numbers of forces, perhaps even an approach that relied essentially on special forces. (Cornwell 2002; Daalder and Lindsay 2002; Landay 2002; Ricks, 2002a,b). Of course, either approach would mean a major war, so it is not quite fair to describe the civilian-preferred plan as constrained or circumscribed. Nevertheless, the military preference for larger and the civilian preference for smaller—the pattern evident in the TISS data—reemerged in modified form in the debate over Iraq.

Not surprisingly, September 11th only reinforces our basic finding on casualties: that only a minority of the public can be considered truly casualty phobic, and that the president can count on the public to support a military operation even if that operation involves terrible human costs—provided that the operation is brought to victory. Although our data cannot address this issue directly, our analyses in chapter 5 showed that respondents' willingness to tolerate casualties is a function of the extent to which they feel that American interests are at stake in the conflict. Citizens at both the mass and the elite levels view terrorism as an issue that touches the core security interests of the United States. In fact, the TISS data indicate that the American public viewed terrorism as a significant threat even two years prior to the September 11th attacks. For instance, 63 percent of the public responded that terrorist attacks on the United States represented a "very serious" threat, whereas somewhat lower percentages of elite civilians (54 percent) and elite military (57 percent) concurred. The public's desire to protect American soil even extends to one "threat" that does not seem to pose physical dangers to the safety of U.S. citizens, namely, "large numbers of immigrants and refugees coming to the U.S." On this question, fully 33 percent of the general public responded that this was a "very serious" threat, compared with only 14 percent of civilian elites and 8 percent of military elites.[2]

These expectations have been borne out by the extensive polling done by others since September 11th. As figure 6.1 indicates, the military operations conducted in Afghanistan were supported by strong majorities. Polling support did not drop off substantially with actual casualties. Mentions of hypothetical casualties did reduce support, but almost never below a very high baseline of 60 percent. The one exception was a single Washington Post/ABC poll taken in the first week of November 2001, just before the total collapse of the Taliban forces, arguably the low point of the war for the United States with concerns that the extensive bombing was not leading to any success. As was seen in chapter 4, the polls do suggest that some small fraction of the public supported the war in Afghanistan only insofar as it involved few U.S. casualties, but the administration could count on a solid base of support provided that it saw the operation through to victory.

[2] See also Feaver (2000).

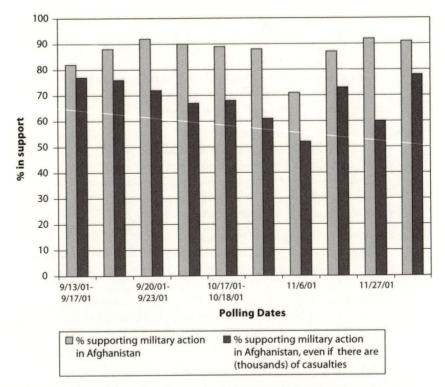

Figure 6.1. Public support and casualty sensitivity for U.S. War with Afghanistan.

Question Wording for Polling Data on Afghanistan:

9/13/01–9/17/01: Princeton

Do you favor or oppose taking military action, including the use of ground troops, to retaliate against whoever is responsible for the terrorist attacks (on the World Trade Center in New York and the Pentagon in Washington, D.C., September 11, 2001)?

Do you favor or oppose taking military action, including the use of ground troops, to retaliate against whoever is responsible for the terrorist attacks (on the World Trade Center in New York and the Pentagon in Washington, D.C., September 11, 2001) even if it means that U.S. armed forces might suffer thousands of casualties?

9/14/01–9/15/01: Gallup/CNN/U.S.A Today

Do you think the U.S. should—or should not—take military action in retaliation for the attacks on the World Trade Center and the Pentagon?

Would you support or oppose the U.S. military taking action if you knew each of the following would happen? How about if 5,000 U.S. troops would be killed?

9/20/01–9/23/01: CBS/NYT

Do you think the U.S. should take military action against whoever is responsible for the attacks?

What if that meant that thousands of American military personnel will be killed, then do you think the United States should take military action against whoever is responsible for the attacks?

9/25/01–9/27/01: Washington Post

If the U.S. can identify the groups or nations responsible for the attacks, would you support or oppose taking military action against them?

Would you support or oppose taking military action against the groups or nations responsible for these attacks, if you knew that it meant getting into a long war with large numbers of U.S. troops injured or killed?

10/17/01–10/18/01: Opinion Dynamics

Do you support or oppose the U.S. military action (in Afghanistan) being taken in response to the terrorist attacks (on the World Trade Center and the Pentagon, September 11, 2001)?

Would you support or oppose the U.S. military action (in Afghanistan) being taken in response to the terrorist attacks (on the World Trade Center and the Pentagon, September 11, 2001) even if it means thousands of American soldiers' lives would be lost?

10/25/01–10/28/01:CBS/NYT

Do you approve or disapprove of the military attacks led by the U.S. against targets in Afghanistan?

Suppose several thousand American troops lose their lives in Afghanistan—do you think the war in Afghanistan would be worth that cost or not?

11/6/01: ABC/Washington Post

Would you support or oppose sending a significant number of U.S. ground troops into Afghanistan?

What if it meant getting into a long war with large numbers of U.S. troops killed or injured—in that case would you support or oppose sending a significant number of U.S. ground troops into Afghanistan?

11/10/01–11/12/01: LA Times

Do you support the military attacks on Afghanistan, or do you oppose them?

Would you support the military attacks in Afghanistan, even if they result in a substantial number of casualties among American troops, or would you oppose them in that case?

11/27/01: ABC/Washington Post:

> Do you support or oppose U.S. military action in Afghanistan?
>
> Do you think it's worth risking a large number of U.S. military casualties (in Afghanistan) in order to capture and kill Osama bin Laden, or not?

3/12/02–3/13/02: Opinion Dynamics

> Do you support or oppose the U.S. military action being taken (in Afghanistan) in response to the terrorist attacks (on the World Trade Center and the Pentagon, September 11, 2001)?
>
> In recent weeks, there have been increased numbers of American battle casualties (in the military action being taken in Afghanistan in response to the terrorist attacks on the World Trade Center and the Pentagon, September 11, 2001). Will you support or oppose the military action if this trend continues and increasing numbers of American soldiers' lives are being lost?

Polling data includes a representative selection of polls from the time period following the September 11th attacks and through the Afghanistan campaign. Anomalous and low polling results were specifically included in this data set.

The polling on a possible war with Iraq followed this same pattern (see figure 6.2). The overall numbers are lower than the conflict in Afghanistan, which in historical terms was surely the most popular war the United States ever fought. Nevertheless, the hawks in the Bush administration could count on a sizable base of support for an Iraqi war, even if casualties mounted. In some polls, the casualty question seems to drive support below the 50 percent mark. But as we argued in chapter 4, the 50 percent mark is not the decisive threshold; public support has only really collapsed when it drops below 40 percent. Of course, none of this is dispositive on whether a war against Iraq is actually in the best interests of the United States, but it does suggest that casualty phobia need not be the decisive factor in weighing the issue.

To our knowledge, there has been no polling of the military on these issues in the post-September 11th environment, and so we can only speculate about military attitudes toward casualties since then. Chapter 5 identified confidence in the political leadership as a major factor in shaping military attitudes toward casualties, and it is plausible that the shift from President Bill Clinton to President George W. Bush shored up military tolerance of casualties early in the Bush administration. Of course, Bush's willingness to contemplate using force in Iraq, over the apparent objections of his senior military advisors, might have undercut that confidence somewhat; and certainly Rumsfeld's stormy relations with the Pentagon further complicate this picture (Loeb and Ricks 2002). Nevertheless, on balance we would not be surprised to learn that civilian and military attitudes on casualties converged slightly after September 11th.

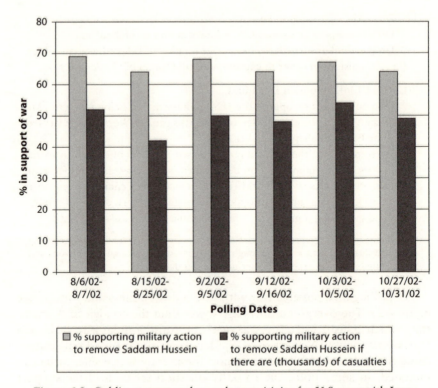

Figure 6.2. Public support and casualty sensitivity for U.S. war with Iraq.

Question Wording for Polling Data on Iraq:

6/1/02: Gallup

Would you favor or oppose taking military action to end Saddam Hussein's rule?

Would you favor or oppose taking military action to end Saddam Hussein's rule, even if it meant that US forces might suffer thousands of casualties?

8/6/02–8/7/02: Fox/Opinion Dynamics

Do you support or oppose U.S. military action to remove President Saddam Hussein?

Would you support or oppose the military action even if it means thousands of American soldiers' lives would be lost?

8/7/02–8/12/02: ABC/Washington Post

What if (a U.S. invasion with ground troops) caused a significant number of U.S. military casualties—in that case would you support or oppose a U.S. invasion with ground troops?

What if (a U.S. invasion with ground troops) caused a significant number of U.S. military casualties—in that case would you support or oppose a U.S. invasion with ground troops?

8/15/02–8/25/02: Pew
Would you favor or oppose taking military action in Iraq to end Saddam Hussein's rule?
Would you favor or oppose taking military action in Iraq to end Saddam Hussein's rule (even if it meant that U.S. forces might suffer thousands of casualties)?

9/2/02–9/5/02: CBS/NYT
Do you approve or disapprove of the U.S. taking military action against Iraq to try and remove Saddam Hussein from power?
Suppose the U.S. military action in Iraq would result in substantial U.S. military casualties, then would you favor or oppose the U.S. taking military action against Iraq?

9/12/02–9/16/02: Princeton
Would you favor or oppose taking military action in Iraq to end Saddam Hussein's rule?
Would you favor or oppose taking military action in Iraq to end Saddam Hussein's rule, even if it meant that U.S. forces might suffer thousands of casualties?

10/3/02–10/5/02: CBS/NYT
Do you approve of the U.S. taking military action against Iraq to try and remove Saddam Hussein from power?
If military action in Iraq would result in substantial American military casualties, would you favor or oppose it?

10/27/02–10/21/02:CBS/NYT
Do you approve of the U.S. taking military action against Iraq to try and remove Saddam Hussein from power?
If military action in Iraq would result in substantial American military casualties, would you favor or oppose it?

Polling data includes a representative selection of polls from the time period between June 1, 2002, and November 1, 2002. Anomalous and low polling results were specifically included in this data set.

In sum, there is nothing in our argument that would expect sharp civil-military differences on the novel issue of how to handle homeland defense or the real prospect of ongoing attacks on the continental United States. At such an extreme level of national security threat, civil-military differences are probably not crucial. But as one moves beyond the obvious threats—from Al Qaeda to the Taliban to Iraq to Colombia—the civil-military differences may matter more. And even on high-salience issues like Afghanistan and Iraq, unfolding events continue to conform to the pattern we observed.

Limitations of Our Findings

Even though developments since the TISS survey seem to conform to our argument, it is important to note several inherent limitations. We have presented these findings to scores of audiences inside the national security policymaking community and throughout academia and have confronted a fairly standard menu of skeptical responses that fall into two broad categories. The first category of objections point to misunderstandings about what we are claiming, about the methods we have used, or about the limitations that are inherent in any social science research. The second category are worthy objections that generally fall outside the scope of our project, or were unanswerable given the limits of existing data, but point to fruitful lines of future inquiry. We briefly discuss the first set of objections before moving on to proposing a research agenda for addressing the second set.

Critiques of survey research are well known and need not be reviewed in detail here.[3] We are perforce measuring respondents' expressed opinions, which may only uncertainly relate to their true opinion. Moreover, we are limited to measuring the expressed opinions of people who responded to our survey—a subset of the group to whom we sent the survey which is itself a subset of the group we are purporting to study. We took reasonable steps to avoid pitfalls inherent in this kind of research, and we have good reasons to be confident about many of our survey findings: for instance, the findings about a civil-military difference on the use of force is consistent with other research on the topic, and our findings that the public is not casualty phobic is consistent with other scholarly research (though not with the conventional wisdom) on the topic. But in the end, there are only two responses to this limitation. First, we acknowledge that our survey analysis only imperfectly captures true civil-military attitudes on the topic. Second, we urge others to do secondary analysis of our data to determine whether we erred in some way, and we urge others to do additional surveys on this topic to test the reliability and validity of our broader claims.

We recognize that we cannot answer definitively the selection-effect question: does civilian and military experience condition the differences of opinion we observe or do people who hold these differences of opinion naturally gravitate to the civilian or military life? Undoubtedly, there are

---

[3] For a careful review of the arguments, see Zaller (1994).

selection effects in our survey data, which for the most part measure the attitudes of people who voluntarily joined or refused to join an all-volunteer force. For current analyses, the selection-effect possibility is interesting but somewhat beside the point; it matters less why we observe the differences than that we observe them in the first place. For the historical aspect of our study, however, the selection effect could be more important. If opinion differences are entirely a result of selection and no socialization whatsoever is going on, then the meaning of being a veteran is fundamentally modified during periods of a draft, and our assumption that we can treat veterans as more or less equivalent over time is called into question.

As a first cut, we are prepared to defend our assumption that the selection versus socialization question does not matter, although we recognize that future analyses may require some reinterpretation of our findings. We think this is unlikely, however, because, as mentioned in chapter 2, we were able to distinguish between respondents (active duty and veterans) who joined the military because they were drafted or in order to avoid a draft and those who joined for other reasons. Similarly, in the analysis of casualty sensitivity in chapter 5, we were able to control for the reasons that active duty officers had for joining the military. These differing reasons had no impact on officers' tolerance for casualties. Though not perfect, this allows for a partial test of the selection-effect hypothesis. The draft or no-draft status never affected the results of our analyses of the opinions of elite civilians or elite military. This of course does not prove that draft versus volunteer status did not ever matter for public opinion in other historical periods, only that the selection effect does not appear to be decisive in our opinion data. Our measures of military experience in chapter 3, however, are not precise enough to distinguish between draftees and other forms of military experience. As we discuss below, exploring that question should be a priority for future research.

We use a snapshot survey of civil-military attitudes in 1998 to 1999 to shape a behavioral study of over 175 years of American foreign policy conduct. Obviously we do not have survey data extending back that far in time, and so we are, to some extent, mixing apples and oranges. We do so via our "veterans in the political elite variable," which is an admittedly rough and ready proxy that others may improve upon in future research. We can all think of prominent examples, both current and historical, that seem to cut against the general pattern we purport to find; undoubtedly there are some military officers who are willing to try out gradual escalation on apparently low-priority conflicts and some civilian politicians who advocate the all-or-nothing approach to the use of force. If such exceptions are really the norm, especially for large periods of U.S. history, then we are clearly erring in assuming otherwise. In the end, our final defense against this critique is a methodological one. If our assumptions about the general construct of civilian and military/veteran opinion in the past are unwarranted, this fact will show up as "noise" in the data; if civil-military opinions have varied widely or randomly over time, then statistical tests looking for a consistent correlation would fail. The limitations of our method, in other words, bias our analysis against finding *any* relationship.

The fact that chapter 3 finds such a strong statistical relationship therefore increases our confidence in what we have found. It is always possible that we have a spurious finding, but we have gone to great lengths to ensure that this is not the case. As we document at length in chapter 3, we have controlled for other factors that are clearly shaping decisions on the use of force, including virtually every counterinterpretation proposed by critics of the "veteran's effect" finding. For instance, is the apparent veteran's effect merely an artifact of general war weariness, for example, the recency of a great war? No. General war weariness may indeed shape decisions on the use of force, but veterans in the political elite have an independent effect. Is this simply an artifact of the cold war and the unique role the United States has played since 1945? No. The statistical results are undoubtedly shaped by the cold war period, but the pattern is statistically evident before and during the cold war. Are our results meaningless because measurement of interesting social variables is always difficult, and impossibly so when it is necessary to code those variables far back in time—the garbage-in-garbage-out critique? We recognize the measurement problems inherent in our project, but again these problems should bias our analysis against finding any relationship. Since we do find a relationship with our crude measurements, better measurements should lead to even stronger findings. Of course, we cannot persuade those willing to uphold the most extreme radical critique, one that rejects all quantitative analysis of history. We have found, however, that those who appear to be holding that line (usually for reasons of personal taste or disciplinary bias) are not themselves consistent with the logical implications of the critique. They still talk about "historical patterns" or "trends," and their evidentiary basis is always at some level quantitative, using, for example, multiple historical illustrations to buttress their case (King, Keohane, and Verba 1994). A rejection of all quantitative analysis is a rejection of all generalizations from history, which is a rejection of any attempt to learn something from history to apply it today. We have nothing to offer critics willing to go that far; for everyone else, we are only talking about disagreements of degree and we believe we have taken adequate steps to ensure that our findings are sufficiently plausible, reliable, and valid to merit entry into the debate.

The findings on attitudes toward casualties are especially subject to limitations. We measured casualty sensitivity with a series of hypothetical questions, not by measuring attitudes during an actual use of force. Obviously a public that claims it will tolerate casualties ex ante may change its mind dramatically when the horror of the human costs of war becomes all too evident in a real conflict. Certainly no one should expect that the raw numbers of "acceptable casualties" we report for various respondent groups reflect the precise level of casualties that would be tolerated before support for an intervention would dissipate. But as we argued in chapter 4, the answers to our hypothetical questions are surely not meaningless. There are good reasons to believe that responses to hypothetical questions understate a public's willingness to pay the human costs of war. Hypotheticals do not benefit from the rally 'round the flag phenomenon and can only uncertainly capture the boost that comes from a president who actively mobilizes support for the mission. Moreover, there is internal validity to the responses; the professed casualty acceptance of individual respondents rationally lines up with those individuals' answers to other questions on the survey, such as the foreign policy priority they assign to missions like the ones asked about in the casualty scenario. There is also external validity in that the broad findings are consistent with analyses of polling data taken during actual conflicts. At some point the burden of proof shifts to those who insist on claiming that the public emotionally and uncontrollably abandons support for military operations at the first hint of casualties, and insist on making these claims without much data to support them. Of course, we are not claiming that the public will support any military operation, regardless of casualties, nor are we claiming that the military is so casualty phobic as to oppose all missions. The wording of our question made public support conditional on achieving the goal, that is, on being successful. We believe the public will tolerate casualties when victory is in sight. Not explicit in our question, but evident from other studies (especially Larson 1996, 2000), are some sort of minimal leadership requirements; political leaders must mobilize public opinion and expend political capital to gird support for the mission. If such a leadership effort is lacking, or is stymied by deep divisions within the political leadership (as evidenced by a bitter debate between Congress and the president or across parties over the wisdom of the mission itself), then it is reasonable to expect that public support for the mission will erode, and hence public sensitivity to the human costs of the mission will intensify.

Suggestions for Further Research

This book is clearly not the last word on the subject. Perhaps the simplest claim we are making is that our research has demonstrated the value of using tools—survey research and statistical analysis of the historical record—that are rarely used by political scientists to study political phenomena related to civil-military relations.[4] The chief value is that we have generated interesting findings that call out for further research to build upon, clarify, and, as necessary, revise the findings we put forward. Future research should be directed along four broad lines.

First, there is an obvious need for additional surveys of civilian and military opinion.[5] The bulk of our opinion data comes from a single snapshot survey of opinion. Although we have some historical survey data from the Foreign Policy Leadership Project elite surveys (which ran from 1976 to 1996), the questions were limited. Many of our most provocative findings concern first-of-a-kind queries from the TISS survey. Obviously, our confidence in the validity and reliability of our results will increase (or be justly shaken) only with additional surveys asking these questions in a variety of settings. Future surveys should also seek to expand the subsamples, especially of military personnel: the survey could be administered to enlisted personnel; the officer sample could be larger to permit more subsample demographic analysis, for example, on race and gender; the mass survey could include more questions to permit more mass-elite comparisons; and so on. Additional surveys are necessary to answer one of the most common criticisms of our research: that our opinion findings are merely an artifact of the peculiar time in which we surveyed.[6] We have gone to great lengths to establish the external validity of our findings— comparing our results with the FPLP series of surveys, with other opinion surveys, and, most obviously, testing hypotheses derived from the opinion analyses against 177 years of U.S. history—but we recognize that additional surveys might be necessary to convince skeptics.

Additional surveys are especially important for questions that we asked for the first time. In this regard, we would highlight the casualty sensitivity question as a priority for future survey work. It must be noted that casualty sensitivity is itself a sensitive issue. We found high refusal rates on

[4] Surveys are, of course, a staple of sociological research on civil-military relations, such as studies of military morale, propensities to join the military, and so on.

[5] It goes without saying that a top priority for future research is simply reanalyzing the TISS database itself. For reasons of space and scope, we did not make use of all the subsamples in the TISS data—comparing, for instance, precommissioned to older officers—and for some subsamples that we did analyze, like reserves, we only skimmed lightly over the results. Even in those subsamples we analyzed closely, like elite veterans and elite nonveterans, we did not consider all the possible attitudinal correlates contained in the survey. The interested reader is encouraged to review Feaver and Kohn (2001b) to get a feel for the richness of the TISS data. Moreover, replicating our basic approach but using other statistical tools or controls is a standard way social science progresses and should be considered as a priority for future research.

[6] Of course, every time is "peculiar" at some level, but we recognize that surveying opinion on civil-military relations during the troubled second term of the Clinton administration introduced special concerns about idiosyncrasies.

our casualty questions, especially in the military sample, a modal response of zero, and a fair number of what might be called sabotaged ballots, that is, responses that were clearly absurd, such as casualty estimates larger than the population of the United States. During pretesting we encountered some resistance to the wording of the question—are casualties ever "acceptable"—and found similar problems with other wordings like "tolerable" or "reasonable." In the text, we treat acceptance and tolerance as synonyms but recognize that some respondents may draw subtle distinctions. We are confident, however, that our measure is valid and that our findings about the underlying determinants of casualty sensitivity are robust. As explained in chapters 4 and 5, we did extensive sensitivity analyses, treating nonresponses and zeros in different ways, and the underlying phenomena did not change. Our study therefore can provide a reliable point of departure for follow-on studies that could seek to refine the measure and supplement aggregate analysis with focus groups to unpack the issue further.

Yet our study must remain agnostic on certain related issues because we simply have not collected data on them. Future surveys and analyses of surveys could explore two intriguing questions left hanging by our research: how willing is the public to take U.S. civilian casualties and how willing is the public to tolerate enemy casualties? U.S. civilian casualties were not a focus of our study, since the most likely uses of the U.S. military have been and will continue to be in foreign operations. But the devastating attacks of September 11th and the continuing specter of terrorism on U.S. soil, whether involving weapons of mass destruction or conventional means, raise important questions about the willingness of the U.S. population to suffer the collateral damage of war hitherto paid only by other countries.

Another unanswered question concerns casualties sustained by the enemy. The literature is less developed on this issue, but the phenomenon seems no less present, especially with regard to enemy noncombatants. The distinctive feature of the Kosovo operation was precisely the twin effort to reduce NATO casualties to unprecedented levels and the effort to avoid Serbian civilian casualties. As the air war continued with scant evidence of political results, NATO gradually became less sensitive to Serbian civilian casualties, and by the third month of bombing NATO began striking a range of civilian infrastructure facilities in an effort to put pressure on the Milosevic regime by increasing the suffering of the civilian population (Becker 1999). But even in the wake of the September 11th attacks, American concern over enemy civilian casualties appears to have a significant impact on American military operations against the Taliban and Al Qaeda in Afghanistan.

Compared with American practices during World War II, or even with discussions about hypothetical nuclear wars during the cold war, there has been a marked change in attitudes about civilian casualties in war. One might call the effect "creeping just war-ism," the gradual solidifying of the just war norm against killing noncombatants and against using disproportionate force. This observation may be more descriptive than explanatory—it is hard to argue that the change is entirely due to a realization that the norm is right in some philosophical sense. There has been over the same period, for instance, a parallel increase in the use of economic sanctions that have precisely the opposite effect, "targeting" civilians with pain in an effort to coerce decision makers. Indeed, such sanctions are defended on the just war grounds of using all available alternatives before resorting to force. Moreover, increased attention to civilian casualties in war has come alongside a spread of democracy, which undercuts the moral logic of just war theory that holds noncombatants as immune because they do not bear any responsibility for the war; a democratic population shares, in some senses, culpability for what its government does and is therefore a more justifiable target than a population suffering under a dictator (or, hearkening back to the setting that gave rise to just war theory, a medieval regent). It is also fair to say the norm is hardly universal, as the continued use of ethnic cleansing as both a goal and a means of war suggests. Nevertheless, at least in the U.S. case, it is plausible that there has been a growing sensitivity concerning inflicting enemy civilian casualties in war.

How might civilian and military preferences diverge on these questions? The conventional wisdom—if there is such a thing on this topic— would probably expect U.S. civilians to be more sensitive to enemy civilian casualties than the U.S. military would be. The logic the conventional wisdom expects to see with respect to U.S. military casualties applies here: civilians would be more inclined to believe that war can be antiseptic, while the military specialists in violence would understand that war is unavoidably messy. Thus, Luttwak (1999) argues, civilians try for a clean war and impose restrictive rules of engagement and other constraints on a reluctant military in the vain quest for an antiseptic war. Our findings of a fair degree of casualty tolerance on the part of the American public suggest the opposite speculation: that the public will in fact tolerate enemy collateral damage provided it is necessary for victory. Classical realist concerns about the moody democratic public would reinforce this view. Since public support can be mobilized only if the enemy is demonized, civilians would be prone to the utter devastation of total war while the realpolitik military would accept limited aims (and a professionalized military would accept just war restrictions) that result in fewer civilian casualties. It is possible, however, that the U.S. military is more opposed to restrictions that aim to reduce enemy civilian casualties but that raise risks to the U.S. military. Indeed, because of the inherent trade-off, at some point the casualty-averse U.S. military must accept greater enemy collateral damage to sustain low U.S. combatant deaths (Schmitt 1999a, b).

Casualty sensitivity may even extend so far as a reluctance to inflict casualties on enemy combatants. The Clinton administration's reliance on cruise missiles as its weapon of choice had the possibly intended side effect of reducing enemy military casualties to a minimum. Consider, for example, Clinton's decision to strike the Iraqi targets in the dead of night when few Iraqis of any stripe, civilian or military, would be at risk; Iraqi casualties were so low, and sensitivities so high, that President Clinton was able to memorize the names of those who died (Bernstein 1993; Cockburn 1993; Jehl 1993; Broder 1999). The sensitivity almost certainly predates Clinton. During the final days of Desert Storm, General Powell intervened to press for a quick end to the fighting before the Republican Guard had been thoroughly destroyed. This effort is partly attributable to a desire to end the war while U.S. casualties were very low. But it is also attributable to what Powell called the "warrior's code," the desire to limit enemy military casualties and to avoid, again in Powell's words, the appearance of "slaughter for slaughter's sake" (Powell 1995, 505–14).[7] Significantly, accounts suggest that the view was shared equally by civilians and the military.

A comprehensive analysis of casualty sensitivity should consider all of these aspects, because at some fundamental level, combat decisions involve making trade-offs across all of these issues. To the extent that technology is driving changing attitudes toward casualties, it should affect enemy and friendly casualties alike. Technology brings a standoff strike capability that reduces our casualties and a precision-strike capability that reduces collateral damage. The same media can dramatize U.S. casualties and also (perhaps even especially) can dramatize the unintended destruction of enemy civilian society. The possibility for greater precision (and perhaps the illusion that the precision is greater than it is) means that this moral calculus will be central to every military mission. As ethical theory suggests, if "ought" implies "can," so, too, "can" implies "ought." Even absent an advance in technology, many efforts to reduce U.S. casualties raise the risk of increasing enemy civilian casualties and vice versa. One way to reduce collateral damage is to require visual identification before striking the target, to remain in the vicinity of the target longer so as to keep the target lit with laser tracking devices, or to use ground troops that directly engage enemy military forces and avoid civilian centers—

[7] See also Schwarzkopf (1992, 542–47), and Gordon and Trainor (1995, 404–19).

measures that increase risks to U.S. pilots and soldiers.[8] In Kosovo especially, critics claimed that the casualty aversion policy of the Clinton administration showed up in increased enemy collateral damage—that is, Clinton traded off enemy civilian casualties in order to reduce American combatant deaths.[9]

The second broad area for future research is historical case studies, to flesh out the causal mechanism described in chapter 3. Statistical research on conflict behavior has two inherent limitations: in finding general patterns in aggregate data it obscures interesting and potentially important details about the phenomenon under study, and at a basic level it demonstrates correlation, not causation. The remedy to both limitations is to conduct historical case studies. Case studies of civil-military interactions would allow researchers to determine whether the actors actually held the opinions the statistical results imply they held and whether these opinions and the relative weight thereof seemed to shape how decisions were made. Undoubtedly the case studies will uncover exceptions to the general rule we are positing, but at some point an accumulation of exceptions will erode confidence in our interpretation of our results. Strong conclusions from such case studies that veterans and nonveterans were not interacting as our model assumes, however, would not invalidate our statistical findings; on the contrary, such a result would beg the follow-on question of what else is going on to produce such an enduring statistical result. Case studies would also help show that the correlations we observe are indeed causally associated. The qualitative/quantitative critique and its link to issues of causation should not be exaggerated. After all, any causal claim—whether supported by historical or statistical data—inevitably rests on counterfactual assumptions and is therefore at some level always

---

[8] Of course, a ground operation that did not avoid urban centers might actually increase collateral damage, as the battle for Grozny between Russian and Chechen separatists demonstrated.

[9] See, for example, Cook (2000); Hodge (2000); Coll (2001). For a contrary view, see Meilinger (2001). The definitive treatment of this issue is the Human Rights Watch review of the Kosovo operation, which claims that "insufficient evidence exists" to settle the question of whether this trade-off in fact occurred. See Human Rights Watch (2000). Charles Dunlap (2000) argues that the Kosovo campaign did not involve this trade-off, more precisely that the decision to bomb at higher altitudes did not result in appreciably greater collateral damage among Serbs and Kosovars. Moreover, he claims, a ground assault might have involved even more collateral damage because he assumes, without justification, that any ground invasion would have devolved into a Grozny-like siege. Dunlap does not address the broader point that the reluctance to engage the Serbs close-in (a reluctance he claims was not held by the tactical officers but concedes was the driving strategy) prolonged the war and allowed the Serbs to conduct the ethnic cleansing that produced the greatest civilian casualties of the war.

uncertain (Fearon 1991). Moreover, statistical correlations can indicate causation if the correlations have a theoretical grounding (as do ours) and if care has been taken to control against a spurious result (as we have). And, of course, case studies have their own inherent limitations—subjectivity of interpretation of evidence, difficulty in accounting for complex or multicausal phenomena—and so do not prove causal mechanisms. Nevertheless, our confidence that we understand the causal relationship between civil-military interactions and the use of force would increase if case studies supported the statistical results.

We have not yet done these case studies, because we believe the results are sufficiently compelling to merit public consideration on their own. But we support further research along these lines, because it will increase our understanding of the way civil-military relations affects the use of force over time.[10] Indeed, there is a natural, cyclical interaction between the various methods used to examine this phenomenon. We were inspired to ask the questions we asked on the survey and to explore certain hypotheses with quantitative data precisely because of our reading of the existing case study literature. Now our findings can perhaps inspire other scholars to explore other questions in additional case studies. Just as the earlier case studies could stand on their own while leading to additional research, so can our work stand on its own while leading to additional research.

Such an effort would naturally lead to the third broad area for future research, refining the measures used in chapter 3, especially those of the civil-military gap and the use of force. The gap measure could be refined by differentiating the nature of military service and further differentiating the position of influence of military veterans within the policymaking system. The most frequent objection to our findings is that our analysis in chapter 3 treats all veterans as equal; the draftee who served as a cook is coded the same as the reserve intelligence officer who only served in an office on weekends, and both are coded the same as the special forces veteran who earned the Medal of Honor for bravery and saw multiple tours of combat. Moreover, veterans from "good" wars like World War II are treated the same as veterans from "bad" wars like Vietnam, and, indeed, both are treated the same as veterans whose entire service coin-

---

[10] One initial effort to explore our findings in a case study format is Demske (2001), which compared civil-military relations in the 1898 Spanish-American War and in the 1909–10 limited intervention in Nicaragua. Demske concluded that military experience or the lack thereof profoundly shaped the preferences of the key civilian policymakers in each case. However, not all the details of the Spanish-American intervention conformed to the expectations of the model we develop here. Specifically, President William McKinley, a veteran, was able to override pressure he was receiving from the larger percentage of nonveterans in the political elite to intervene early in the Cuban conflict.

cided with peacetime. And what about service differences (which we un-cover in the opinion data in chapter 5)? Is it reasonable to treat Navy veterans as necessarily approaching the use of force in the same way as Army veterans? At an intuitive level, such an aggregation of military experience is jarring. Shouldn't different kinds of service result in different kinds of opinions and different causal relationships to the propensity to use force? We share this intuitive expectation and were simply unable to test it because we did not have data to differentiate the kinds of service experienced by members of the political elite. As reported in chapters 2 and 3, we were able to assess the impact of one very important distinction—officer versus enlisted—and determined that it had no effect, at least at the elite level. Future research could be directed at other distinctions, at a minimum by differentiating combat from noncombat (or wartime with peacetime) service within the political elite. We would not be surprised if that research found that type of military service also has an independent effect on attitudes and therefore on behavior. We would be surprised, however, if differentiating military service in this way invalidated our findings by erasing the civil-military effect altogether.

In a similar vein, surely not all veterans' in the political elite are equal; are not some by dint of their personality more influential than others? We use a fairly crude measure of veterans' influence: percentage of veterans in Congress and the cabinet, as well as the independent effect of a veteran as president and veterans as secretary of state and war/defense. Sensitivity analyses showed that our results were robust even to different specifications of the veterans' influence variable; the results were essentially the same whether one used only veterans in national security posts in the cabinet or all the veterans in the House of Representatives. But our sensitivity analyses were limited by the nature of the data we had available. Future research should determine the extent to which the position of the veteran in the political elite matters, especially once one is able to differentiate between various forms of military service. Likewise, other scholars may find better ways of measuring veterans' influence than we did.

At the same time, our measure of escalation is fairly crude, only a four-point scale that distinguishes between four crisis strategies: threaten militarized force; present a show of militarized force (defined as the threatening movement of troops); use militarized force (defined as any combat that results in less than 1,000 battle deaths); and major war (any combat with more than 1,000 battle deaths). This only uncertainly captures the underlying concept we mean to test, which is incrementalism versus an all-out use of force. It is possible that using force decisively, as we argue military officers prefer, would result in less than 1,000 battle deaths whereas using force incrementally would result in a slow war of attrition that passed the

1,000-death hurdle to qualify as a major war. If so, then these coding anomalies are confounding our interpretation of our results. A priority for future research is developing a better measure of incrementalism.[11]

The fourth broad line of future inquiry concerns how generalizable our results are beyond the U.S. case. Of course, studying civil-military relations within a case as important as the United States is a worthy effort in itself, and discovering that our results are only true for the United States would not constitute much of a rebuttal. Nevertheless, at a fundamental level, there is no a priori reason to believe that our results should only hold for the United States. Or rather, there are good reasons to expect similar results for other countries, especially other advanced democracies. The underlying problem of civil-military relations holds in every country, and civil-military conflicts over how to use force are ubiquitous. To our knowledge, there are as of yet no systematic data on civil-military opinions in other countries, so a priority for research would be collecting that data. Other aspects of our project, particularly measuring the veteran's effect on the use of force, should be easier to replicate, and we look forward to seeing the results of such studies.

Implications for Policy

The most obvious implication of our research is that analysts and journalists should bring civil-military relations back to the forefront of their treatment of national security policymaking. Most existing discussions emphasize partisanship and personality. Consider the way the Clinton-to-Bush transition is conventionally understood. The partisan story line had prudent (or, depending on one's predilections, hopelessly cold war–bound) Republicans vying with promiscuous (or progressive) Democrats on how cautious the United States should be in using military force. The personality story line looked at the idiosyncrasies of the individuals who hold the senior-most positions—Colin Powell as the most popular military figure of our day wielding unprecedented clout from his new perch as secretary of state is contrasted with his predecessor, the academic and voluble Madeleine Albright. Dick Cheney, the über-Vice President, contrasts with President Bush, the son who draws inevitable contrasts with the father, and so on.

Certainly partisanship and personality matter in the formation of policy in the United States, but our research shows that another story line, a civil-military one, deserves more scrutiny than most treatments gave it, at least until very recently. To make sense of debates ongoing within the

[11] We are grateful to Phillip Demske for helping us to clarify our thinking on this point.

Bush administration, say between the relatively dovish Powell and the relatively hawkish Cheney or Paul Wolfowitz (deputy secretary of defense), observers need to factor in the enduring division between civilians and the military over when and how to use military force. The civil-military story line helps to shape policy and, in so doing, is following a pattern that obtains for most of U.S. history. In short, our results demonstrate convincingly that the civil-military gap is an important issue for those who study international conflict, for those who study American foreign policy, and for the American people in general.

A second broad policy implication flows naturally from the first: expect friction on decision making on the use of force. Some of the friction will merely be the next chapter in the enduring story of civil-military disputes about how to use force. But some of the friction will be due to the particular nature of elite military opinion on the appropriate role of the military in use-of-force decisions. Chapter 2 demonstrated that civilian and military elites disagree on the proper way to use force. The TISS data also show that at the same time large majorities of military elites believe that the proper role for the military is to advocate or even to insist on their preferred approach to the implementation of use-of-force decisions. The elite military believe that they should advocate and insist on matters such as setting rules of engagement, developing an "exit strategy," and deciding what kinds of military units (air versus naval, heavy versus light) will be used to accomplish all tasks.[12]

Still more friction will result from the peculiar civil-military mix of the current era. Consider the interaction between two of our findings: that the veteran status of the secretary of state has a statistically discernible independent impact on the propensity of the United States to use force and that the percentage of veterans in the political elite likewise affects the use of force. Changing the secretary of state from a nonveteran to a veteran decreased the number of military disputes initiated by the United States by an average of two disputes over a three-year period. Interestingly, however, the veteran status of the president did not influence American military behavior. The president's choice of advisors may be more consequential for the kinds of policies he will implement than the choice of the president himself. In short, changing the guard in Foggy Bottom from the quintessential elite civilian who never served in the military, Madeleine Albright, to the quintessential retired general, Colin Powell,

---

[12] Feaver and Kohn (2001b), pp. 464–65. Interestingly, to a surprising degree, elite civilians seem to endorse military advocacy and insistence on these matters. The friction that results, therefore, may not be perceived as issues of civilian control even if it raises concerns about civil-military cooperation.

was likely more than simply a shift in style and demeanor. Other things being equal, it could have augured a return to a less bellicose American foreign policy agenda. That, at least, was the administration's plan until September 11th rendered other things decidedly not equal.

Yet other things were not equal even before the terrorist attacks. On the one hand, Bush's cabinet is far more veteran-heavy than his predecessor's—37 percent versus Clinton's low of barely 20 percent—but by historical standards the percentages do not indicate an overwhelming dominance of military views. Bush's appointments return us to the level of veteran representation found in his father's cabinet, which was marked by conflicts over intervention in places like Panama, Iraq, and Somalia. On the other hand, regardless of the makeup of the younger Bush's cabinet, he has continued to face a powerful force beyond his control: vanishing veterans in Congress. In 1973 more than 70 percent of those serving in Congress had also served in the U.S. military. By 1990 that percentage had dropped to just over 40 percent. Today barely 32 percent of Congress (38 percent of senators and 31 percent of representatives) have any military experience. If 175 years of history is any guide, the disappearance of veterans from the political elite in Congress is likely to put upward pressure on the propensity of the United States to use force. The secular decline in the representation of veterans in politics is probably a direct result of the decision to move to an all-volunteer force in 1973. The end of the draft changed the career trajectories of those entering politics and in doing so altered the landscape of American politics. In this sense, American foreign policy after the cold war began in the Nixon administration and its decision to abandon the draft. Thus the combination of these two cross-cutting civil-military divides may simply be returning us to another round of civil-military debates of the early 1990s. Indeed, the round of debates began in earnest immediately after September 11th—triggered, of course, by the terrorist attacks, but shaped, we would argue, by the civil-military dynamic.

A third broad policy implication is a nonimplication: we are not making a judgment one way or the other about whether civil-military differences are inherently wrong or whether one side has an inherently superior vision of how to use force. Our survey data do not speak one way or the other to whether civilian elite views are a reflection of näiveté about the military and the limits of its capabilities or are based on a superior understanding of geopolitics. We note, however, that on some issues where the naïveté hypothesis might expect to find big gaps, in fact we find none. For instance, there is not much difference between civilian and military elite responses to questions concerning how effective military tools are compared with nonmilitary tools for coping with a variety of threats to national security. Likewise, the elites seem to share a consensus on the determinants of military effectiveness and the kinds of problems that might have a corrosive impact on military effectiveness. Although this apparent consensus should be investigated further, it does suggest that different opinions about when and how to use force are more reflective of different value judgments about what is worth doing rather than dramatically different beliefs about the efficacy of force. In a similar way, we are not making any judgments regarding whether the United States should be willing to initiate militarized disputes, or whether the United States should be willing to initiate disputes against the interventionist threats that dominated the agenda in the first decade after the cold war, or whether force should be used massively or gradually. These are important normative issues that lie outside the scope of our research.

Regardless of where one comes down in evaluating the merits of the interventionist versus the realpolitik vision of how the United States should engage in the world, however, our research points to the factors that will affect the likelihood of either position's holding sway. If, for example, one wants to reduce the propensity of the United States to initiate the use of force, then tinkering with the civil-military mix inside the government may have influence. Importantly, our results do not suggest that the president must be a veteran. We would expect that a nonveteran president who was surrounded by veterans in the Congress and in his administration would be less likely to initiate militarized disputes. Conversely, we would expect that even a president with military experience would be likely to have a relatively high incidence of military conflict if the rest of his administration and the Congress was composed of nonveterans.

Likewise, an advocate of the return to a draft, or perhaps to some kind of national service, might find support for his or her views in our findings. A draft that did not allow for many exemptions would likely increase military experience among the political elite and thereby dampen the propensity of the United States to initiate the use of force, other things being equal. But a draft might not be necessary; a similar effect could be achieved by increasing veteran representation among the political elite, regardless of whether the pool of veterans remains small because of the continuance of the all-volunteer force. For example, a recent study found that throughout most of the twentieth century, Congress was populated by a larger proportion of veterans than existed in the comparable age cohort in the country at large (Bianco and Markham 2001). This "veterans' premium" had the effect of dampening the likelihood that the United States would use force. However, the study also finds that the veterans' premium has evaporated over the past decade. As the premium disappears, so too should the dampening effect.

In this light, Congressman Charles Rangel's recent proposal to revive the draft as a way of protesting an alleged cavalier attitude in Congress and the Bush administration is equal parts wrong-headed and on point (Fears 2003; Glastris 2003; Rangel 2003). It is wrong-headed, because there is no evidence that political leaders have been cavalier about casualties; on the contrary, the record of the past decade or so is that political leaders have been excessively preoccupied with combat casualties. At the same time, our study supports Congressman Rangel's broader intuition about a link between a personal connection to the military and one's attitudes about the use of force. The historical record clearly shows that the presence of veterans in Congress and the senior executive branch does have a significant effect on the likelihood that the United States will initiate the use of force. And it is also true that having friends or loved ones in the military makes respondents more sensitive to casualties in opinion surveys. The revive-the-draft movement is probably wrong to want to make political leaders even more wary about U.S. casualties, but they have stumbled on a plausible way to do it—increasing those political leaders' personal connections to the military.

Of course, all of these policy goals and measures—reducing the propensity of the United States to initiate the use of force, adopting criteria for senior appointments, or returning the draft—have other costs and benefits that lie beyond the scope of this study. Our research cannot tell us what is the correct way to value any of these goals, but it can point to the policy implications of our choices.

By contrast, a fourth broad policy implication does allow for an unambiguous value judgment, at least one that we find compelling. It is plainly dangerous for the United States to act as if the public is casualty phobic when the public is not. It is clear that the perception of American casualty phobia encourages American adversaries and puts American troops at greater risk. Slobodan Milosevic, Saddam Hussein, and Osama bin Laden have all explicitly premised their policies on the assumption that the United States could be paralyzed by the infliction of relatively few casualties on American forces. Milosevic knew, and Hussein and bin Laden know, that they cannot prevail against American power, and they have anticipated that American power might be brought to bear against them. But they have believed that casualties are America's Achilles heel and so they have been emboldened. America's deterrent threats are more likely to be challenged, even by hopelessly overmatched adversaries, if those adversaries hear U.S. leaders endorse the myth of the American public's casualty phobia.[13]

---

[13] The Chinese have, apparently, drawn precisely the same inference about the United States. An unidentified Chinese scholar reportedly claimed, "The People's Liberation Army

Moreover, strategic planning is hamstrung by the erroneous belief that the public will demand that the U.S. military cut and run at the first American combat deaths. It remains important, of course, to prevent or limit American casualties as much as possible. No one is clamoring for more American casualties or thinking it is a good thing to suffer the terrible human costs of war. But it would be a grave mistake to believe that the United States can provide global leadership without risking military casualties. It is also a mistake to believe that the American public is unwilling to take risks when its leaders are persuasive that risks are appropriate.

The United States is tying its own hands and thereby making it more difficult to exercise its global leadership role responsibly. If the additional requirement of limiting all casualties is levied on an operation, the paralysis becomes even more pronounced. Our study cannot answer whether America ought to be intervening in conflicts around the world, or whether we ought to be willing to suffer casualties in order to do so. But we can recommend that policymakers start listening more carefully to the expressed—not mythical—views of the American people. A myth is hardly sound footing for American foreign policy in the twenty-first century.

A fifth broad policy implication of our research also concerns the civil-military sensitivity gap on casualties. The gap is likely to grow over time, since it is most pronounced between the active military and the "pure civilian" groups, that is, civilians without any military experience. The declining force structure and long-standing changes in the structure of the civilian elite ensure that fewer and fewer citizens will have military service. Absent efforts to change military or civilian elite opinion, we can expect that on a prominent category of missions the military elite will seem increasingly casualty sensitive relative to the civilian elite.

As we explain in chapter 5, elite military casualty sensitivity is not simply due to a natural military desire for self-preservation, because the categories of elite military respondents most likely to be in combat are often the ones most willing to accept casualties. Yet as a body, the elite military officer corps is considerably more casualty sensitive on so-called interventionist missions than is the civilian elite or the mass public. Skeptics might argue that casualty sensitivity itself is not a relevant or important variable, dismissing survey results by arguing that private views do not matter. According to this view, when the order to go comes, the members of the military will obey regardless of whether they say they view low or high numbers of casualties as acceptable. In other words, an analysis of survey

genuinely feels that Americans can't tolerate death. . . . They look at your yellow ribbons for these servicemen and your casualty-free Kosovo and they think you don't have the will" (Pomfret 2001, A1). See also Blechman and Wittes (1999); Byman and Waxman (1999); Christenson (2001); and Tarzi (2001).

responses must be set against the long record of civilian control in the United States. Nevertheless, since these missions are likely to remain central to American foreign policy, policymakers may be faced with ever more reluctant warriors. Either civilian policymakers will have to change their priorities, the military will have to change their perceptions of the costs they are willing to pay for these missions, or military professionalism will face an ever more severe array of challenges.

Should the elite military become more casualty acceptant in these non-traditional missions? One could argue that a reluctant military is a useful brake on over-eager civilian hawks. This normative judgment is beyond the scope of our study. But our sense is that the gap is problematic for several reasons. A persistent gap could skew the advisory role of the military. Military advisors who believe certain missions are hardly worth any sacrifice have a strong incentive to give biased advice on what is feasible and how. In this regard, it is interesting that civilian elites and military elites differ markedly in their expectation of military obedience when civilian leaders order the military to do something that it opposes. According to the TISS survey, only about one-quarter of the elite military expect that the military will seek ways to avoid carrying out the order some of the time, most of the time, or all of the time (19 percent, 4 percent, and 2 percent, respectively); in contrast, almost twice as many civilian elites expect some kind of shirking (37 percent some of the time, 9 percent most of the time, and 2 percent all of the time). If civilian elites lose confidence in the quality of the advice they receive from military professionals, the quality of policymaking is sure to suffer.

It is also possible that the strong military reluctance to take casualties will undermine the moral authority of the civilian leadership, especially if the civilian leaders themselves have no military experience. Our data permit a conclusive rejection of Moskos's (1998) claim that the public does not believe the elite has the moral authority to order casualties because the elite is not willing to serve. The data show that the mass public are not the most casualty-sensitive group and, in any case, are not casualty phobic across the board; if Moskos's conjecture were correct, the mass would oppose all casualties instead of giving varying estimates based on other considerations like perceived stakes.[14] But the data do not permit a decisive assessment of the alternative moral authority hypothesis: that political elites are reluctant to take casualties in these operations for fear of having to reconcile the sacrifices of other soldiers with their own unwillingness to risk it themselves. The finding that elite civilians are the most casualty acceptant suggests that elites as a whole do not confront

---

[14] A modified Moskos hypothesis might hold, namely that the mass public challenges the elite's moral authority only on military missions of secondary importance.

such a self-imposed constraint. The effect should be most pronounced, however, among the political elite who would be held responsible for any deaths, and we do not have their views captured in our sample. The extraordinary lengths to which the Clinton administration went to reduce U.S. casualties is strong evidence that self-restraint was operating at the highest levels of policymaking. It is still plausible that this was a function of the administration's self-doubt regarding the moral authority it held in this arena. In any case, the wide gap between those who serve and those who did not serve, and the willingness of people like Congressman Rangel to exploit the issue, both indicate that the moral authority issue is likely to remain in play. A wide and growing gap on what might be considered the core moral question of the military function—is this mission worth dying for—augurs ill for policymaking on the use of force.

Further, these factors could result in a "zero defects" mentality in which the nontraditional mission can go forward provided it is carried out with zero or minimal casualties. Thus the civil-military casualty gap can paralyze policymakers when it comes to the actual use of force, thereby exacerbating the problems associated with the myth about the public attitudes as discussed above. Indeed, the record of how the government acts (as opposed to how elites think) suggests that it is beginning to view military casualties the way the public might view fireman or police casualties. Rather than a tragic but also an expected and inherently unavoidable part of the job, military casualties are treated as a cause for great hand-wringing, to be avoided at all costs. Precisely this phenomenon occurred in the Kosovo operation (Graham 1999). In 2001 the Bush administration went to some lengths to correct this problem during the Afghanistan operation. President Bush repeatedly emphasized that American casualties were tragic but expected and necessary, and the deaths that did occur did not generate the same degree of hand-wringing that was evident in the Clinton administration. Nevertheless, unease remains. Since there is a trade-off between our casualties and the other costs of war, especially collateral damage in the enemy civilian population, these cleavages could drive the United States into wars where we place increasing numbers of enemy civilians at risk in order save ever-smaller numbers of American soldiers. Such a military might begin to resemble the mercenary forces of an earlier era rather than the professional military of modern times. The problem, therefore, is not so much that military elites are casualty phobic on certain missions but rather that military elites may be highly casualty sensitive on missions that an influential portion of the larger policymaking community is nevertheless willing to embrace. Unless the gap is closed, policymakers will be whipsawed by contradictory pressures.

The foregoing implies that excessive casualty sensitivity is corrosive to the professional military ethic. The military is built on the principles of self-sacrifice and mission accomplishment (Snider, Nagl, and Pfaff 1999).[15] Troops are supposed to be willing to die to defend the nation and its interests so that civilians do not have to risk their lives. In the Bosnian peacekeeping operation, casualty aversion reached an unprecedented level. "Force protection," meaning the prevention of U.S. casualties, became an explicit mission goal, on a par with, if not superseding, the primary mission of restoring peace to Bosnia. As a result, war criminals were not aggressively pursued and arrested, community-building activities were curtailed, and every stray movement of a U.S. peacekeeper was a mission-threatening event. In short, the risk is that force protection will supplant mission accomplishment as a goal (Hyde 2000).

Importantly, our analysis suggests that the gap need not be permanent. Casualty sensitivity may be learned and unlearned. On either side of the civil-military divide, there are interesting pockets of respondents who resemble the profile of the other side. There are, for example, "interventionist" soldiers, on the basis of their confidence in American political leadership and their lack of alienation from civilian society. Presumably, a determined society could cultivate both viewpoints within the military through increased emphasis on building civil-military trust and indoctrination on the value of the nontraditional missions.

Our data point to an even more intriguing possibility for convergence in the other direction. It is striking how civilians in the professional military education system diverge from other civilian elites to fit the military profile. The sample consists of civilians, primarily drawn from the civil service, whose professional responsibilities involve national security and who therefore would benefit from an advanced educational course at a military institution. Arguably, they share a professional orientation with the "State Department" and more distantly the "foreign policy author" subsamples of the general civilian elite. Nevertheless, on most of the dimensions we studied they differ significantly from these subsamples and the larger civilian elite. We cannot rule out selection effects, since we did not survey them before and after their tenure at the school. Nevertheless, it is just as plausible that participation in a course of study designed to give civilian elites an appreciation for the military point of view is in fact shaping their viewpoints. The implication is clear: if civilian elite attitudes on the use of force and casualty acceptance are a matter of concern, then the views of a strategically positioned subsection of the civilian elite can be influenced through the PME system or some other systematic program of study in military/strategic affairs involving some exposure to the active duty military.

---

[15] See also similar discussions in Eikenberry (1996) and Grossman (1999). For a contrary view, see Dunlap (2000).

A Last Word

We began by asking two simple questions. Do civilians and the military in the United States hold differing opinions on the use of force? Do these differences matter? Our answer is yes on both accounts. Civilians and the military do play to type, and typecasting has mattered for the way the United States has performed its role on the global stage. Students and practitioners of American national security policy must therefore make civil-military relations a central preoccupation if they are going to correctly understand and effectively manage U.S. foreign policy.

REFERENCES

Achen, Christopher. 1986. *The Statistical Analysis of Quasi-Experiments*. Berkeley: University of California Press.

Alvarez, R. Michael, and John Brehm. 2002. *Hard Choices, Easy Answers: Values, Information, and American Public Opinion*. Princeton: Princeton University Press.

Alvis, Michael W. 1999. "Understanding the Role of Casualties in U.S. Peace Operations." Landpower Essay Series, no. 99–1. Institute of Land Warfare, Association of the United States Army.

Andreski, Stanislav. 1980. "On the Peaceful Disposition of Military Dictatorships." *Journal of Strategic Studies* 3, no. 3 (December): 3–10.

Atkinson, Rick. 1996. "Warriors without a War: U.S. Peacekeepers in Bosnia Adjusting to New Tasks: Arbitration, Bluff, Restraint." *Washington Post*, 14 April, p. A1.

Avant, Deborah D. 1994. *Political Institutions and Military Change: Lessons from Peripheral Wars*. Ithaca, N.Y.: Cornell University Press.

———. 1996/97. "Are the Reluctant Warriors out of Control? Why the U.S. Military Is Averse to Responding to Post–Cold War Low-Level Threats." *Security Studies* 6, no. 2: 51–90.

Axelrod, Robert. 1984. *The Evolution of Cooperation*. New York: Basic Books.

Backstrom, Charles Herbert, and Gerald Hursh-César. 1963. *Survey Research*. Chicago: Northwestern University Press.

Baker, William D., and John R. Oneal. 2001. "Patriotism or Opinion Leadership? The Nature and Origins of the 'Rally 'Round the Flag' Effect," *Journal of Conflict Resolution* 45, no. 5 (October): 661–87.

Bamford, James. 2002. "Untested Administration Hawks Clamor for War" *USA Today*, 9 September, p. 15.

Beck, Nathaniel, Jonathan Katz, and Richard Tucker. 1988. "Taking Time Seriously: Time-Series-Cross-Section Analysis with a Binary Dependent Variable." *American Journal of Political Science* 42, no. 4.

Becker, Elizabeth. 1999. "NATO Calls Transformers a Key Target in War Plan." *New York Times*, 25 May, p. 16.

Bennett, Scott D., and Allan C. Stam III. 1998. "The Declining Advantages of Democracy: A Combined Model of War Outcomes and Duration." *Journal of Conflict Resolution* 42, no. 3: 344–67.

———. 2000. EUGene: A Conceptual Manual. *International Interactions* 26, no. 2: 179–204.

Bernstein, Richard. 1993. "U.S. Presents Evidence to U.N. Justifying Its Missile Attack on Iraq." *New York Times*, 28 June, p. 7.

Betts, Richard K. 1991. *Soldiers, Statesmen, and Cold War Crises*. New York: Columbia University Press, Morningside Edition.

———. 1995. "What Will It Take to Deter the United States?" *Parameters* 25, no. 4: 70–79.

Bianco, William, and Jamie Markham. 2001. "Vanishing Veterans: The Decline in Military Experience in the U. S. Congress." In Peter D. Feaver and Richard H. Kohn, eds., *Soldiers and Civilians: The Civil-Military Gap and American National Security.* Cambridge: MIT Press.

Biddle, Stephen. 1996. "Victory Misunderstood: What the Gulf War Tells Us about the Future of Conflict." *International Security* 21, no. 2: 139–79.

Biddle, Stephen, and Robert Zirkle. 1996. "Technology, Civil-Military Relations, and Warfare in the Developing World." *Journal of Strategic Studies* 19, no. 2: 171–212.

Blainey, Geoffrey. 1973. *The Causes of War.* New York: Free Press.

Blechman, Barry M., and Tamara Cofman Wittes. 1999. "Defining Moment: The Threat and Use of Force in American Foreign Policy." *Political Science Quarterly* 114, no. 1 (Spring): 1–30.

Brecher, Michael. 1996. "Crisis Escalation: Model and Findings." *International Political Science Review* 17, no. 2 (April): pp. 215–30.

Brehm, John. 1993. *The Phantom Respondents: Opinion Surveys and Political Representation.* Ann Arbor: University of Michigan Press.

Bremer, Stuart. 1992. "Dangerous Dyads: Conditions Affecting the Likelihood of Interstate War, 1816–1965." *Journal of Conflict Resolution* 36, no. 2: 309–41.

Broder, John M. 1999. "Crisis in the Balkans: White House Memo: From Baptism of Fire to Kosovo: Clinton as Commander in Chief." *New York Times*, 8 April, p. 16.

Brody, Richard. 1984. "International Crises: A Rallying Point for the President?" *Public Opinion* 6, no. 6: 41–43.

Brooks, Risa. 2000. "Institutions at the International and Domestic Nexus: The Political-Military Origins of Strategic Integration, Military Effectiveness, and War." Ph.D. dissertation, University of California, San Diego.

Bueno de Mesquita, Bruce. 1981. *The War Trap.* New Haven: Yale University Press.

Bueno de Mesquita, Bruce, and David Lalman. 1992. *War and Reason: Domestic and International Imperatives.* New Haven: Yale University Press.

Bueno de Mesquita, Bruce, James D. Morrow, Randolph Siverson, and Alastair Smith. 1999. "An Institutional Explanation for the Democratic Peace." *American Political Science Review*, 93: 791–808.

———. 2000a. "Political Institutions, Political Survival, and Policy Success." In Bruce Bueno de Mesquita and Hilton Root, eds., *Governing for Prosperity*, pp. 59–84. New Haven: Yale University Press.

———. 2000b. "Testing the Selectorate Explanation of the Democratic Peace." Manuscript.

Bueno de Mesquita, Bruce, and Randolph M. Siverson. 1995. "War and the Survival of Political Leaders: A Comparative Study of Regime Types and Political Accountability." *American Political Science Review* 89, no. 3: 841–55.

Bueno de Mesquita, Bruce, Randolph M. Siverson, and Gary Woller. 1992. "War and the Fate of Regimes: A Comparative Analysis." *American Political Science Review* 86, no. 3: 638–46.

Bueno de Mesquita, Bruce, Alastair Smith, Randolph Siverson, and James Morrow. 1999. "Policy Failure and Political Survival: The Contribution of Political Institutions." *Journal of Conflict Resolution* 43: 147–61.

———. 2000. "The Logic of Political Survival." Manuscript.

Burk, James. 1999. "Public Support for Peacekeeping in Lebanon and Somalia: Assessing the Casualties Hypothesis." *Political Science Quarterly* 114, no. 1: 53–78.

Burns, Robert. 2000. "Top Brass Focus on Safety." *European Stars and Stripes*, 27 October, p. 2.

Byman, Daniel, and Matthew Waxman. 1999. "Defeating U.S. Coercion." *Survival* 41, no. 2 (Summer): 107–20.

Choi, Seung-Whan, and Patrick James. 2002a. "The Impact of Civil-Military Relations on Militarized Interstate Disputes, 1887–1991: Words of Warning for a Neo-Kantian World." Manuscript.

———. 2002b. " 'Quadrangulating' the Peace? Civil-Military Dynamics, Political Communications, and Militarized Interstate Disputes." Manuscript.

Christenson, Thomas J. 2001. "Posing Problems without Catching Up: China's Rise and Challenges for U.S. Security Policy." *International Security* 25, no. 4 (Spring): 5–40.

Clark, Richard, and Kenneth Dautrich. 2000. "Who's Really Misreading the Public? A Comment on Kull and Ramsay's 'Challenging U.S. Policymaker's Image of an Isolationist Public.' " *International Studies Perspectives* 1, no. 2: 195–98.

Clark, Wesley K. 2001. *Waging Modern War: Bosnia, Kosovo, and the Future of Combat.* New York: Public Affairs.

Cockburn, Patrick. 1993. "Clinton Acclaims Iraq Strike." *The Independent*, 28 June, p. 1.

Cohen, Eliot A. 2001. "The Unequal Dialogue: The Civil-Military Gap and the Use of Force." In Peter D. Feaver and Richard H. Kohn, eds., *Soldiers and Civilians: The Civil Military Gap and American National Security.* Cambridge: MIT Press.

———. 2002a. "Hunting 'Chicken Hawks.' " *Washington Post*, 5 September, p. 31.

———. 2002b. *Supreme Command: Soldiers, Statesmen, and Leadership in Wartime.* New York: Simon and Schuster.

Coll, Alberto R. 2001. "Kosovo and the Moral Burdens of Power." In Andrew Bacevich and Eliot A. Cohen, eds., *War over Kosovo: Politics and Strategy in a Global Age.* New York: Columbia University Press.

Collins, Joseph. 1998. "The Complex Context of American Military Culture: A Practitioner's View." *Washington Quarterly* 21, no. 4: 213–28.

Conversino, Mark J. 1997. "Sawdust Superpower: Perceptions of U.S. Casualty Tolerance in the Post-Gulf War Era." *Strategic Review* 25, no. 1: 15–23.

Cook, Martin L. 2000. "Immaculate War: Constraints on Humanitarian Intervention." *Ethics and International Affairs* 14: 55–65.

Cornwell, Rupert. 2002. "Analysis Iraq: The Inside Out Solution to the Problem of Saddam." *The Independent*, 30 July, p. 11.

Cox, Matthew. 1999. "America Willing to Risk Your Life: Despite Possible Casualties, Most Surveyed Believe Ethnic Cleansing Must Stop." *Army Times*, 7 June, p. 10.

Cuningham, Henry. 2000. "Shelton Says Test Necessary: Death Potential Considered Factor." *Fayetteville Observer*, 27 January, p. 1F.

Daalder, Ivo H., and James M. Lindsay. 2002. "It's Hawk vs. Hawk in the Bush Administration." *Washington Post*, 27 October, p. B03.

Daalder, Ivo H., & Michael E. O'Hanlon. 2000. *Winning Ugly: NATO's War to Save Kosovo*. Washington, D.C.: Brookings Institution.

Dauber, Cori. 1998. "The Practice of Argument: Reading the Condition of Civil-Military Relations." *Armed Forces & Society* 24, no. 3: 435–46.

———. 2001. "The Role of Visual Imagery in Casualty Shyness and Casualty Aversion." In "Media and Education in the U.S. Civil-Military Gap," special edition of *Armed Forces & Society* 27, no. 2: 205–30.

Davis, James A. 2001. "Attitudes and Opinions among Senior Military Officers and a U.S. Cross-Section, 1998–99." In Peter D. Feaver and Richard H. Kohn, eds., *Soldiers and Civilians: The Civil-Military Gap and American National Security*. Cambridge: MIT Press.

Demske, Phillip. 2001. "Civilian Hawks, Military Doves?" Manuscript.

Desch, Michael. 1999. *Civilian Control of the Military: The Changing Security Environment*. Baltimore: Johns Hopkins University Press.

Dewar, Helen. 2002. "For Wellstone, Iraq Vote Is Risk But Not a Choice; Principles May Be Costly in November." *Washington Post*, 9 October, p. A08.

Dixon, Paul. 2000. "Britain's 'Vietnam Syndrome'? Public Opinion and British Military Intervention from Palestine to Yugoslavia." *Review of International Studies* 26: 99–121.

Dowd, Maureen. 2002. "Coup De Crawford." *New York Times*, 8 August, p. 17.

Doyle, Michael J. 1986. "Liberalism and World Politics." *American Political Science Review* 80, no. 4: 1151–69.

Drozdiak, William, and Dana Priest. 1999. "NATO's Cautious Air Strategy Comes under Fire." *Washington Post*, 16 May, p. 26.

Dunlap, Charles. 2000. "Kosovo, Casualty Aversion, and the American Military Ethos: A Perspective." Manuscript.

Eichenberg, Richard C. 2002. "Gender Differences and the Use of Force in the United States, 1990–2002." Paper prepared for the annual meeting of the American Political Science Association, Boston, August 29–September 1.

Eikenberry, Karl W. 1996. "Take No Casualties." *Parameters* 26, no. 2: 109–18.

Ekirch, Arthur A., Jr. 1956. *The Civilian and the Military*. New York: Oxford University Press.

Erdmann, Andrew P. N. 1999. "The U.S. Presumption of Quick, Costless Wars." *Orbis* 43, no. 3: 363–82.

Everts, Philip. 2002. *Democracy and Military Force*. London: Palgrave.

Fearon, James. 1991. "Counterfactuals and Hypothesis Testing in Political Science." *World Politics* 43, no. 2: 169–95.

Fears, Darryl. 2003. "Draft Bill Stirs Debate over the Military, Race, and Equity." *Washington Post*, 4 February, p. 3.

Feaver, Peter D. 1995. "Civil-Military Conflict and the Use of Force." In Donald Snider and Miranda A. Carlton-Carew, eds., *U.S. Civil-Military Relations: In Crisis or Transition?* Washington, D.C.: Center for Strategic and International Studies.

———. 1996a. "The Civil-Military Problematique: Huntington, Janowitz, and the Question of Civilian Control." *Armed Forces & Society* 23, no. 2: 149–79.

———. 1998. "Crisis as Shirking: An Agency Theory Explanation of the Souring of American Civil-Military Relations." *Armed Forces & Society* 24, no. 3: 407–34.

———. 1999. "Civil-Military Relations." In Nelson Polsby et al., eds., *Annual Review of Political Science, 1999.*

———. 2000. "The Public's Expectations of National Security." In Max G. Manwaring, ed., *To Insure Domestic Tranquility, Provide for the Common Defense.* Carlisle, Pa.: Strategic Studies Institute.

———. 2003. *Armed Servants: Agency, Oversight, and Civil-Military Relations.* Cambridge: Harvard University Press.

Feaver, Peter D., and Christopher Gelpi. 1999a. "Civilian Hawks and Military Doves: The Civil-Military Gap and the American Use of Force, 1816–1992." Paper prepared for the TISS Conference on the Gap between the Military and Civilian Society.

———. 1999b. "The Civil-Military Gap and Casualty Aversion." Paper prepared for the TISS Conference on the Gap between the Military and Civilian Society.

———. 1999c. "How Many Deaths Are Acceptable? A Surprising Answer." *Washington Post*, 7 November, p. B3.

———. 2000. "Myths and Realities: Casualty Aversion in the United States." *Foresight*, no. 4 (April/May). In Japanese.

Feaver, Peter D., and Richard H. Kohn. 2001a. "Special Issue: Media and Education in the U.S. Civil-Military Gap." *Armed Forces & Society* 27, no. 2: 177–82.

Feaver, Peter D., and Richard H. Kohn, eds. 2001b. *Soldiers and Civilians: The Civil-Military Gap and What It Means for National Security.* Cambridge: MIT Press.

Finer, Samuel Edward. 1962. *The Man on Horseback—The Role of the Military in Politics.* London: Pall Mall.

Fordham, B. O., and C. C. Sarver. 2001. "Militarized Interstate Disputes and United States Uses of Force." *International Studies Quarterly* 45, no. 3 (September): 455–66.

Friedman, Thomas. 2001. "A Memo from Osama." *New York Times*, 26 June, p. A19.

Gacek, Christopher. 1994. *The Logic of Force: The Dilemma of Limited War in American Foreign Policy.* New York: Columbia University Press.

Gartner, Scott Sigmund, and Gary M. Segura. 1998. "War, Casualties, and Public Opinion." *Journal of Conflict Resolution* 42, no. 3: 278–320.

Gartner, Scott Sigmund, Gary M. Segura, and Michael Wilkening. 1997. "All Politics are Local: Local Losses and Individual Attitudes toward the Vietnam War." *Journal of Conflict Resolution* 41, no. 5 (October): pp. 669–94.

Gaubatz, Kurt. 1999. *Elections and War: The Electoral Incentive in the Democratic Politics of War and Peace*. Stanford: Stanford University Press.

Gelpi, Christopher, and Peter D. Feaver. 2002. "Speak Softly and Carry a Big Stick? Veterans in the Political Elite and the American Use of Force." *American Political Science Review* 96, no. 4: 779–93.

Gentry, John. A. 1998. "Military Force in an Age of National Cowardice." *Washington Quarterly* 21, no. 4: 179–92.

George, Alexander L., and Richard Smoke. 1974. *Deterrence in American Foreign Policy: Theory and Practice*. New York: Columbia University Press.

Gertz, Bill, and Rowan Scarborough. 2002. "Inside the Ring." *Washington Times*, 11 October, p. 10.

Glastris, Paul. 2003. "First Draft." *Washington Monthly*, 1 March.

Goemans, Hein E. 2000. *War and Punishment: The Causes of War Termination and the First World War*. Princeton: Princeton University Press.

Goodpaster, Andrew Jackson, and Samuel P. Huntington. 1977. *Civil-Military Relations*. Washington, D.C.: American Enterprise Institute. 1977.

Gordon, Michael R. 1992. "Powell Delivers a Resounding No on Using Limited Force in Bosnia." *New York Times*, 28 September, p. 1.

Gordon, Michael R., and Bernard E. Trainor. 1995. *The Generals' War*. Boston: Little, Brown and Company.

Gowa, Joanne. 1999. *Ballots and Bullets: The Elusive Democratic Peace*. Princeton: Princeton University Press.

Graham, Bradley. 1999. "War without 'Sacrifice' Worries Warriors." *Washington Post*, 29. June, p. 12.

Gronke, Paul, and Peter D. Feaver. 2001. "Uncertain Confidence: Civilian and Military Attitudes about Civil-Military Relations." In Peter D. Feaver and Richard H. Kohn, eds., *Soldiers and Civilians: The Civil-Military Gap and American National Security*. Cambridge: MIT Press.

Grossman, Elaine. 1999. "For the U.S. Commander in Kosovo, Luck Played Role in Wartime Success." *Inside the Pentagon*, 9 September, p. 1.

Hallion, Richard. 1999. "How Many Deaths?" *Washington Post*, 15 November, p. 22.

Halperin, Morton. 1972. "The President and the Military." *Foreign Affairs* 50, no. 2: 311–24.

Herrmann, Richard K., Philip E. Tetlock, and Penny S. Visser. 1999. "Mass Public Decisions to Go to War: A Cognitive-Interactionist Framework." *American Political Science Review* 93, no. 3: 553–75.

Hillen, John. 1999. "Must U.S. Military Culture Reform?" *Orbis* 43, no. 1: 1–15.

Hines, Cragg. 1999. "Pity, Not U.S. Security, Motivated Use of GIs in Somalia, Bush Says." *Houston Chronicle*, 24 October p. A11.

Hinich, Melvin J., and Michael C. Munger. 1997. *Analytical Politics*. Cambridge and New York: Cambridge University Press.

Hoagland, James. 1999. "Shades of LBJ." *Washington Post*, 7 April, p. 21.

Hodge, Carl Cavanagh. 2000. "Casual War: NATO's Intervention in Kosovo." *Ethics and International Affairs* 14: 39–54.

Holsti, Ole. 1996. *Public Opinion and American Foreign Policy.* Ann Arbor: Michigan University Press.

———. 1999. "A Widening Gap between the U.S. Military and Civilian Society? Some Further Evidence, 1998–99." Paper prepared for the TISS Conference on the Gap between the Military and Civilian Society.

———. 2001. "Of Chasms and Convergences: Attitudes and Beliefs of Civilians and Military Elites at the Start of the New Millennium." In Peter D. Feaver and Richard H. Kohn, eds., *Soldiers and Civilians: The Civil-Military Gap and American National Security.* Cambridge: MIT Press.

Huelfer, Evan Andrew. 2000. "Sacred Treasures: How the Casualty Issue Shaped the American Military Establishment, 1919–1941." Ph.D. dissertation, University of North Carolina, Chapel Hill.

Human Rights Watch. 2000. "Civilian Deaths in the NATO Air Campaign." Human Rights Watch. February. Available at *http://www.hrw.org/reports/2000/nato/.*

Huntington, Samuel. 1957. *The Soldier and the State.* Cambridge: Harvard University Press.

Huth, Paul. K. 1988. *Extended Deterrence and the Prevention of War.* New Haven: Yale University Press.

Huth, Paul K., Christopher Gelpi, and D. Scott Bennett. 1993. "Escalation of Great Power Disputes: Deterrence versus Structural Realism, 1816–1984." *American Political Science Review* 87, no. 3: 609–23.

Hyde, Charles. 2000. "Casualty Aversion: Implications for Policy Makers and Senior Military Officers." *Aerospace Power Journal* 14, no. 2: 17–27.

Ignatieff, Michael. 2000. *Virtual War: Kosovo and Beyond.* New York: Holt and Company.

Jaggers, Keith, and Ted Robert Gurr. 1996. Polity III: Regime Change and Political Authority, 1800–1994 [computer file]. 2nd ICPSR version. Boulder, Colo.: Keith Jaggers / College Park, Md.: Ted Robert Gurr [producers], 1995. Ann Arbor, Mich.: Inter-university Consortium for Political and Social Research [distributor].

James, Patrick, and John Oneal. 1991. "The Influence of Domestic and International Politics on the President's Use of Force." *Journal of Conflict Resolution* 35 (June): 307–32.

Janowitz, Morris. 1960. *The Professional Soldier: A Social and Political Portrait.* Glencoe, Ill.: Free Press.

Jehl, Douglas. 1993. "U.S. Says It Waited for Certain Proof before Iraq Raid." *New York Times,* 29 June, p. A1.

Jentleson, Bruce W. 1992. "The Pretty Prudent Public: Post-Vietnam American Opinion on the Use of Military Force." *International Studies Quarterly* 36, no. 1: 49–74.

———. 1998. "Still Pretty Prudent." *Journal of Conflict Resolution* 42, no. 2: 395–417.

Jones, Daniel M., Stuart A. Bremer, and J. David Singer. 1996. "Militarized Interstate Disputes, 1816–1992: Rationale, Coding Rules, and Empirical Patterns." *Conflict Management and Peace Science* 15, no. 2: 163–213.

Kelly, Michael. 2002. "Return of the 'Chicken Hawks.' " *Washington Post*, 30 October, p. A23.

Kennan, George F. 1993. "Somalia, through a Glass, Darkly." *New York Times*, 30 September, p. A25.

Kessler, Glenn. 2002a. "Powell Treads Carefully on Iraq Strategy." *Washington Post*, 2 September, p. 1.

———. 2002b. "Powell Cites 'Real' Divide Internally on Iraq Policy." *Washington Post*, 4 September, p. 1.

———. 2002c. "On Iraq, Powell Is Front and Center." *Washington Post*, 17 September, p. 17.

Kiely, Kathy. 2002. "Iraq War Vote Looms as a Battle of the Heart." *USA Today*, 8 October, p. 1.

King, Gary, James Honacker, Anne Joseph, and Kenneth Scheve. 2001. "Analyzing Incomplete Political Science Data." American Political Science Review 95, no. 1: 49–69.

King, Gary, Robert O. Keohane, and Sidney Verba. 1994. *Designing Social Inquiry: Scientific Inference in Qualitative Research*. Princeton: Princeton University Press.

King, Gary, and Langche Zeng. 2001. "Explaining Rare Events in International Relations." *International Organization* 55, no. 3.

Klarevas, Louis. 2000. "Trends: The United States Peace Operation in Somalia." *Public Opinion Quarterly* 64, no. 4 (Winter): 523–40.

Kohn, Richard H. 1975. *Eagle and Sword: The Beginnings of the Military Establishment in America*. New York: Free Press.

———. 1994. "Out of Control: The Crisis in Civil-Military Relations." *National Interest*, no. 35: 3–17.

———. 2002. "Erosion of Civilian Control of the Military in the United States Today." *Naval War College Review* 55, no. 3 (Summer): 8–59.

Korb, Lawrence J. 1997. "The Use of Force." *Brookings Review* 15, no. 2: 24–25.

Krauthammer, Charles. 1999. "Bombing Empty Buildings." *Washington Post*, 8 April, p. 31.

Kretchik, Walter E. 1997. "Force Protection Disparities." *Military Review* 77, no. 4: 73–78.

Kull, Steven, and I. M. Destler. 1999. *Misreading the Public: The Myth of a New Isolationism*. Washington, D.C.: Brookings.

Kull, Steven, and Clay Ramsay. 2000. "A Rejoinder from Kull and Ramsay." *International Studies Perspectives* 1, no. 2: 202–5.

Landay, Jonathan. 2002. "Iraqi Force May Exceed 100,000." *Philadelphia Inquirer*, 1 November, p. 1.

Lanman, Eric. 1998. "Wither the Warrior?" *Proceedings of the U.S. Naval Institute* 124, no. 4: 26–29.

Larson, Eric V. 1996. *Casualties and Consensus: The Historical Role of Casualties in Domestic Support for U.S. Military Operations*. Santa Monica, Calif.: Rand.

———. 2000. "Putting Theory to Work: Diagnosing Public Opinion on the U.S. Intervention in Bosnia." In Miroslan Nincic and Joseph Lepgold, eds., *Being*

Useful: Policy Relevance and International Relations Theory. Ann Arbor: University of Michigan Press.

Lee, Jong Sun. 1991. "Attitudes of Civilian and Military Leaders toward War Initiation: Application of Richard Betts' Analysis of American Cases to Other Countries." Ph.D. dissertation, Ohio State University.

Leng, Russell. 1993. *Interstate Crisis Behavior, 1816–1980.* New York: Cambridge University Press.

Levy, Jack S. 1989. "Diversionary Theory of War: A Critique." In Manus I. Midlarsky, ed. *Handbook of War Studies.* Ann Arbor: University of Michigan Press.

Lian, Bradley, and John R. Oneal. 1993. "Presidents, the Use of Military Force, and Public Opinion." *Journal of Conflict Resolution* 37, no. 2: 277–300.

Loeb, Vernon, and Thomas Ricks. 2002. "Rumsfeld's Style, Goals Strain Ties in Pentagon," *Washington Post*, 16 October, p. 1.

Luttwak, Edward N. 1994. "Where Are the Great Powers?" *Foreign Affairs* 73, no. 4: 23–29.

———. 1995. "Towards Post-Heroic Warfare." *Foreign Affairs* 74, no. 3: 109–22.

———. 1999. "From Vietnam to Desert Fox: Civil-Military Relations in Modern Democracies." *Survival* 41, no. 1: 99–112.

Mandelbaum, Michael. 1996. "Foreign Policy as Social Work." *Foreign Affairs* 75, no. 1: 16–32.

Mansfield, Edward. 1994. *Power, Trade, and War.* Princeton: Princeton University Press.

Mansfield, Edward, and Jack Snyder. 1995. "Democratization and the Danger of War." *International Security* 20, no. 1: 5–38.

Maoz, Zeev. 1997. "The Controversy over the Democratic Peace: Rearguard Action or Cracks in the Wall?" *International Security* 22, no. 2: 162–98.

Maoz, Zeev, and Nasrin Abdolali. 1989. "Regime Types and International Conflict, 1816–1976." *Journal of Conflict Resolution* 33, no. 1: 3–35.

Maoz, Zeev, and Bruce M. Russett. 1993. "Normative and Structural Causes of Democratic Peace." *American Political Science Review* 87, no. 3: 624–38.

Marquis, Christopher. 2002. "Bush Officials Differ on Way to Force Out Iraqi Leader." *New York Times*, 19 June, p. 7.

McGregor, Deborah. 2002. "Republican Leaders Find McCain an Unlikely Bedfellow." *Financial Times*, 17 September, p. 10.

Mearsheimer, John. 1983. *Conventional Deterrence.* Ithaca, N.Y.: Cornell University Press.

Meilinger, Phillip. 2001. "A Matter of Precision." *Foreign Policy* 123 (March/April): 78–79.

Milbank, Dana. 2002a. "Bush's Summer Reading Hints at Iraq." *Washington Post*, 20 August, p. 11.

———. 2002b. "Powell Aide Disputes Views on Iraq." *Washington Post*, 28 August, p. 16.

Millett, Allan R., and Williamson Murray. 1988. *Military Effectiveness, vol. 1: The First World War.* Boston: Allen and Unwin.

Morgenthau, Hans J. 1985. *Politics among Nations.* New York: Alfred A. Knopf.

Moskos, Charles C. 1977. "From Institution to Occupation: Trends in the Military Organization." *Armed Forces & Society* 4, no. 1: 41–50.

———. 1998. "Grave Decision: When Americans Accept Casualties." *Chicago Tribune*, 12 December, p. 25.

Moskos, Charles C., and Frank R. Wood, eds. 1988. *The Military: More Than Just a Job?* Washington, D.C.: Pergamon-Brassey's.

MSNBC. 2002. Transcript of "Hardball with Chris Matthews." 26 August.

Mueller, John. 1973. *War, Presidents, and Public Opinion.* New York: John Wiley and Sons.

———. 1994. *Policy and Opinion in the Gulf War.* Chicago: Chicago University Press.

Mueller, Karl. 2000. "Politics, Death, and Morality in U.S. Foreign Policy." *Aerospace Power Journal* 14, no. 2: 12–16.

Murray, Shoon Kathleen. 2000. "Bringing the Majority Back In." *International Studies Perspectives* 1, no. 2: 198–202.

Neuman, Johanna. 1996. *Lights, Camera, War: Is Media Technology Driving International Politics?* New York: St. Martin's Press.

Newcity, Janet. 1999. "Description of the 1998–1999 TISS Surveys on the Military in the Post–Cold War Era." Paper prepared for the TISS conference on the Gap between the Military and Civilian Society.

Nincic, Donna J., and Miroslav Nincic. 1995. "Commitment to Military Intervention: The Democratic Government as Economic Investor." *Journal of Peace Research* 32, no. 4: 413–426.

Noonan, Michael. 1997. "The Illusion of Bloodless Victories." *Orbis* 41, no. 2: 308–20.

O'Hanlon, Michael. 2002. "Decision Could Be Tougher than President Thought," *Milwaukee Journal Sentinel*, 4 October, p. J01.

Oneal, John R., and Anna Lillian Bryan. 1995. "The Rally 'Round the Flag Effect in U.S. Foreign Policy Crises, 1950–1985." *Political Behavior* 17: 379–401.

Oneal, John R., and Bruce Russett. 1997. "The Classical Liberals Were Right: Democracy, Interdependence, and Conflict, 1950–1985." *International Studies Quarterly* 41, no. 2: 267–94.

Organski, A.F.K., and Jacek Kugler. 1980. *The War Ledger.* Chicago: University of Chicago Press.

Ostrom, Charles W., and Brian L. Job. 1986. "The President and the Political Use of Force." *American Political Science Review* 80, no. 2: 541–66.

Pape, Robert. 1996. *Bombing to Win.* Ithaca, N.Y.: Cornell University Press.

Peffley, Mark, Ronald E. Langley, and Robert Kirby Goidel. 1995. "Public Responses to the Presidential Use of Military Force: A Panel Analysis." *Political Behavior* 17, no. 3: 307–36.

Petraeus, David H. 1987. "The American Military and the Lessons of Vietnam." Ph.D. dissertation, Princeton University.

———. 1989. "Military Influence & the Post-Vietnam Use of Force." *Armed Forces & Society* 15, no. 4: 489–505.

Pomfret, John. 2001. "In Beijing's Moves, a Strategy on Taiwan." *Washington Post*, 6 April, p. A1.

Posen, Barry R. 1984. *The Sources of Military Doctrine: France, Britain, and Germany between the World War.* Ithaca, N.Y.: Cornell University Press.

Powell, Colin L. 1992. "Why Generals Get Nervous." *New York Times,* 8 October, p. 35.

————. 2000. " 'No Casualties' Is Political, Not Military." *Wall Street Journal,* 14 September, p. A27.

Powell, Colin, with Joseph E. Persico. 1995. *My American Journey.* New York: Ballantine.

Priest, Dana. 1995. "1,400 U.S. Troops Part of Advance Group." *Washington Post,* 28 November, p. A9.

Puddington, Arch. 1991. "Black Leaders vs. Desert Storm." *Commentary* 91, no. 5: 28.

Rangel, Charles. 2003. "Military Conscription: Mandatory Service Might Make Hawks Think Twice." *Atlantic Journal-Constitution,* 14 January, p. 21A.

Raspberry, William. 2002. "Unasked Questions." *Washington Post,* 30 September, A19.

Ray, James Lee. 1995. *Democracy and International Conflict: An Evaluation of the Democratic Peace Proposition.* Columbia: University of South Carolina Press.

Record, Jeffrey. 2000. "Failed States and Casualty Phobia: Implications for Force Structure and Technology Choices." Occasional Paper no. 18. October. Center for Strategy and Technology, Air University, Maxwell Air Force Base, Alabama.

Reilly, John. 1999. "Americans and the World: A Survey at Century's End." *Foreign Policy,* no. 114: 97–114.

Richburg, Keith B. 1993. "Rangers Net 17 but Miss Aideed Again; Mogadishu Warlord Frustrates Elite GIs." *Washington Post,* 8 September, p. A1.

Ricks, Thomas E. 1997. *Making the Corps.* New York: Scribner.

————. 2000. "Containing Iraq: A Forgotten War." *Washington Post,* 25 October, p. 1.

————. 2002a. "Some Top Military Brass Favor Status Quo in Iraq." *Washington Post,* 28 July, p. 1.

————. 2002b. "Timing, Tactics on Iraq War Disputed." *Washington Post,* 1 August, p. 1.

Rizer, Kenneth R. 2000. "Military Resistance to Humanitarian War in Kosovo and Beyond: An Ideological Explanation." Fairchild Paper. Air University Press, Maxwell Air Force Base, Alabama.

Roman, Peter J., and David W. Tarr. 2001. "Military Professionalism and Policymaking: Is There a Civil-Military Gap at the Top?" In Peter D. Feaver and Richard H. Kohn, eds. *Soldiers and Civilians: The Civil-Military Gap and What It Means for National Security.* Cambridge: MIT Press.

Rousseau, David L., Christopher Gelpi, Dan Reiter, and Paul K. Huth. 1996. "Assessing the Dyadic Nature of the Democratic Peace, 1918–88." *American Political Science Review* 90, no. 2: 512–33.

Russett, Bruce. 1990. *Controlling the Sword: The Democratic Governance of National Security.* Cambridge: Harvard University Press.

Sagan, Scott D. 1986. "1914 Revisited: Allies, Offense, and Instability." *International Security* 11, no. 2 (Fall): 166–71.

Sagan, Scott D. 1994. "The Perils of Proliferation: Organization Theory, Deterrence Theory, and the Spread of Nuclear Weapons." *International Security* 18, no. 4: 66–107.

Salinero, Mike. 2002. "Gen. Zinni Says War with Iraq Is Unwise." *Tampa Tribune*, 24 August, p. 1.

Sapolsky, Harvey, and Jeremy Shapiro. 1996. "Casualties, Technology, and America's Future Wars." *Parameters* 26, no. 2: 119–27.

Schelling, Thomas. 1960. *The Strategy of Conflict*. Cambridge: Harvard University Press.

———. 1966. *Arms and Influence*. New Haven: Yale University Press.

Schmitt, Eric. 1999a. "What Price Civilian Deaths?" *New York Times*, 15 April, p. 13.

———. 1999b. "It Costs a Lot to Kill Fewer People." *New York Times*, 2 May, p. 5.

Schofield, Julian. 2000. "Militarized Decision-Making for War in Pakistan: 1947–1971." *Armed Forces & Society* 27, no. 1 (Fall): 131–48.

Schultz, Kenneth. 1999. "Do Democratic Institutions Constrain or Inform? Contrasting Two Institutional Perspectives on Democracy and War." *International Organization* 53, no. 2: 233–66.

Schwarz, Benjamin C. 1994. *Casualties, Public Opinion, and U.S. Military Intervention: Implications for U.S. Regional Deterrence Strategies*. Santa Monica, Calif.: Rand.

Schwarzkopf, H. Norman. 1992. *It Doesn't Take a Hero*. New York: Bantam.

Segal, David R. 1986. "Measuring the Institutional/Occupational Change Thesis." *Armed Forces & Society* 12, no. 3: 351–76.

Shelton, Henry H. 2000. "National Security and the Intersection of Force and Diplomacy." Remarks to the ARCO Forum, Kennedy School of Government, 19 January.

Signorino, Curtis S. 1999. "Strategic Interaction and the Statistical Analysis of International Conflict." *American Political Science Review* 93, no. 2 (June): pp. 279–98.

Singer, J. David, Stuart Bremer, and John Stuckey. 1972. "Capability Distribution, Uncertainty, and Major Power War, 1820–1965." In Bruce Russett, ed., *Peace, War, and Numbers*. Beverly Hills, Calif.: Sage Publications.

Smith, Alastair. 1999. "Testing Theories of Strategic Choice: The Example of Crisis Escalation." *American Journal of Political Science* 43 (4): 1254–83.

Smith, Louis. 1951. *American Democracy and Military Power*. Chicago: University of Chicago Press.

Smith, Michael. 2001. "American 'Body-Bag Syndrome Is Holding Back NATO.'" *London Daily Telegraph*, 21 March, p. 15.

Smith, R. Jeffrey. 2000. "West Tires of Struggle to Rebuild Bosnia." *Washington Post*, 25 November, p. 1.

Snider, Don, John Nagl, and Tony Pfaff. 1999. "Army Professionalism, the Military Ethic, and Officership in the 21st Century." Available at *http://carlisle-www.army.mil/usassi/ssipubs/pubs99/ethic/ethic.htm*.

Snyder, Glenn Herald, and Paul Diesing. 1977. *Conflict among Nations: Bargaining, Decision Making, and System Structure in International Crises*. Princeton: Princeton University Press.

Snyder, Jack. 1984. *The Ideology of the Offensive: Military Decisionmaking and the Disasters of 1914*. Ithaca, N.Y.: Cornell University Press.

Sobel, Robert. 1990. *Biographical Directory of the United States Executive Branch, 1774–1989*. New York: Greenwich Press.

———. 2001. *The Impact of Public Opinion on Foreign Policy since Vietnam: Constraining the Colossus*. Oxford: Oxford University Press.

Stevenson, Charles A. 1996. "The Evolving Clinton Doctrine on the Use of Force." *Armed Forces & Society* 22, no. 4: 511–36.

Stimson, James. 1976. "Public Support for American Presidents: A Cyclical Model." *Public Opinion Quarterly* 40: 1–21.

Strobel, Warren P. 1997. *Late-Breaking Foreign Policy: The News Media's Influence on Peace Operations*. Washington, D.C.: U.S. Institute of Peace.

———. 2001. "Public Shows Support for U.S. Aggression; but Sentiments Could Change over Time, Analysts Say." *Milwaukee Journal Sentinel*, 28 October, p. A10.

Szanya, Thomas, and Kevin McCarthy. 2002. Civil-Military Relations: A Framework for Assessing the "Gap" and Implications for the Military. Draft presentation.

Tarzi, Shah. 2001. "The Threat of the Use of Force in American Post–Cold War Policy in the Third World." *Journal of Third World Studies* 18, no. 1 (Spring): 39–64.

Thurman, James N. 1999. "An Uneasy Tolerance of Civilian Casualties." *Christian Science Monitor*, 10 May, p. 2.

Toffler, Alvin, and Heidi Toffler. 1993. *War and Anti-War*. New York: Warner Books.

Unattributed. 1992. "National Military Strategy." *Defense Daily*, 13 February, p. S1(6).

———. 1993. "Excerpts from Clinton Interview Transcript." *San Diego Union-Tribune*, 6 October, p. A12.

———. 2000. "What Will America Risk?" *Wilson Quarterly* 24, no. 4: 97–98.

———. 2002. "Excerpts from Iraqi President Saddam Hussein's Speech on Thursday, the Anniversary of the End of the 1980–88 Iran-Iraq War, as Provided by the Official Iraqi News Agency." Associated Press. August 8.

Upton, Emory. 1917. *Military Policy of the United States*. Washington, D.C.: Government Printing Office.

Vagts, Alfred. 1937. *A History of Militarism: A Romance and Realities of a Profession*. New York: W. W. Norton and Company.

Van Deerlin, Lionel. 2002. "Behind-the-Desk Brigade Promotes War Others Fight." *San Diego Union-Tribune*. 4 September, p. B7.

Van Evera, Stephen. 1984. "The Cult of the Offensive and the Origins of the First World War." *International Security* 9, no. 1: 58–107.

Vogel, Steve. 2000. "Death Miscount Etched into History." *Washington Post*, 25 June, p. C01.

Waltz, Kenneth. 1958. *Man, the State, and War*. New York: Columbia University Press.

———. 1979. *Theory of International Politics*. Reading, Mass.: Addison-Wesley Publishing Company.

Watson, Paul. 1993. "Aideed Hunt's Still On, Peacekeepers Insist." *Toronto Star*, 29 September, p. A4.

Webb, James. 1998. "Military Leadership in a Changing Society." Naval War College Conference on Ethics, 16 November.

Webb, James. 2002. "Heading for Trouble." *Washington Post*, 4 September, p. 21.

Weigley, Russell F. 1973. *The American Way in War*. New York: Macmillan.

———. 1993. "The American Military and the Principle of Civilian Control from McClellan to Powell." *Journal of Military History* 57, no. 5: 27–58.

———. 2001. "The American Civil-Military Cultural Gap: A Historical Perspective, Colonial Times to the Present." In Peter D. Feaver and Richard H. Kohn, eds., *Soldiers and Civilans: The Civil-Military Gap and American National Security*. Cambridge: MIT Press.

Weiner, Tim, and Jane Perlez. 1999. "How Clinton Approved the Strikes on Belgrade." *New York Times*, 4 April, p. 1.

Wheatcroft, Geoffrey. 1999. "A Land of Reluctant Warriors." *New York Times*, 14 April, p. A25.

Wittkopf, Eugene R. 1990. *Faces of Internationalism: Public Opinion and American Foreign Policy*. Durham, N.C.: Duke University Press.

Worthington, Peter. 1999. "Bill's Push-Button, Play-Safe 'War': The U.S. Military Is Ready to Kill for Its Country But Not Die for It." *Toronto Sun*, 27 May, p. 17.

Zaller, John. 1994. *The Nature and Origins of Public Opinion*. New York: Cambridge University Press.

NAME INDEX

SUBJECT INDEX